Software Licensing

Second Edition

David Bainbridge
Barrister
BSc, LLB, PhD, CEng, MICE, MBCS

CLT Professional Publishing Ltd
A Member of the Central Law Training Group

© David Bainbridge 1999

Published by
CLT Professional Publishing Ltd
A Member of the Central Law Training Group
Stonehills House
Howardsgate
Welwyn Garden City
Herts AL8 6PU

ISBN 1 85811 191 9

Typeset by Cheryl Zimmerman
Printed in Great Britain by The Book Company Ltd.

Contents

Preface

The scope, extent and power of computer software continues to advance at breathtaking pace. The term "computer software" now includes such a wide and diverse range of works that one could almost claim that "everything is software now". It is true that every imaginable form of work, in the copyright sense, can be converted to, represented in or stored in a digital form and we are already seeing the power of digital representation in the growth of the Internet, telecommunications and networks and, more lately, even broadcasting. In the early days of computers, licences were in the main restricted to computer programs. Now they have to encompass all manner of works. Consider, for example, a multimedia encyclopaedia with its vast number of individual works and compilations. There are likely to be literary works, photographs, drawings, films, sounds and music at the very least. Then there are the programs that are used to manipulate these various works. These programs may well be opaque to the user but, nevertheless, they exist and are of prime importance. All these various works, to the extent that rights subsist in them (and rights will subsist in most of them), will be the subject matter of any licence to use them or otherwise exploit them.

Another issue is that there are often additional rights in a collection of works, for example, as compilations or databases. The law relating to databases has recently changed and it is important to recognise the effect of the changes, especially as many databases will now enjoy a further right in addition to copyright. It must also be noted that the individual items within a database may have their own separate and independent rights. Furthermore, unlike computer programs, databases may be subject to moral rights under copyright law which may have to be addressed by any licence agreement in respect of software including them (and other works such as literary and audio-visual works).

Computer software plays a central role in the operation of most organisations whether of a commercial or public nature. Not only do large companies and public authorities make considerable use of computer technology but many sole traders and individuals also extensively use computer software. In many cases, utility has now grown in dependency. The demand for reliable and high quality software is ever increasing and the legal arrangements that govern the acquisition and use of the software are of prime importance.

Anyone drafting a software licence must have an understanding of the technical environment surrounding the use and operation of the software concerned and the attendant technical implications. However, that in itself is insufficient and full account must also be taken of the legal environment. Some 20 or 30 years ago, software licences used to be fairly rudimentary agreements, in some cases, occupying less than one side of A4 paper (or even foolscap for those of us with longer memories) with terms which seemed to warrant very little if anything and to exclude everything. It was common for software licences to restrict liability for defects to the licence fee, if not to exclude liability whatsoever. Software companies, perhaps influenced by the view that the law had not caught up with the computer revolution, thought they could draft their licences as they wished. It was a sort of digital "Wild West".

Things have changed dramatically. We now have a considerable number of legal constraints on what can or cannot be included in software licences. For example, the Unfair Contract Terms Act 1977 has particularly sharp teeth here. Copyright law makes certain types of terms in software licences void and unenforceable. Other areas of law may be appropriate, including data protection law and criminal law. The person drafting a software licence now has to feel his or her way through this legal minefield as well as attempting to produce a licence which will provide a sensible framework. That will not always be the end of the story. The software company is likely to try to "call the shots" when it comes to the licence but more often nowadays, clients want their say. There may be a significant amount of negotiation before the agreement is finalised.

Liability for defective software has been an issue that has concentrated many minds in the software industry and elsewhere. The "Millennium Bug" or "Year 2000 problem", which at first seemed to be of little serious consequence, became the subject of wild hysteria and is now appreciated by many as the most serious issue ever to affect computers. The consequences of a failure to meet this problem in particular cases could be catastrophic. It is vital, therefore, that any licences for new software or modifying existing software take account of this problem as best they can. Unfortunately, there are no golden bullets, even contractually. One major problem for software companies is now the growing reluctance or, in many cases refusal, by insurers to underwrite risks concerning errors attributable to dates. As European monetary union comes ever closer, another problem is whether computer software will be able to perform the complex currency conversions that will be required. The software licence itself can provide only part remedies to such problems. It is of the utmost importance that any specification for new or modified software contains comprehensive mechanisms governing the duty of the software company to demonstrate that the software performs as it should do in respect of these matters. At the end of the day, full and satisfactory technical compliance is far more desirable than contractual provision for when things go wrong. Of course, that is not to say that there should be no such provision.

Two forms of licence agreement especially are considered in this book. The first is for bespoke software; that is, software that is specially written or modified for a client, usually on the basis of a detailed specification. The second form is for licences used with off-the-shelf software, ready-made software that includes a vast range and variety of types of software. Typical are the popular word processing, spreadsheet, database, desk top publishing, graphical and statistical packages.

This book is arranged in such a way that, after an introductory chapter, the intellectual property rights that may subsist in software are described with particular emphasis on the application of those rights to software. Next, the legal nature of software is described including a thorough consideration of the potential liabilities resulting from defective software. This is an important aspect when one considers that any significant item of software is almost certain to contain errors, some of which may not be discovered for a long time. Even the Court of Appeal has recognised this fact of life in the business of software writing and accepted that software may be fit for its purpose yet still contain errors.

The latter part of the book is concerned with the detail of software licences and there are descriptions of the two main forms of licences together with example licence terms. There are also chapters on some aspects of software procurement, negotiation and facilities management. There then follows a glossary of software terms and two sample licence agreements in the Appendices based on the examples discussed earlier in the book. Readers are free to use or modify these agreements whether in whole or in part providing that they accept the agreements for what they are – examples based on hypothetical situations that may not be appropriate in a particular case. Neither the author nor the publisher can accept any responsibility whatsoever for any loss or damage, whether direct or indirect and howsoever caused resulting from the use of this book or the use of the sample licences, in whole or in part. Indeed, the author's view is that it is always best to go back to first principles when drafting a software licence agreement although some standard terms usefully may be employed. This view is particularly true of bespoke software licences.

During the preparation for and writing of this second edition of this book, I have been helped enormously by discussions with lawyers practising in this area, clients (including a number of computer software companies), colleagues and students. I thank them all - they have all proved to be a source of stimulation. I hope readers find this second edition both informative and useful. The law is stated as I believe it to be as at 1 October 1998.

David I Bainbridge
October 1998

Table of Cases

Table of Legislation

Directives

Legal protection of computer
programs, OJ [1991]
L122/42   30, 31, 43
Article 1(1)   42

Legal protection of databases,
OJ [1996] L77/20   50, 52
recital 15   58

Protection of individuals with
regard to the processing of
personal data and on the free
movement of such data, OJ
[1995] L281/31   108

Term of protection of copyright,
OJ [1993] L290/9   19

Proposals

Directive on the patentability of
biotechnological inventions, OJ
[1998] C110/17   70

International Conventions

Agreement on Trade-Related
Aspects of Intellectual
Property Rights (TRIPs
Agreement)   40

Berne Copyright
Convention   21, 41, 191

Brussels Convention   191

European Patent Convention 67

Lugano Convention   191

Patent Cooperation Treaty   67

Rome Convention   41

Sans Sebastian Convention   191

Universal Copyright
Convention   21, 41

List of Figures

List of Tables

Introduction

Introduction

The use of information technology has grown at an incredible rate. In the space of a few years, computers have changed from being something of a rarity only owned by very large organisations to being so commonplace in business and the home that it is now unusual to find even a sole trader who does not have a computer or a young person that is not proficient in the use of computers, if only for playing games. The growth of computer hardware has stimulated an equally impressive development in the variety and sophistication of computer software including computer programs, files and databases. Now, as we embark on the information super-highway with electronic publishing, multimedia, electronic mail, cable TV, video on demand, home shopping and information services, the need for high quality software is ever increasing, as is the need for fair and workable legal provisions concerning the protection and licensing of computer software.

A great deal of software is acquired by means of a licence agreement. It is essential that the licence agreement provides the proper balance between protecting the owner's rights and giving the client software that performs well with adequate recourse if it does not. The owner must also be shielded to some extent from any potential losses resulting from use of the software. It must be noted that now software is fulfilling many important and critical roles, the consequences of defects can be enormous. To take some examples:

- a simple mistake in poll-tax software resulted in a local authority receiving £1.3 million less than it should have done in one year; *St Albans City & District Council* v *International Computers Ltd* [1997] FSR 251;
- the London Ambulance Service's computer-aided despatch system went haywire forcing the service to revert to the old semi-manual system. Delays of up to 90 minutes were reported and it was alleged that a number of people died as a result of the delays (*The Times*, 29 October 1992, p 3);
- software that had been specially written for a client after a feasibility study proved to be unusable leading to an award of £663,000 in damages; *The Salvage Association* v *CAP Financial Services Ltd* [1995] FSR 654;

- an alleged error in a computer program resulted in nearly 1,000 cancer patients receiving radiotherapy doses below the required level. The problem only came to light 10 years after the system had been installed (*Computing*, 13 February 1992, p 4);
- even the humble spreadsheet can be at the root of massive losses. It is estimated that one company paid £10 million more than it should have done for an acquisition because a mistake in a spreadsheet was not spotted until too late (*Computing*, 28 August 1997, p 6);
- new software to help people complete their self-assessment tax returns had an error which confused pounds and pence in some places, meaning that some of the 50,000 users of the software would wrongly assess their tax indebtedness. The company responsible for the software said that it would pay fines incurred and would also consider paying interest where users had overpaid (*Computing*, 13 August 1997, p 5);
- the European Space Agency's Ariane-5 rocket was destroyed when its guidance software went wrong. The rocket automatically self-destructed when the software fault caused the rocket to veer wildly off-course. It transpired that the software had not been fully tested (*Computing*, 25 July 1996, p 1).

Other stories of poorly performing software abound. One sobering thought is that the computer controlled nuclear reactor shut-down system at Sizewell B contains approximately 100,000 lines of code. The source code for equivalent software in a Canadian power station was only 10,000 lines long, took 35 person-years to test and some serious errors were found (*The Times*, 20 March 1992, p 25). Add to this the fact that software of this complexity is continually being modified and updated and it becomes apparent that it is impossible to claim that software does not contain errors with any degree of conviction.

It is likely to get much worse. Everyone must by now have heard of the "Millennium bug" also known as "Year 2000" or "Y2K". This is the enormous difficulty facing computer users and software developers of ensuring that their computers and software systems will still work effectively on and after 1 January 2000. It seems incredible now, but it was common for programmers only to use the last two digits of the year of a date, so instead of allowing four digits in their programs for the year, they only used two. Thus, 14 September 1982 was stored and manipulated as 14/09/82 rather than 14/09/1982. The consequences could be grave if this problem is not dealt with. It also has massive implications in terms of liability for defects and for some time now every wise client has been demanding the inclusion of appropriate warranties in agreements for the acquisition, modification or development of software. Those with software of an older pedigree may have less recourse.

As an example, consider an industrial process which, timed to last 36 hours, might deduct the present time and date from the time and date the process started. If the process is started at 6 pm on 31 December 1999, at the stroke of midnight the computer will think it has been in operation for 00.00 hours on 01/01/00 minus 18.00 hours on 31/12/99, that is, six hours short of 100 years. The software will be thrown into confusion. Another example might be where a bank's computer works out interest payable on a loan. If the Millennium problem is not cured, the computer could decide that the bank owes the borrower an enormous amount of interest. The problems are exacerbated when the software is used in a safety critical situation, such as in air traffic control or controlling hospital equipment.

Many large organisations, such as banks, are spending literally hundreds of millions of pounds modifying their software to make sure that there will be no problems. The Halifax is reputed to have estimated that curing the problem will require a total of 300 man years, at a cost of £15 milliion but this figure is reckoned by some to be too low as the Abbey National has costed the exercise at £75 million (*Computing*, 28 August 1997, p 4). However, the tremendous size and complexity of many software systems makes it extremely difficult to be absolutely certain that all date references have been picked up and corrected. So serious is the problem that insurers are tending to exclude liability for losses caused by the Millennium bug (*Computing*, 13 November 1997, p 1).

Although hyped as the Millennium problem, other dates could also give rise to software failures. It was common practice for programmers to use 9/9/99 to mark the end of a data file and 01/01/01 was sometimes used where a date of birth was not known. Other glitches are sure to surface.

Another issue is that software is subject to copyright (and sometimes other intellectual property rights). This has two implications. First, because of the existence of these rights, the use of another person's software will generally require a licence, for example, to perform acts restricted by copyright. Simply running and using computer software involves the making of copies. Even if those copies are transient only, for example, where the software is operated from a floppy disk, this falls within the meaning of copying for copyright purposes. In many cases, permanent copies will be made also by loading a copy of the software onto a hard disk or other storage media.

The second point relates to the question of infringement of copyright. The licence agreement circumscribes the use which the licensee may make of the software. Any use beyond that will be a breach of the agreement and may also be an infringement of copyright. For example, a company with a single user licence may make and use several copies. Unauthorised use is rife and although the problem of software piracy has been largely dealt with, there remains the thorny issue of use of software by organisations in excess of the terms of the licence agreement under which the software has been obtained. The loss due to unauthorised copying of computer programs is estimated at £1.7 billion per year in Europe alone (*The Computer Bulletin*, March 1998, p 24). Even Her Majesty's Prison Service has been caught operating unlicensed software, having to settle with a payment of nearly £40,000 in respect of one prison, despite the requirement for all prisons to carry out annual software audits (*Computing*, 2 July 1998, p 3).

It is unlikely to be satisfactory simply to take a standard agreement based on US law and modify it for use in the United Kingdom. This practice was criticised by Harman J in *Andersen Consulting* v *CHP Consulting Ltd* (unreported) 26 July 1991, Chancery Division. The plaintiff supplied computer software to clients and provided copies of the source code comprising some 100,000 lines of code. The defendant offered to maintain this software for those clients and the plaintiff's earlier licence agreements did not prevent third party maintenance. In refusing the injunctions sought, the judge, Harman J, criticised the plaintiff's licence agreement. He gave one example: "... exclusive owner of the programs which are proprietary and copyrighted" and described this as an obscure phrase followed by an Americanism. He said that it was obviously an American agreement which had been modified for the UK market and it would be very difficult to determine whether there had been a breach of the agreement or whether there was any prima facie breach. The benefit of doubt was given to the defendant.

Equally, it may be unsatisfactory to take a standard form licence agreement or precedent and use it without addressing the particular nature of the software, its purposes, subsequent use and future maintenance and development. The varied nature of software, expectations and the interests of the client and software developer mean that their respective interests often can only be adequately protected by modifying and tailoring standard forms and precedents to the particular circumstances.

What is software?

The term "software" covers a great many items but, unfortunately, there is little agreement as to its precise meaning. It is always taken to include computer programs in source code form but it will also cover computer databases and documents, drawings and other works stored or transmitted electronically. It may extend to things produced by the operation of a computer program, such as a report or document stored electronically or even printed out on paper and to electronic signals or messages generated by the program. Computer programs in object code form stored in integrated circuits are sometimes referred to as firmware because of the permanence of this mode of storage, although others still refer to such programs as software. However, object code programs stored on magnetic disks or tape are always described as software. Sometimes, printed documentation accompanying a computer program or database is included in the definition of software.

The Oxford University Press *Dictionary of Computing* (3rd ed, 1990) describes software as: "A generic term for those components of a computer system that are intangible rather than physical" and then goes on to distinguish software from hardware, being physical computer equipment. In this book, a generous definition is taken and "software" includes computer programs (in whatever form) and data stored (or intended to be stored) in a computer, preparatory design materials (such as written specifications, flowcharts, screen layout designs, etc), computer programming languages and associated documentation such as user guides, manuals and other printed documentation; and information generated by a programmed computer and stored or transmitted electronically, whether or not of transient existence; see Figure 1.1.

How is a computer program developed?

Conventionally, computer programs are written by a team of professionals comprising systems analysts and programmers. Following a decision to write a program to perform a particular task or tasks, some amount of research will be undertaken, studying

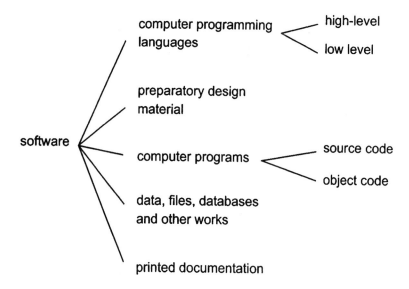

Figure 1.1 Computer software

existing manual methods (if applicable), ascertaining functional and operational requirements and the interaction between the new program and databases or other programs. Specifications will be written, stating the perceived requirements, the functions to be performed by the software, the technical aspects and the standards of performance. Flowcharts will be drawn up indicating the structure of the program, the inter-relationship between its various sub-elements (often referred to as modules or sub-routines) and the sequence of operations to be performed. In practice, several flowcharts will be produced representing various levels of detail. Other material to be produced before programming work commences will include designs for screen displays and reports to be generated by the program and details of the methods by which the program will interface with the user. Diagrams and tables showing the structure and format for any data files or databases to be used in conjunction with the program will also be produced. Typically, this work will be carried out by systems analysts (who will liaise with and discuss the requirements with the client) and it will form the basis for the program to be written by the programmers.

All of the preparatory materials described above will be used by the programmers who produce a source code program which may be written in a high-level language such as BASIC or COBOL or in a low-level language, normally termed assembly language. Increasingly, "fourth-generation" languages are used. These reduce the amount of program writing required by automating a number of the tasks. The program code must be converted into the computer's machine language before it can be run (operated in the computer). This is done by the use of a compiler program (or assembler program in the case of an assembly language source code program) The converted form is known as object code. The distinction between high-level languages and low-level languages is that one statement of the former represents many statements in machine language while one statement of a low-level language is directly equivalent to one statement of machine language. The process of conversion to object code from a high-level source code program is known as compilation and the reverse process, obtaining the source code from an object code program, is known as decompilation. For low-level languages, the equivalent processes are known as assembly and disassembly respectively, though for the purposes of understanding the legal provisions, the terms compilation and decompilation are apt to cover both forms of conversion.

In writing the source code program, the programmer might make use of known sub-routines that are common in the industry or which have been developed and used over time by the programmer, being part of the programmer's "toolkit". A programmer will collect a library of useful routines that can be incorporated into new computer programs. Once the program has been written, there will follow a period of testing, error correction and modification. Two stages of testing are common, "alpha testing" and "beta testing". The latter refers to testing after the software has been installed on the client's computer equipment and should make use of "live data", that is, data of a kind which the client will use once the software has been accepted. It is common for changes to be made to the specification during the development of a new computer program and these must be incorporated into the licence. The process of writing a computer program is shown diagramatically in Figure 1.2.

The above description inevitably is a simplification of the process and, in practice, a computer software system will contain a great many individual computer programs, database files and other information stored, for example, on magnetic disks. An examination of the number of programs and various files that come with a modern word processing package will confirm this. Also, manuals and other documentation must be produced to help users of the system and to assist in the ongoing maintenance of the software. A log book should

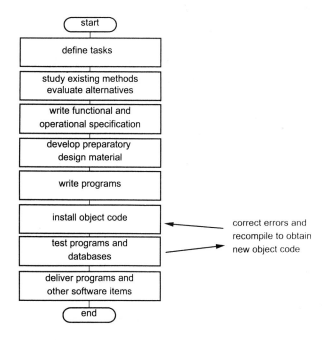

Figure 1.2 Writing a computer program

also be kept of the development of the software and its subsequent maintenance and modification. Although "fourth-generation languages", such as Oracle are being used increasingly to develop software systems, the basic principles of software development described above still hold true.

How software is obtained

One option open to some organisations is to develop the required software in-house, using its own staff or hiring in freelance staff to do the work. Where the organisation has suitably qualified and experienced individuals, this may present the best way forward. The persons involved in writing the software will be familiar with the organisation's business and its methods. However, there may be some pitfalls also. For example, it is difficult to impose strict budgetary control over the work and some in-house projects end up costing far more than the equivalent system written by a specialist software company would have done. In some cases, this extra expense may be justified if it results in a superior system. If it is decided to develop software in-house, the need to set deadlines, hold regular meetings with the commissioning department and encourage a sense of discipline cannot be stressed too highly. One way of doing this is to allocate funds for the project and to develop a contractor-client relationship between the staff developing the software and the department or departments that will use it. A final point for anyone thinking of adopting this approach is that there will be no-one else to blame (or sue) should the software turn out to be useless.

In the majority of cases, the development of software in-house will not be feasible or desirable. The question then becomes one of how to procure the desired software. A number of options exist:

- the software may be specially written for a client by a software company (sometimes referred to as a software house). The software may be produced in accordance with a tightly drawn specification, perhaps after a feasibility study. Prototyping might be carried out (a preliminary version is made to test out certain aspects of the proposed software or it may even be used to develop the final software). Specially written software is sometimes referred to as bespoke software. It will certainly be the most expensive solution compared to those below but in many cases will be the only approach open to the client;

- existing software may be modified (more procedures and facilities added, errors corrected, converted to run on other hardware, etc). In many respects this is similar to bespoke software and the same contractual considerations apply. It is likely to be significantly less expensive than having completely new software developed;

- existing software may be obtained "off-the-shelf", for example, word processing programs, spreadsheet programs, computer games and graphics programs. Huge numbers of copies of these ready-made programs are licensed and their quality is extremely high. The cost varies from a few pounds to tens of thousands of pounds.

An important factor for the client in the first two cases is whether the source code is to be made available to him. This will be important in maintaining the software and correcting any errors that come to light. It will also enable the client to improve and enhance the software later either by using its own staff or by engaging a different software company. In the case of off-the-shelf software, the source code is not made available and only a copy of the object code is given to the customer. Off-the-shelf software usually cannot be modified by the client (although options as to how it is to operate may be built in) and this constraint is not normally present in the case of bespoke software. The analogy with buying a new suit is apt. One can buy a suit off-the-peg or have one tailor made. It is the same with software but the constraints are even more rigid (it is usually possible at least to have the trousers of an off-the-peg suit shortened!).

Another possibility is for an organisation to employ a contractor to operate its computer operations for it. This is known as facilities management and applies to other aspects of business activity also. A company may, for example, call in a facilities management contractor to take over all its processing activities, often transferring the staff of the organisation's computer department to the contractor. Apart from anything else, this has implications in terms of employment law. It may also result in significant efficiency and cost savings for the client as the contractor may be in a position to make other hardware and software available in respect of processing the client's data. Where the client transfers existing software licences to the contractor, this may cause problems, especially if the licence states that the software is non-transferable.

A number of considerations are important when obtaining, developing or distributing software. For example, the nature of the use to which the software may be put, ownership of the copyright, method and timing of delivery and payment, maintenance and error correction and liability for defects all must be dealt with in the licence agreement. Of course, some are more relevant to bespoke software than off-the-shelf software but, in either case, the scope and content of the licence agreement is of primary importance. It forms the basis by which the software is created, acquired or distributed.

Purpose of this book

The purpose of this book is to provide practical guidance in the drafting of licence agreements. Where possible, examples are provided together with draft clauses based on realistic scenarios to give context. It must be noted by the reader that it is dangerous to over-generalise, hence the need for context. The construction of a licence agreement for an important piece of software should always start with first principles. That is not to say that standard terms may not be used; certainly they will prove useful but they must be used with caution and only after the essential mechanism of the agreement has been defined and clarified. With this in mind, it should be possible to produce a fair and workable agreement that will focus on the parties' obligations yet have ample provision for the things that can go wrong but to treat this as an exercise in risk apportionment rather than an attempt to evade liability at all costs. A confrontational licence will result in an adversarial atmosphere rather than one of co-operation which is so important to the final goal of timely delivery of software that performs satisfactorily in all respects in return for reasonable payment.

The structure of the book is to look at the legal background first, followed by an examination of terms typically found in licence agreements. In Chapter 2, the basic principles of copyright law are described with special focus on computer programs, databases and other computer works. Industrial property rights, including the law of confidence, patents, designs, trade marks and passing off are looked at in Chapter 3. The following two chapters consider the legal environment of software licensing with Chapter 4 concentrating on the contractual aspects and Chapter 5 looking to the liability for loss or damage resulting from defective software. Chapter 6 concentrates on bespoke software and includes examples of clauses based on a hypothetical situation together with commentary on the terms and their significance. Off-the-shelf software licences are considered in Chapter 7 including a look at the legal status of these contracts, something which has still to be finally resolved. In Chapter 8 issues relating to software procurement are dealt with including feasibility studies and the invitation of tenders. Chapters 9 and 10 are new and deal with negotiation of software agreements and facilities management respectively. There follows a Glossary of common software terms and an example software licence based on the terms discussed in Chapter 6 with some additional terms added.

Chapter 2

Copyright and Computer Software

Copyright and Computer Software

Introduction

The heart of any agreement concerning the use or exploitation of computer software is a licence to perform specific acts under copyright law. The mechanism of copyright law is based upon giving the copyright owner the right to perform or authorise the performance of a number of particular acts in relation to the copyright work. The most obvious of these acts being the exclusive right to make copies of the work. Any person who performs any of the owner's exclusive rights in respect of a substantial part of the work, whether directly or indirectly, without the licence of the copyright owner will infringe the copyright and be liable to remedies such as an injunction, damages, an account of profits, additional damages and delivery up. The agreement must, therefore, deal fully with the copyright position and whilst the agreement will cover many other matters (such as training, indemnity and liability issues), the copyright owner's permission to carry out the acts envisaged by the parties is the central plank upon which the rest of the agreement is founded.

Copyright law has existed since Tudor times and was an early response to the problems associated with the ease of publishing and copying works of literature and other written materials as a result of the invention of the printing press and moveable type. Although initially concerned with the control of the dissemination of information as much as protecting authors and publishers from unauthorised copying, copyright law came to be the primary legal form for protecting all manner of creative works from piracy. Copyright law developed in a very pragmatic way and, as advances in technology brought about new forms of creative works, copyright law eventually extended its protection to them. Thus, photographs, sound recordings, films and broadcasts all became works of copyright.

With the advent of computer technology, computer programs also came within the copyright club, albeit somewhat belatedly. Most recently databases are recognised as works of copyright in their own right. The traditional forms of copyright works may also be stored in digital form in a computer or on computer storage media and also fall within the meaning of software. In many cases, a software licence will have to address the copyright issues not only in relation to computer programs delivered to the licensee but also in respect of other types of work provided in digital form. A good example is a modern word processing package. Apart from the word processing programs, the software will contain a thesaurus, dictionary, style sheets, macros and other works such as digitised versions of graphic works. A very high proportion of programs that are specially written for a client (bespoke programs) make use of databases of one form or another. The copyright position as regards these other works and databases must also be addressed thoroughly in the drafting of the agreement.

In the description of copyright that follows, emphasis is placed first on the copyright position of computer programs. This is discussed comprehensively, using computer programs as a platform from which to view the principles of copyright law. Then, particular issues relating to preparatory design material, programming languages, computer-generated works and other works stored in computers are discussed. Special attention is given to the protection of databases by copyright and by the database right, which can best be described as a right *sui generis* but which has some similarity to copyright.

Copyright law and computer programs

The question of subsistence of copyright in computer programs was not finally and conclusively decided until the Copyright (Computer Software) Amendment Act 1985 which amended the Copyright Act 1956. There had been a number of interlocutory hearings prior to the amending legislation but none of these had put the matter beyond doubt. The 1985 Act was seen as a temporary measure and the Copyright, Designs and Patents Act 1988 fully dealt with the copyright issues relating to computer programs and new and evolving forms of storage media. Even so, this Act has been amended since, particularly as a result of the implementation of a number of EC Directives including those on the legal protection of computer programs and the legal protection of databases. Other Directives, concerned with the duration of copyright and rental and lending rights have had an impact on software copyright.

Subsistence of copyright

Part I of the Copyright, Designs and Patents Act 1988 governs copyright and it states in section 1(1) that copyright subsists in original literary, dramatic, musical or artistic works; sound recordings, films, broadcasts or cable programmes; and the typographical arrangement of published editions. For copyright to subsist in a work it must, by section 1(3) satisfy the qualification requirements. These are contained in Chapter IX of the Act (ss 153 to 162) and there are further provisions for qualification in sections 163 to 169 (Crown and Parliamentary copyright, etc).

Basically, a work may qualify for copyright protection in one of two ways, either by virtue of the person who creates the work, the author (for example, if the author is a British citizen or resident in the UK), or by virtue of the country of first publication. Thus, for a work to be a work of UK copyright, it could either have been created by a British citizen or first published in the United Kingdom. In terms of first publication, there is a period of grace of 30 days. The work must be published in the United Kingdom or other country to which the provisions apply within 30 days of its first publication if this occurred in another country. By publishing a work in a number of countries simultaneously, a copyright owner may acquire a bundle of national copyrights. However, international conventions provide for reciprocal protection; for example, the provisions relating to qualification for copyright in the Copyright, Designs and Patents Act 1988 have been extended to many other countries that are parties to the relevant conventions or otherwise give adequate protection under their law.

Literary works are defined as meaning any work, other than a dramatic or musical work, which is written, spoken or sung and includes a table or compilation (other than a database), a computer program, preparatory design material for a computer program and a database; section 3(1). The Act does not define "computer", "computer program" nor "preparatory design material". This is probably just as well because a rigid definition could be very soon outdated in this fast moving technology. The meaning is best left to the courts to develop in the light of evolving and unpredictable technological change. However, "database" is defined and that definition is reproduced in the section on databases later in this chapter. Prior to the changes to the protection of databases, which came into force on 1 January 1998, there is no doubt that databases would have been protected as compilations. The exclusion of databases from the meaning of compilations is a result of those changes and did not apply before they took effect.

Literary, dramatic, musical or artistic works must be original for copyright to subsist in them. It should be noted that this has been applied in a very liberal manner in the past in the United Kingdom and neither literary merit nor novelty has been required. It has simply been a question of whether the work has originated from the author as a result of his skill, effort and judgment. Examples of works denied copyright protection on this basis are rare, one example being *G A Cramp & Sons Ltd* v *Frank Smythson Ltd* [1944] AC 329 in which it was held that the work in selecting five pages containing tables of the usual information to be placed at the front of a diary was insufficient to attract copyright because the commonplace nature of the tables left no room for skill and judgment in their selection.

Another way of looking at the requirement of a minimum of skill, effort and judgment is that it is evidence of the existence of a "work". Small or trivial items will not be afforded copyright and there is, accordingly, a *de minimis* threshold to be attained. For example, it has been held that the phrase "Beauty is a social necessity, not a luxury" is not protected by copyright (*Sinanide* v *La Maison Kosmeo* (1928) 139 LT 365) nor is the word "Exxon" (*Exxon Corp* v *Exxon Insurance Consultants International Ltd* [1981] 3 All ER 241).

An additional requirement that applies to literary, dramatic and musical works (but not artistic works) is that copyright does not subsist unless and until the work is recorded in writing or otherwise; section 3(3). "Writing" is generously defined by section 178 of the Copyright, Designs and Patents Act 1988 as including "any form of notation or code, whether by hand or otherwise and regardless of the method by which, or medium in or on which, it is recorded, and "written" shall be construed accordingly". This will extend to storage on magnetic disks or tape, silicon chips or other forms of storage such as Read Only Memory (ROM). It is more difficult to tell whether it applies to transient memory such as a computer's volatile memory (Random Access Memory – RAM). In *R* v *Gold* [1988] 2 WLR 984, the phrase "recorded or stored" in section 8(1) of the Forgery and Counterfeiting Act 1981 was held by the House of Lords to connote some permanent form of storage and did not apply to a password used to gain access to a computer file. However, it should be noted that a transient copy of a work may be an infringing copy notwithstanding its temporary nature.

As noted above, copyright can subsist in a compilation as a form of literary work. This fact is very important as it is increasingly rare for a software application to contain just one single program. More likely, several programs, data files and databases will be linked together and as such there can be an additional copyright in the entire suite of programs and other materials as a compilation, without prejudice to the copyright subsisting in each individual program. So it was held by

Jacobs J in *Ibcos Computers Ltd* v *Barclays Mercantile Highland Finance Ltd* [1994] FSR 275.

To summarise, for copyright to subsist in a computer program or other literary, dramatic or musical work, the work must exhibit the following qualities:

- it must satisfy the qualification requirements (author or country of first publication);
- it must be original;
- it must be a "work" and not be *de minimis*;
- it must be recorded in writing or otherwise.

At this point it should be noted that the test for originality for databases is somewhat different to that for other works. A database is original for copyright purposes only if it is the author's own intellectual creation. This certainly seems to be a higher standard than the traditional test of originality and it is discussed further in the section on databases later in this chapter. Strictly speaking, the same test should be used for computer programs as the same standard was in the Directive on the legal protection of computer programs. However, the implementing regulations did not use this phrase and, to that extent at least did not fully comply with the Directive. In practice, this anomaly should make little difference as all but the very simplest sub-routine in a computer program can be described as an intellectual creation. The same cannot be said of all databases as many are quite simple in their design, such as a mailing list. A new form of protection is provided for such databases which, in spite of their design simplicity, may be commercially valuable.

The basic requirements for subsistence of copyright in artistic works are similar to the position for literary works except there is no express requirement that they be recorded. The very existence of an artistic work suggests some tangible form of expression.

Duration of copyright

The duration of copyright is generous. This can be justified on the grounds that copyright does not grant true monopolies as the independent creation of a similar work will not infringe. That is because infringement, as will be seen later, is based on specific acts in relation to the copyright work or copies of the work. Copyright in computer programs, as with other types of literary works (and dramatic, musical or artistic works), subsists for a period of 70 years from the end of the calendar year during which the author died; section 12(1). This was increased from "life plus 50 years" on 1 January 1996 as a result of compliance with the Directive on the term of copyright and neighbouring rights. As computer-generated works are created in circumstances such that there is no human author, the term of copyright for such works is unchanged at 50 years from the end of the calendar year during which they were created.

If the work is one of joint authorship, as will often be the case in terms of computer programs and other software items, the period of 70 years runs from the end of the calendar year during which the last surviving author dies under section 12(4). There are special provisions in the case of anonymous works and the copyright in such works expires at the end of the period of 70 years from the end of the calendar year in which the work was made. However, if during that period the work was made available to the public, the copyright expires at the end of the period of 70 years from the end of the calendar year in which it was first so made available.

In view of the rapid pace of change and development in the computer industry, the duration of copyright is largely irrelevant as regards computer programs especially as it has been recognised that modifying a computer program can give rise to a fresh copyright; Jacob J in *Ibcos Computers Ltd* v *Barclays Mercantile Highland Finance Ltd* [1994] FSR 275. It will be almost beyond doubt, even in years to come, that a computer program that is still in use will be subject to some unexpired copyrights. However, it could be relevant in terms of other forms of computer software such as where a publisher wishes to publish on CD-ROM substantial extracts from some old music or a novel or a compilation of old works. The publication of older works on computer media is becoming increasingly common, for example, in the case of a multimedia encyclopaedia.

Authorship and ownership of copyright

The identity of the author of a work, being the person who created the work, is important for two reasons. In most cases, for the original works, it is the life of the author upon which the duration of copyright is determined. Secondly, the basic rule is that the author will be the first owner of the copyright by section 11(1) of the Copyright, Designs and Patents Act 1988. To this, however, there are some exceptions. The major exception is where the work has been created by an employee in the course of his employment in which case the employer will be the first owner of the copyright; section 11(2). This is subject to agreement to the contrary and such agreement may be implied as in *Noah* v *Shuba* [1991] FSR 14 where copyright remained with the employee because, in the past, it was accepted that employees could publish works they had created during their employment without interference by the employer.

There are also exceptions in the case of Crown and Parliamentary copyright and works created for certain international organisations such as the United Nations. Thus, by section 163, a work made by Her Majesty or by an officer or servant of the Crown in the course of his duties will be Crown copyright. Such a work will qualify for copyright regardless of the normal rules for qualification. Parliamentary copyright applies where a work is made under the direction or control of either House and, again, the normal qualification requirements do not apply.

Section 91 provides for prospective ownership of copyright and is especially important where a work is being created by a person who is not an employee such as a self-employed consultant. Freelance staff and self-employed consultants are commonplace in the computer software industry and the importance of this provision must not be underestimated. Where such a person is commissioned to create a work of copyright, that person should be asked to assign the future copyright. The agreement must be in writing and be signed by or on behalf of the prospective owner (in this case, the person who will create the work). On the work coming into existence, the copyright subsisting in it will automatically vest in the assignee.

Failure to provide properly for ownership of copyright in works created by a person who is not an employee can cause problems. That person will be the first owner of the copyright at law. Depending on the circumstances, the courts may be prepared to accept that the person who commissioned the creation of the work is the owner of the copyright in equity; that is, the beneficial owner. However, this is far from being a certainty and, in *Saphena Computing* v *Allied Collection Agencies* [1995] FSR 616, the court held at first instance that beneficial ownership would not be appropriate where the creator of the software would want to grant licences to others to use the software. A useful guide to whether beneficial ownership is likely is where the price paid by the person commissioning the work is of the order to be expected if that person was to be granted exclusive rights in the software. If the price is significantly lower than that, an implied non-exclusive licence might be the most apposite result.

Relying on beneficial ownership is unsatisfactory and it is far better to have a formal written assignment of copyright signed by the person commissioned to create the software. A beneficial owner cannot obtain a permanent injunction or damages unless he joins the legal owner in the court action. In any case, the acceptance of beneficial ownership by the courts is uncertain and unpredictable.

The rights of the copyright owner

Section 16 of the Copyright, Designs and Patents Act 1988 lists the acts which only the copyright owner has the exclusive right to do in the United Kingdom. Those acts, referred to as the acts restricted by the copyright, are:

- to copy the work;
- to issue copies of the work to the public;
- to rent or lend the work to the public;
- to perform, show or play the work in public;
- to broadcast the work or include it in a cable programme service;
- to make an adaptation of the work or do any of the above in relation to an adaptation.

Although the Act talks in terms of the United Kingdom only, by virtue of the Berne Copyright Convention and the Universal Copyright Convention, some degree of reciprocity is granted between members of the conventions (the UK belongs to both) and the same rights are granted to nationals from the other states so that, effectively, the copyright owner has the above rights, or their equivalent, in all the other countries in the conventions. There may still be some difficulty, for example, where a member country does not have an equivalent act restricted by copyright or where the duration of the right is less. Nevertheless, a copyright owner will seek to exploit his work on an international scale.

As from 1 December 1996, there is a publication right. This gives a right that lasts for 25 years in respect of unpublished works in which copyright has previously expired and which are subsequently published for the first time. "Publication" includes any communication to the public; in particular, the issue of copies to the public, making the work available by means of an electronic retrieval system, renting or lending copies to the public, performing, exhibiting or showing the work in public, or broadcasting it or including it in a cable programme service.

The right belongs to the person who first published the work with the permission of the person who owns the physical medium on which the work is embodied or recorded; for example, the person who owns an ancient manuscript. This right will be relevant in the context of computer software where previously unpublished old works are made available in digital form.

Infringement of copyright

Copyright is infringed by any person who without the licence of the copyright owner, does or authorises another to do, any of the acts restricted by the copyright; section 16(2). By section 16(3) infringement may be direct or indirect and must involve the whole or any substantial part of the work. Substantiality is generally taken to be a question of quality not quantity; see the judgment of Lord Pearce in *Ladbroke (Football) Ltd* v *William Hill (Football) Ltd* [1964] 1 All ER 465.

For computer programs, the most important acts are those of copying and making an adaptation and these will be dealt with comprehensively below. Issuing copies to the public and rental may also be relevant. However, the right to issue copies to the public only relates to the first issue of the relevant copy and will not apply if the copy has already been issued by the copyright owner or with his consent. For example, a person who buys a copy of a sound recording may resell that copy. The copyright owner's rights are said to be exhausted by the first sale. The same will apply to a computer program providing the licence agreement does not prohibit the assignment of the licence and transfer of the copy of the program and other items supplied. However, a person acquiring a copy of a program, sound recording or film may not rent it or lend it without the copyright owner's permission.

The Act provides for secondary infringements of copyright, some of which (though not all) may also give rise to criminal offences; sections 22 to 26. These infringements can be said to be largely of a commercial nature such as dealing with or importing infringing copies of works (often described as "piracy") or providing premises or apparatus for infringing performances. Also covered is providing the means for making infringing copies, for example, by being in possession of a plate or master copy from which multiple copies will be made. The criminal penalties vary depending on whether the offence is triable either way or summarily only. The maximum penalty that can be imposed for a conviction in the Crown Court is two years' imprisonment and/or a fine; section 107(4). The courts appear to be more willing to sentence software pirates to custodial sentences and some judges have described the activity as a form of theft.

Copying computer programs

For computer programs (and other literary, dramatic, musical and artistic works) copying means reproducing the work in any material form including storing the work in any medium by electronic means; section 17(2). "Electronic" is widely defined in section 178 as being actuated by electric, magnetic, electro-magnetic, electro-chemical or electro-mechanical energy. Copying also includes the making of copies which are transient or incidental to some other use of the work.

The act of reproducing a work in any material form would seem to extend to loading a computer program into a computer. In *Bookmakers' Afternoon Greyhound Services Ltd* v *Wilf Gilbert (Staffordshire) Ltd* [1994] FSR 723, it was held that displaying a work on a display monitor was a reproduction in a material form for the purposes of the Copyright Act 1956. The 1988 Act should not be any different in this respect and, in any case, under the 1988 Act, loading a program into a computer would be making a transient copy which itself infringes.

The scope of the act of copying will not be in doubt where a duplicate copy of a program is made, say, by disk to disk copying. In such cases, it will be simply a matter of whether a substantial part has been taken. Where difficulties can and do arise is where the second program is not an exact copy. This may be a result of a program being re-written in a different computer language by a process of manual conversion by a programmer. The programmer will use, analyse and inspect the first program to find out what it does and how it does it and, from the knowledge so gleaned, he will write the second program using a different language. It will be a case of copying the structure of the first program, screen displays, data structures and such like and, rather than translating on a line by line basis, it will be more a matter of writing new sub-routines and modules to emulate those in the first program. There will be no or little literal similarity when print outs of the two programs are compared. For obvious reasons, this is known as non-literal copying or, sometimes, look and feel copying. Figure 2.1 shows the difference between literal and non-literal copying. Whether the copying is literal or non-literal, there are important issues to be resolved and both forms of copying deserve further attention. Literal copying will be examined first.

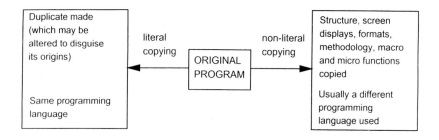

Figure 2.1 Literal and Non-literal Copying of Computer Programs

Literal copying

If it is alleged that a computer program (or a suite of computer programs) has been copied without authorisation there are only the following issues to consider:

- does copyright subsist in the plaintiff's program;
- has the defendant copied from the plaintiff's program; and
- does the part taken represent a substantial part of the plaintiff's program?

If the answer to all of these questions is in the affirmative then, unless the defendant can rely on a defence to infringement such as one of the permitted acts, infringement is proved. In practice, seldom will the answer to the first question be negative as even relatively small programs will be the result of skill, effort and judgment.

In *Ibcos Computers Ltd* v *Barclays Mercantile Highland Finance Ltd* [1994] FSR 275, the plaintiff's computer software comprised 335 programs, 171 record layout files and 46 screen layouts. Jacob J said that copying was a question of fact and could be proved by showing that something trivial or unimportant had been copied. There were a number of spelling mistakes common to both the plaintiff's and defendant's programs and, in the absence of a plausible explanation, this was sufficient to prove disk to disk copying. Both sets of programs also contained the same redundant code. On the question of substantiality, Jacob J stressed the importance of expert evidence in this respect. He decided that 28 out of 55 of the defendant's programs infringed the plaintiff's copyrights. He also found that a later version of the defendant's programs infringed the plaintiff's copyrights. Additionally, it was held that the defendant was guilty of a breach of confidence.

Whilst thoroughly reviewing copyright law in the context of computer programs and commenting on earlier cases (often in a critical way) Jacob J made some other interesting points as follows:

- US copyright law is different from UK copyright law and the use of US precedents was of doubtful value. In particular, the US test for non-literal copying was not helpful (however, on this point it should be noted that the *Ibcos* case was concerned with literal copying);
- fresh copyright may be created when a program is modified;
- a file record may not be a program within the Act but it will be a compilation;
- the inclusion of functional elements that could only be expressed in one, or a limited number of ways, does not affect the fact of copyright subsistence;
- where the evidence clearly indicates copying but this is denied by the defendant, the court should infer that similarities are the result of copying and not due to programming style unless independent evidence suggests otherwise (this is particularly relevant where the defendant previously was involved in creating the plaintiff's programs, as is often the case);
- the data division of a COBOL program can be a substantial part of a program; and
- the right to repair principle in *British Leyland* (see Chapter 4) did not permit the copying of a file transfer program.

Non-literal copying

As regards non-literal copying, the scope of copyright protection for computer programs remains a difficult and controversial issue, for example, where the flow or structure of a program is copied along with other elements such as a menu system or sequence of operations. An important test for giving effect to copyright protection, particularly in the United States (though not without some judicial approval in the UK) is the classification of a work, or parts of it, as idea or expression. A basic, though some would say, naive, rule is that copyright protects expression not idea. Ideas alone are not protected by copyright and, consequently, if a particular thing can only be expressed in one way because the form and character of the expression is dictated by an idea, then even that expression is not protected by copyright. However, it is true to say that this approach, popular as it is in the United States, is not on all fours with UK law. Nevertheless, it will be useful to consider the distinction between idea and expression.

Idea/expression dichotomy

It could be said that denying copyright to ideas is implicit in UK law as the Copyright, Designs and Patents Act 1988 requires that literary, dramatic or musical works are recorded in writing or otherwise. They must, therefore, have some form of tangible expression. There are also a number of judicial statements to this effect, for example, in *University of London Press Ltd* v *University Tutorial Press Ltd* [1916] 2 Ch 601, Peterson J said:

> "Copyright Acts are not concerned with the originality of ideas, but with the expression of thought."

In an earlier case, *Kenrick* v *Lawrence* (1890) 25 QBD 93, it was held that there was no infringement of copyright in a drawing showing a hand marking a ballot paper which was intended to show people how to vote. Any artist set the same task, that is, to create a drawing to show semi-literate persons how to vote, would come up with a similar drawing. (The law report states that the intention of the drawing was to show *illiterate* persons how to vote. But, if they were truly illiterate, how would they know who they were voting for?) However, it was said, that there would have been an infringement if the plaintiff's drawing had been slavishly copied. This shows a distinction between UK and US copyright law. In the United Kingdom it is more to do with the weight to be given to evidence of similarity rather than whether the work is protected by copyright.

"Look and feel"

If it is accepted that copyright protects expression but not idea, it is important to be able to distinguish between them. If parts of a computer program have been copied, the court must be able to apply a test to determine whether those parts are idea or expression. This issue first was considered in relation to computer programs in the US case of *Whelan Associates Inc* v *Jaslow Dental Laboratory Inc* [1987] FSR 1. The same person had been involved in the development of the two programs (the function of which was to administer dental laboratories) but, as they had been written in different languages, a line for line comparison was of no assistance. The court had to focus attention on non-literal elements such as the program's structure; its look and feel.

In finding for the plaintiff, the court held that, in relation to a computer program designed to carry out a mundane task anything which was essential to the task was idea whilst anything which was not essential, and could have been written in different ways, was expression. If these latter parts were copied, then copyright would be infringed because the expression had been copied. If the programmer had no option but to write a part of the program the way he did because it was dictated by the task then that part was idea and not protected by copyright. Similarly, the purpose of a utilitarian program was idea but the structure of the program, if there were several different possible structures which could have been adopted, was expression. The existence of design freedom, therefore, is indicative of copyright subsistence.

The look and feel test as enunciated in *Whelan* v *Jaslow* was criticised strongly by the New York Court of Appeals in *Computer Associates International Inc* v *Altai* (1992) 20 USPQ 2d 1641. The defendant had a program called "Oscar", a job scheduling program for controlling the order in which tasks are carried out by a computer. The program contained a common interface component permitting it to be used with different operating systems. The plaintiff had an equivalent program. One of the plaintiff's programmers was very familiar with this and even took the program home to work on. He left the employment of the plaintiff to work for the defendant and when he was asked to assist in writing "Oscar", he made use of parts of the plaintiff's program. When the plaintiff complained of copyright infringement, the defendant re-wrote "Oscar", using different programmers in a "clean-room" environment in an effort to avoid infringing the plaintiff's copyright. However, the plaintiff still complained of infringement even though the defendant had agreed not to challenge an award of $364,444 damages in respect of the earlier version of "Oscar". The trial judge held that the later version of "Oscar" did not infringe the plaintiff's copyright and the plaintiff appealed to the Court of Appeals which confirmed the decision of the trial judge but, in doing so, the court laid down an important new test for infringement by non-literal copying. The test requires a three-step procedure.

- Abstraction – discovering the non-literal elements of the plaintiff's program by a process not unlike reverse engineering, beginning with the code and ending with the program's ultimate function. The designer's steps are retraced and mapped. This produces structures and other non-literal elements of different detail at varying levels of abstraction.
- Filtration – the separation of protectable expression from non-protectable material. Some elements will be unprotected being idea, dictated by considerations of efficiency (therefore necessarily incidental to idea), required by external factors or taken from the public domain. These elements are filtered out leaving a core of protectable material (this is the program's "golden nugget").
- Comparison – a determination of whether the defendant has copied a substantial part of the protected expression – whether any aspect has been copied and, if so, an assessment of the copied portion's relative importance in respect of the plaintiff's overall program.

The judges in the Court of Appeals recognised that, initially, this new test would be difficult to apply and further case law would be needed before its application could be predicted with any certainty.

Look and feel in the United Kingdom

The decision in *Computer Associates* v *Altai* was expressly approved and partly applied in the United Kingdom in the case of *John Richardson Computers Ltd* v *Flanders* [1993] FSR 497. The plaintiff's program was written in assembly language (a low-level language) and the defendant's program was written in QuickBASIC (a high-level language). Because of the differing nature of the programming languages there could be no significant literal similarities between the two programs Therefore, the judge had to consider non-literal elements, such as structure, sequence, input and output routines and formats, facilities and options. Ferris J said:

> "There is thus nothing in any English decision which conflicts with the general approach adopted in the Computer Associates case ... in my judgment it would be right to adopt a similar approach in England. This means that consideration is not restricted to the text of the code."

He did not, however, otherwise apply the test as set out in the US Court of Appeals he simply used it as authority for the protection of non-literal elements of computer programs.

Ferris J identified 17 objective similarities in the non-literal elements of the programs and then went on to consider the reasons for the similarities which he classified as follows:

- similarities that were the result of copying a substantial part of the plaintiff's program, it was in respect of these parts that copyright infringement was found;
- similarities that were the result of copying but not in relation to a substantial part of the plaintiff's program;
- similarities that *might* have been the result of copying but, in any case, only related to an insubstantial part of the plaintiff's program;
- similarities that were not the result of copying.

The line editor, amendment routines and dose codes were deemed to have been copied and to represent a substantial part of the plaintiff's program. Thus, there was a partial infringement of the copyright subsisting in the plaintiff's program. Possible explanations for an objective similarity are indicated in Figure 2.2.

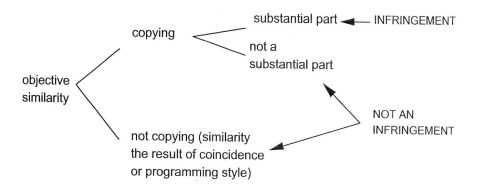

Figure 2.2 Explanations for an Objective Similarity

Making an adaptation of a computer program

The meaning of making an adaptation was altered as a result of compliance with the EC Directive on the legal protection of computer programs (OJ 1991 L122/42). Now, by section 21(3)(ab) of the Copyright, Designs and Patents Act 1988, an adaptation of a computer program means: "an arrangement or altered version of the program or a translation of it."

Previously, an adaptation was simply a translation. For computer programs, by section 21(4), a translation includes (the words in square brackets were repealed by the Copyright (Computer Programs) Regulations 1992 which implemented the Directive):

> "a version of the program in which it is converted into or out of a computer language or code or into a different computer language or code[, otherwise than incidentally in the course of running the program]."

It is arguable that the look and feel approach to non-literal copying is not required as such copying would fall within the meaning of making an adaptation. The new program would fall to be treated as an arrangement or altered version of the first program. However, where the restricted act of making an adaptation is particularly useful is where a copy of a program is automatically translated into a different form of computer code; for example, where a source code program is converted into object code and vice versa. Thus, compilation and decompilation of computer programs will infringe unless done with the authorisation of the copyright owner. The ability to control decompilation is particularly important as this act makes the ideas, principles and interfaces in a program more transparent. It also assists in the process of correcting errors in the program. However, the ability of the copyright owner to control decompilation has been prejudiced by the inclusion of a new permitted act allowing a lawful user to decompile a computer program under certain tightly drawn circumstances, as will be seen later.

Remedies for copyright infringement

Remedies for copyright infringement are specified in section 96 of the Copyright, Designs and Patents Act 1988 as damages, injunctions, accounts or otherwise as is available in respect of the infringement of any other property right. By section 97(1), damages are not available if, at the time of the infringement, the defendant did not know, and had no reason to believe, that copyright subsisted in the work. Whether a person has reason to believe is determined objectively by considering whether a reasonable person, with knowledge of the facts known to the infringer, would have believed copyright subsisted in the work.

Additional damages may be available in exceptional cases, taking into account the flagrancy of the infringement and the benefit accruing to the defendant by section 97(2). Additional damages, although not punitive damages strictly speaking, are designed to deter blatant and cynical infringements, where the defendant is likely to benefit to a greater extent than would normally be recoverable in the form of ordinary damages. Orders for delivery up are provided for by section 98. Damages and accounts of profit are alternatives but additional damages may only be claimed where the claim is for damages, not an account; *Redrow Homes Ltd* v *Betts Brothers plc* [1998] FSR 345.

By section 101, exclusive licensees can sue for infringement of copyright. Normally, the copyright owner will be joined in the action and, if not, the leave of the court is required for the exclusive licensee to proceed on his own.

Permitted acts

An infringement of copyright may be excused on the basis of public interest, such as where a person reproduces a computer program designed to assist computer hackers in order to warn computer managers of the dangers. It may also be possible to imply the copyright owner's licence in some cases. However, the Act does contain a large number of permitted acts. These are acts that may be done without infringing copyright and they are of some importance. Of course, where the act complained of does not relate to a substantial part of the work, there is no need to rely on the permitted acts as taking an insubstantial part cannot infringe copyright. Thus, these acts must only be relevant where a substantial part of a copyright work is concerned.

The permitted acts include fair dealing for the purposes of research or private study, for criticism, review and news reporting. Other permitted acts deal with matters such as educational and library use, public administration and a great deal of miscellaneous uses of copyright works. Some specific provisions for computer programs were inserted by the Copyright (Computer Programs) Regulations 1992 made in pursuance of the EC Directive on the legal protection of computer programs. They concern decompilation of a computer program for the purpose of achieving interoperability, making necessary back-up copies and making copies or adaptations which are necessary to the lawful use of the program. It is also possible to use any device or means to observe, study or test the functioning of the program in order to understand the ideas and principles which underlie any element it. These special permitted acts for computer programs apply only in the case of lawful users and are considered in detail below. They are indicated in Figure 2.3.

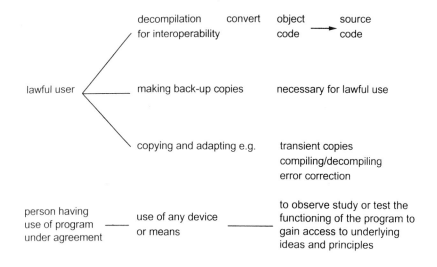

Figure 2.3 The Permitted Acts in Relation to Computer Programs

Lawful users

The three specific permitted acts for computer programs may only be carried out by lawful users. A lawful user is by section 50A(2) of the Copyright, Designs and Patents Act 1988:

> "a person who has a right to use the program, whether under a licence to do any acts restricted by the copyright subsisting in the program or otherwise."

This will extend to licensees and, presumably, to persons acting for the licensee such as employees. Unless prohibited by the licence agreement, it should also apply to agents and independent consultants working for the licensee and to many other persons such as students in respect of a site licence granted to an educational establishment, subscribers to a library or voluntary workers for a charity that has an institutional licence. Others too could fall within the definition of lawful user. It may include a receiver of a company, an external auditor or anyone acting in pursuance of a legal requirement, for example, a person executing a search warrant or Anton Piller Order.

Decompilation of computer programs

Subject to conditions, under section 50B, the permitted act of decompilation allows a lawful user of a copy of a computer program expressed in a low level language:

(a) to convert it into a version expressed in a higher level language, or

(b) incidentally, in the course of so converting the program, to copy it.

The conditions that must apply for decompilation to be permitted by section 50B of the Act are stated in subsection (2) and are that:

"(a) it is necessary to decompile the program to obtain the information necessary to create an independent program which can be operated with the program decompiled or with another program ('the permitted objective'); and

(b) the information so obtained is not used for any purpose other than the permitted objective."

By section 50B(3), those conditions cannot be met if the lawful user has readily available to him the information necessary to achieve the permitted objective; if he does not confine the act of decompiling to that objective; if he supplies the information to any person to whom it is not necessary to supply it in order to achieve that objective or if he uses the information to create a program which is substantially similar in its expression to the decompiled program or to do any act restricted by copyright.

The permitted act of decompilation cannot be prohibited or restricted by any term or condition in an agreement. Any term in a licence agreement purporting to do this is void and unenforceable, unless the agreement was entered into before 1 January 1993, the date these provisions came into force. This is an important point to bear in mind in drafting licence agreements.

Prior to the changes to the Copyright, Designs and Patents Act 1988, it was possible that the fair dealing provisions would have been interpreted so as to allow decompilation broadly in line with that now expressly provided for. In the United States, the fair use defence was available to excuse the decompilation of a whole range of computer games cartridges in *Sega Enterprises Ltd* v *Accolade Inc* (1992) US App LEXIS 26645. The plaintiff was not even allowed to rely on his trade mark to prevent use of the interface information by the defendant in the making of games compatible with the plaintiff's games console. The trade mark was displayed on the screen even when the defendant's games were being played.

Back-up copies of computer programs

Section 50A of the Copyright, Designs and Patents Act 1988 permits the making of back-up copies if necessary for the purposes of the lawful use of a copy of a computer program by a lawful user. As with the decompilation exception to infringement, this cannot be taken away by any term or condition in an agreement and any such term, in so far as it purports to prohibit or restrict the exercise of this act, is void and unenforceable providing the agreement was made on or after 1 January 1993. There may be some question about what is meant by "necessary". It could be interpreted as being "essential" or, if the reader will pardon the pleonasm, "absolutely essential". If this is so, the permitted act will rarely apply as, however desirable and sensible it is to make a back up copy, it could seldom be so described. A better view is to consider the word "necessary" qualified by "reasonably" thereby producing the near oxymoron "reasonably necessary" which accords to the court's approach to the similarly uncompromising word "dictated" which was held by the House of Lords in *Amp Inc* v *Utilux Pty Ltd* [1972] RPC 103 to have a less than dictatorial meaning. Otherwise, the relevant provision in the Registered Designs Act 1949 would have been reduced "almost to vanishing point" in the words of Lord Reid. As this case also involved an exception to an intellectual property right, it would appear to be very good authority for a realistic view to be taken of the word "necessary".

Prior to this amendment, there was no equivalent statutory provision although, in the absence of an express term to the contrary, the courts would probably have been prepared to imply an appropriate term into a software licence where the making of a back-up copy was reasonable in the circumstances. Of course, many software companies make express provision allowing the user to make one or more back-up copies. It is common for the installation instructions to ask the licensed user to make a copy of the program first and use this as the working copy, placing the original disks in a safe place in case the working disks become damaged or corrupted.

Copying and adapting

A licence in respect of a computer program will normally state the acts that may be done by the licensee in relation to the program. If it is silent about some particular act that is within the spirit of the agreement, then the courts would imply the appropriate terms permitting that act and any necessary intermediate acts. Section 50C, in effect, puts this on a statutory footing by allowing a lawful user of a copy of a computer program to copy it or adapt it if that is necessary for his lawful use. Copying or adapting for the purpose of error correction may fall within this exception to infringement and is given as a particular example in section 50C(2) of the Copyright, Designs and Patents Act 1988.

It is common for agreements regulating the lawful use of computer programs to contain a term prohibiting modification by the client and such terms are not controlled by the Act as amended. Unlike the two other permitted acts for computer programs, the Act does not state that it cannot be prohibited or restricted by a term in a licence or otherwise. Therefore, under the provisions of the Act, it would appear that a licence agreement can contain a term prohibiting copying or modification for the purposes of error correction. Indeed, it may become usual for a licence agreement to state that the licensed program may not be decompiled except in accordance with section 50B of the Copyright, Designs and Patents Act 1988. However, such terms, seeking to prevent modification by or on behalf of the licensee, might be controlled in other ways under common law.

In *Saphena Computing Ltd* v *Allied Collection Agencies Ltd* [1995] FSR 616 the Court of Appeal had an opportunity to consider the position at common law with respect to modification and error correction of licensed computer programs. In that case, the licensee had been given a copy of the source code by the licensor and there was, consequentially, an implied undertaking that the licensee could use it for error correction. While the licensor was still testing and modifying the software, the agreement was determined and it was held that the licensee could continue to use the source code for the purpose of error correction but could not use it for other modifications and improvements to the program. However, it was said that there was not an implied duty on a licensor to supply the source code if the agreement only provided for the supply of object code, as is normal practice.

What is the position if the supplier is no longer able or willing to provide error correction? The principle of non-derogation from grant could be applicable with the result that the client can maintain the program himself or approach third parties with a view to their maintaining it. Even if the supplier is prepared to maintain the program and correct errors (for example, by offering a collateral maintenance contract) the licensee may be able to approach others for this service as the non-derogation principle could still apply. Although of worthy pedigree, this principle first saw the light of day in the context of copyright in *British Leyland Motor Corp Ltd* v *Armstrong Patents Co Ltd* [1986] 2 WLR 400, where the House of Lords applied the principle to prevent restriction on a free market in spare parts and extended their refusal to enforce copyright to the manufacturers of spare parts and not just to the purchaser of the relevant article. Their Lordships spoke in terms of articles which, by their nature, would require the fitting of replacement parts during their normal lifespan.

The *British Leyland* principle is most apposite in terms of computer programs as the vast majority contain errors, a number of which might not be discovered for some considerable time, and the lawful user of the program will require work to be done to it in order to correct those errors. The owner of the copyright subsisting in the program should not be able to use his right to prevent the lawful user asking other persons to repair the program otherwise the copyright owner could charge exorbitant prices for this work and the lawful user would have little option but to pay. The alternative would be to abandon using the program, something which might be unthinkable after the client has become dependent upon the program and altered his business methods in reliance of its continued use. However, in *Canon Kabushiki Kaisha* v *Green Cartridge Co (Hong Kong) Ltd* [1997] FSR 817, on appeal from Hong Kong, the Judicial Committee of the Privy Council took a cautious approach to *British Leyland*. It may be more limited in scope than might have appeared. The Privy Council did not apply the principle in a case of copying toner cartridges for photocopying machines and laser printers. It said, unlike the case with replacement exhaust pipes for motor cars, persons buying photocopies and laser printers would take into account the cost of replacement cartridges over the life of the machine when making their buying decision. It is arguable that the same could be said in terms of maintenance of computer software.

If the software company is a large undertaking, licensing software within the European Community, it is possible that a term in a licence agreement prohibiting error correction by the client or a third party would be void by virtue of Article 85(1) or Article 86 of the Treaty of Rome (EC). These provisions control restrictive trading agreements and abuses of dominant trading positions.

On the one hand, there ought to be a free market in the maintenance of computer programs. However, it may be more difficult to rely on the doctrine of non-derogation from grant if the licensee has expressly agreed not to modify or allow third parties to modify the programs covered by the licence agreement. When one contemplates that a licence agreement is not restrictive *per se* because it grants rights that the licensee would not otherwise have (see *Re Ravenseft Properties Ltd's Application* [1978] QB 52 and *Volvo AB v Erik Veng (UK) Ltd* [1989] 4 CMLR 122), dependence upon the doctrine alone is foolhardy. In practice, the question of error correction should be considered fully and provided for in an appropriate fashion at the outset. This is far better than hoping that a court will be prepared to apply the doctrine of non-derogation from grant, particularly after the *Canon* case, which is highly persuasive although not binding on the English courts.

Moral rights

The Copyright, Designs and Patents Act 1988 provides for moral rights for authors and film directors. These are especially important when the author is not the owner of the copyright (previously a film director was not the author of a film but now is, jointly, with the producer). The moral rights apply only to literary, dramatic, musical, artistic works and films and are:

- a right to be identified as the author of a work (or director of a film); section 77;
- a right not to have a work subject to derogatory treatment (such as is prejudicial to the honour or reputation of the author or director); section 80;
- a right not to have a work falsely attributed by section 84 (this was also available under the Copyright Act 1956, see *Moore v News of the World* [1972] 1 QB 441 and *Noah v Shuba* [1991] FSR 14).

There is also a right to privacy in relation to certain commissioned photographs and films. Moral rights survive the death of the right owner. The right to be identified, the right to object to a derogatory treatment of a work and the right of privacy of certain photographs and films last as long as the copyright lasts. The false attribution right lasts for 20 years after the person's death.

Moral rights may not be assigned but will pass on the death of the author or director by testamentary disposition or to the deceased's estate; section 94. Moral rights may be waived by the author or film director. Unfortunately, the moral rights of identification and objection to derogatory treatment do not apply in respect of certain works including computer programs and computer-generated works; see sections 79(2) and 81(2). As other forms of works stored in a computer, including databases, may be subject to moral rights, great care must be taken to ensure that the rights or their waiver are provided for accordingly. For example, if a self-employed computer programmer creates a new program and a database he will have moral rights in respect of the database. It is entirely possible to falsely attribute either a computer program or a computer-generated work.

Employees, as regards things done by or with the authority of the employer, do not have a right to be identified in respect of works created in the course of employment where the copyright originally vested in the employer. To be effective, the right to be identified as author or director must be asserted. This may be done in a licence agreement or otherwise. By section 103, an infringement of a moral right is actionable as a breach of statutory duty owed to the person entitled to the right.

Dealing with copyright

A copyright is a valuable form of intellectual property and, as such, it can be dealt with in a number of ways. It may be assigned or licensed. Alternatively, it may be used as security for a loan. In terms of software, assignments and licensing are most common but there are certain formalities that must be complied with for an assignment or exclusive licence to take effect at law. By section 90, copyright is transmissible by assignment, testamentary disposition or by operation of law. An assignment must be made in writing and be signed by or on behalf of the assignor to be effective; section 90(3). Failure to comply with this simple formality will result, at best, with the purported assignment transferring beneficial ownership only. Whilst this may be satisfactory as between the parties, it can be difficult for the assignee to take effective action against a third party infringer unless the legal owner is joined in any court action.

Prospective ownership of copyright is provided for by section 91. The agreement must be in writing and be signed by or on behalf of the prospective owner. On the work coming into existence, the copyright in it will automatically vest in the assignee or his successor in title. A licence granted by a prospective owner of copyright is binding on his successors in title just as is the case with licences granted by owners of copyright in existing works.

Assignments may be partial and may be limited in terms of duration; section 90(2). Also, an assignment may be limited in geographical scope although this is not mentioned in the Act. For example, the first owner of a copyright subsisting in an item of computer software may grant an assignment to a company in Australia permitting it to grant licences in Australia and New Zealand in respect of the software. This will leave the first owner free to grant licences to others elsewhere.

In a great many cases, the copyright owner will grant licences in respect of the copyright whilst retaining ownership. A licence may be exclusive or non-exclusive and may be partial or restricted in scope just as an assignment. An exclusive licence may be very similar in effect to an assignment and, by section 92, must be in writing, signed by or on behalf of the copyright owner. Failure to comply with this requirement probably will result in a non-exclusive licence being granted instead, although the doctrine of non-derogation from grant might apply. Non-exclusive licences are used when the copyright owner wants to distribute copies of his work to a number of persons when the use of the copies involves an act restricted by the copyright, for example, as is the case with computer programs.

There are some important provisions in respect of exclusive licenses. An exclusive licensee has the same rights and remedies as does the copyright owner as if the licence had been an assignment; section 101. Those rights are concurrent with those of the copyright owner. Normally, an exclusive licensee will sue for infringement after joining the copyright owner. Alternatively, the owner may sue after joining the exclusive licensee. Leave of the court is required for either to proceed without joining the other as plaintiff or adding him as defendant.

An assignment should normally be paid for by way of a lump sum fee whereas it is common for royalties to be paid for a licence. However, these are not hard and fast rules and a number of different payment mechanisms may be used. For example, a licence could be granted for one year renewable for an annual fee of £5,000. One difficulty to be aware of is that of privity of contract, especially in terms of an assignment to be paid for by a royalty. If the copyright is subsequently assigned to a third party or passes by operation of law, such in the case of the bankruptcy of the assignee, it could prove difficult to enforce the royalty against the new owner. In terms of a licence, it is easier to provide that the licence is not assignable or that it terminates on the insolvency, etc of the licensee.

EC and international aspects

The exploitation of any item or product in which intellectual property rights subsist will require, inevitably, a consideration of EC and other international aspects. The world is slowly approaching a global village in terms of minimum standards of recognition of intellectual property rights as witnessed by the "TRIPS" agreement (Agreement on Trade-Related Aspects of Intellectual Property Rights, administered by the World Trade Organisation). The importance of international considerations becomes clear when the fact that most items of software can be transmitted across the world in a few seconds by virtue of computer networks such as the Internet.

EC Law

European Community law may be relevant to the subsistence of rights in copyright and to the exploitation of copyright in a number of ways. Harmonisation has already had a major impact on national copyright laws. Competition law can also be relevant and is likely to grow in importance. This is of particular relevance in terms of licences in respect of the provisions in Article 85(1) of the Treaty of Rome prohibiting restrictive trade practices, concerted practices and the like and Article 86 which controls abuses of dominant positions. Although copyright is not, strictly speaking, a monopoly right in a true sense, Article 86 may be particularly relevant where information has one source only. In *RTE & ITP* v *Commission* [1995] FSR 530, the European Court of Justice held that failure to license advance information relating to forthcoming television programmes to publishers of magazines containing information and timetables of programmes was an abuse under Article 86. The provision may apply, therefore, where someone has a database containing information not available elsewhere and who licenses copies to some organisations but refuses to grant licences to others.

Article 86 could also apply where a supplier of software that has become an officially recognised or *de facto* standard acquires competing companies with a view to driving up the price of its software. The teeth of the Commission of the European Communities and the European Court of Justice are sharp. In a case involving the leading manufacturer of aseptic cartons for drinks, the fine imposed for an abuse under Article 86 was 75 million ECU (approximately £50m at present rates).

Although the prohibitions in Articles 85 and 86 only apply where trade between Member States is likely to be affected, the European Court of Justice has demonstrated impressive imagination in finding this to be possible.

Article 30 of the EC Treaty may also be relevant in appropriate circumstances. It prohibits quantitative restrictions on imports and measures having equivalent effect. This gives rise to the doctrine of exhaustion of rights. Once the right owner has placed items on the market (or they have been put on the market by his consent, for example, by a licensee) his right is said to be exhausted and he can no longer use that right to prevent the subsequent importation and re-sale of the items concerned. He will, however, still be able to control rental and lending unless, of course, he also granted these rights when he put the items on the market.

International

There are two international copyright conventions, the Berne Copyright Convention which dates from 1886 and has well in excess of 100 Member States and the Universal Copyright Convention which is of younger pedigree dating from 1952. The United Kingdom belongs to both conventions. Broadly, the purpose of the conventions is to provide for limited harmonisation and reciprocal protection. For example, the basic copyright provisions of the Copyright, Designs and Patents Act 1988 are extended to countries which are members of the Berne Convention (and the Rome Convention for the Protection of Performers, Producers of Phonograms and Broadcasting Organisations, as appropriate). This is done by extending the provisions relating to qualification for copyright to these countries and others which provide adequate protection to owners of copyright under the 1988 Act. One of the first cases in the United Kingdom brought on the basis of the Berne Convention was *Hanfstaengl* v *Empire Palace* [1894] 2 Ch 1 in which a German citizen sued for an alleged infringement of his artistic copyright, albeit unsuccessfully (although it was accepted that he had the right to sue as a result of the Convention, it was held by the Court of Appeal that there had been no infringement of the copyright).

Harmonisation of copyright is not complete and this weakens international protection. In *Rowe* v *Walt Disney Productions* [1987] FSR 36, heard in the Cour d'Appel in Paris, it was argued that moral rights under French law had been infringed, including the author's right to integrity. However, the plaintiff's claim failed because of a number of factors, none the least being that the original assignment was subject to English law and the then current English copyright legislation, the Copyright Act 1956, unlike the present Act, did not provide for moral rights.

Preparatory design materials

The finished code of the computer program is the culmination of a long and arduous design process which involves the creation of a number of preparatory works. For example, specifications will have been written, flowcharts will have been produced showing the sequence of operations and their structural relationship, diagrams and written descriptions made for the design of any database to be used by the program, layouts designed for the screen displays and reports to be produced by the operation of the program. All of these preparatory materials will represent a considerable amount of work and, before the changes made to the Copyright, Designs and Patents Act 1988, would have been protected by copyright in their own right, providing they were the result of a minimum of skill, effort and judgment. Literary copyright would subsist in written materials and artistic copyright would subsist in diagrams and flowcharts (and, possibly also artistic copyright). However, by virtue of the changes made by the Copyright (Computer Programs) Regulations 1992, in pursuance of the EC Directive on the legal protection of computer programs, preparatory design material for a computer program is now protected by copyright in its own right as a literary work. Such material is now within the definition of literary works in section 3(1)(c). However, there is a conflict here with the wording of Article 1(1) of the Directive which states that the term "computer programs" shall include their preparatory design material although, in practice, this is unlikely to have any significant consequences.

Preparatory design material may be delivered under the licence agreement, particularly where the source code is provided and the licensee is permitted to modify any supplied programs. In terms of modifying computer programs, the presence of good quality preparatory materials makes the operation much easier and less prone to errors. Any licence agreement under which source code is delivered should make it clear whether preparatory design material is also to be delivered to the licensee.

Computer programming languages and instruction sets

In general terms, a programming language is a set of instructions, commands and arithmetical functions that can be used by the programmer to develop a program to perform any task whatsoever. An instruction set can be thought of as a particularised programming language developed for one function or set of functions only; for example, the set of instructions for a microprocessor of a washing machine controller. Considerable skill, effort and judgment is expended in the development of computer programming languages and instruction sets. The question of copyright protection for an instruction set was considered in *Microsense Systems Ltd* v *Control Systems Technology Ltd* (unreported) 17 June 1991, Chancery Division. The plaintiff made traffic control systems and a control unit for pelican crossings. An instruction set of mnemonics (a set of three letter symbols) was devised and these were used to program individual pelican crossings and to monitor their operation. The defendant made similar control units and used 49 of the plaintiff's mnemonics. The defendant submitted that copyright did not subsist in the mnemonics because once the functions to be performed had been decided, there was no room for skill and judgment in devising the mnemonics, some of which were obvious (for example, SUN for Sunday). Judge Paul Baker thought that there was an arguable case that copyright did subsist in the list of mnemonics because of the work in designing the control unit and its functions in the first place.

The EC Directive on the legal protection of computer programs stated that programming languages, at least to the extent that they comprise ideas and principles, should not be protected by copyright. However, there is still an incentive to create new programming languages because usually the program, once written, can only be operated in a computer if it is converted into object code whether temporarily, using an interpreter program, or permanently, using a compiler program. The licensing of these interpreter and compiler programs, together with appropriate documentation describing the syntax, semantics and use of the language is the method by which financial reward for the work of creation of the language is sought.

These programs are, of course, protected by copyright. However, that does not prevent another person writing a competing compiler program providing that person does not copy the first program.

Computer-generated works

The Copyright, Designs and Patents Act 1988 contains provisions for "computer-generated works". These are works generated by a computer in circumstances such that there is no human author; section 178. Because there is no human author by definition, there are special rules dealing with authorship and duration of copyright. The person by whom the arrangements necessary for the creation of the work are undertaken is deemed the author under section 9(3) (this is the same formula as applies to sound recordings) and, under section 12(3), the duration of the copyright in a computer-generated work runs for 50 years from the end of the calendar year during which the work was made. It is questionable whether there can ever be such a thing as a computer-generated work as all works owe their creation to the skill and ingenuity of a human being, albeit indirect in some cases.

Computer-generated works prior to the 1988 Act

Indirect human authorship was recognised prior to the 1988 Act, as a case where letters were selected at random by a programmed computer amply demonstrates. In *Express Newspapers plc* v *Liverpool Daily Post & Echo plc* [1985] 1 WLR 1089, the defendant claimed that grids of letters produced by a programmed computer for a newspaper competition could not be protected by copyright because the grids had no human author. This argument was rejected by Whitford J who said that the programmed computer was no more than a tool with which the winning sequences of letters were produced using the instructions of a programmer who was the author of the grids. He said that the defence submission that there was no human author was as unrealistic as saying that a pen was the author of a work of literature.

What is a "computer-generated work"?

There are two possibilities. First, the provisions in the Act concerning computer-generated works are redundant because there can never be such a thing as a computer-generated work or, secondly, that the Copyright, Designs and Patents Act 1988 overrules the *Express Newspapers* case because it is inconsistent with it. If human authorship can be found in a list of letters drawn randomly by a programmed computer, there seems to be little possibility of a work being considered to be "computer-generated" within the meaning of the Act because it is difficult to think of a work where the direct human contribution is less. On the other hand, if the concept of a computer-generated work within the Act is accepted the problem becomes one of drawing a line between works which are computer-generated and those which are not.

Works created with the aid of a programmed computer

A document produced using a word processing system or a spreadsheet or database of customers' names and address cannot be computer-generated works because the author is the person using the computer, or the person who wrote the material on paper first for entry by a computer operator. The work owes its existence to the person using the system to create it.

Works created by a programmed computer

It is not an easy matter to think of many examples of works that could qualify as computer-generated works. One example might be a weather forecast that has been generated automatically by a programmed computer receiving signals from satellites. The programs might contain a basic model of the world's weather system and rules for developing and enhancing the model based on data recorded by computer over a period of time. A later version of the weather model may bear little relationship to the first model. Either the new model or the forecasts or both could be deemed to be a computer-generated work. The programmed computer will operate with a minimum of direct human intervention, apart from switching it on, checking supplies of paper and printer ink and carrying out mundane housekeeping operations such as making back-up copies of the programs and data. To make a person responsible for such tasks the author of the work is to fly in the face of common-sense but that is what the Act suggests. Surely, the author or authors should be the persons who originally conceived the idea and fleshed out the way in which it was implemented including developing the initial model, the computer programs and data files. Even after the passage of some time, when the model has been re-written by the programs in the computer, these persons can still claim a creative link with the computer output.

Intermediate works and expert systems

Even if the concept of computer-generated works is accepted, a third type of work may prove problematic in terms of identifying the author or authors of the work. Intermediate works can be said to be those in which the human expertise required to produce the work flows from more than one source. The output is the result of a combination of the skill and effort of the person operating the programmed computer and that of the person who wrote the computer program and, in some cases, that of the maker of a database. There are a number of examples of these intermediate works, for example, a specialised accounting system for a particular business or type of business or an estimating program used to create the cost of a project based upon standard rates and prices which are manipulated, modified and added to create an overall cost report. The reports and other output created by the use of such systems cannot be considered as computer-generated works because there is some direct human intervention and decision-making. The difficulty is whether the computer programmer or database creator have any rights in the works created using the particular computer program because of their indirect contribution.

Expert systems are used to provide advice at or approaching the level of an expert. For example, a particular expert system might be used by junior doctors at a hospital to diagnose stomach pains. Expert systems usually comprise a knowledge-base, an inference engine and an explanation interface. The knowledge-base contains the raw material of the expert system; the rules and facts representing the expertise. The knowledge-base will have been developed using experts in the relevant knowledge domain who have worked with knowledge engineers to identify, structure and formalise the knowledge. The inference engine is a computer program which attempts to resolve queries put by the user of the system by using and interacting with the knowledge-base. The inference engine may be either a ready-made program, referred to as a shell, or a program specially written for the particular application. Finally, the interface with the user is simply there to make the system relatively easy to use and to provide a means of inspecting the results and to supply explanations of those results. Typically, the expert system may produce output in the form of a printed report and/or charts and diagrams.

The advice produced by using an expert system is the result of the joint efforts of several persons. For example, the advice may flow from:

- the experts who provided the knowledge contained in the knowledge-base;
- the knowledge engineers who refined and formalised the knowledge;
- the programmers who wrote the computer programs; and
- the person using and interacting with the expert system.

The finished report cannot be computer-generated as the user of the system makes a significant contribution. To attribute authorship solely to the experts and knowledge engineers who developed the knowledge base is unsatisfactory because they have no control over how the system will be used and what responses the user will make. Logically, all those persons listed above are the joint authors. This could lead to all manner of complications regarding the commercial use of expert systems even though the courts might be willing to imply terms, for example, that the licensee is the beneficial owner of the copyright in any output.

In terms of licensing computer software where the identify of the author and hence the first owner of the copyright in any report or other output created using the software is in doubt, it is important to make suitable express provision for ownership in the licence agreement.

Other works stored in computers

All manner of works may be stored in a computer in digital form: documents, music, paintings, drawings, diagrams, sculptures, photographs, sound, video works, etc. In many cases, the storage of such works in a computer or on computer storage media will have no particular consequences in terms of copyright, apart from making them easier to copy and transmit. Collections of such works are likely to have a separate an independent copyright as a database (and/or database right; see p 53). The provider of such a database must, therefore, ensure that all the necessary permissions have been obtained from the owners of rights subsisting in the individual works contained therein. There are, however, some problems in terms of artistic works associated with electronic storage.

The essential feature about a graphic work is that it is something to be looked at; so held Jacob J in *Anacon Corp Ltd* v *Environmental*

Research Technology Ltd [1994] FSR 659. In that case, making electronic circuit boards from circuit diagrams did not infringe the artistic copyright in the diagrams because the finished circuit boards looked nothing like the diagram which was intended to show the logical circuit. However, it was held that the diagram was also a literary work, being something that would be read by the person making a circuit board. Applying the reasoning of Jacob J, digitising an artistic work does not infringe copyright. Converting a painting or other artistic work into a digital representation is not copying because the digitised form looks nothing like the artistic work. Of course, reproducing the work from such digital form will infringe as it is immaterial whether any intermediate acts themselves infringe copyright under section 16(3). The danger is that someone might find a particular use for the work in its digital form. For example, a collection of digitised artistic works created by a particular artist might be used to determine a set of rules defining the style of that artist without the necessity of reproducing the work in visual form. However, it is strongly submitted that the view of Jacob J on the necessity for a copy of an artistic work to look like the original is wrong under the 1988 Act.

The definition of copying in relation to literary, dramatic, musical or artistic works is, under section 17(2), reproducing the work in any material form including storing the work by electronic means. In the *Anacon* case, Jacob J was influenced by the view of the Privy Council in *Interlego AG v Tyco Industries Inc* [1989] AC 217 in which the copying of an artistic work was considered. However, this case was concerned with the Copyright Act 1956 which did not mention electronic storage. From the plain language of section 17(2) it is clear that digitising an artistic work infringes copyright.

Licence agreements must take account of any deficiencies in or doubts about the scope of particular provisions of copyright law and make contractual provision for any use of the work envisaged and place a duty on the licensee not to do anything inconsistent with it. For example the licensor might want to prohibit the distribution of artistic works in digital form, delivered as part of the licensed software, to third parties without the licensor's written consent.

Databases

A database is a collection of data or information stored in a computer or on computer storage media. It may be a list of clients and their addresses, a schedule of rates and prices, a list of a store's current stock, a collection of poems, phrases or other works of literature, a collection of images of works of art, or a collection of music in digital form, and so on. Copyright is important in three senses as far as databases are concerned. First, individual works in which copyright subsists may be included in the database. Secondly, the database as a whole may attract copyright as the "author's own intellectual creation", being the requirement for originality under section 3A(2) of the Copyright, Designs and Patents Act 1988. Thirdly, the structure

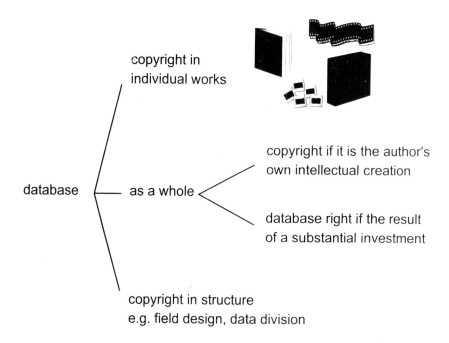

Figure 2.4 Legal Protection of Databases

of the database may be protected as a non-literal element, being its design in terms of the fields allocated to store the various types of information to be contained in the database, see Figure 2.4.

United Kingdom law long since recognised that compilations of non-original matter may be protected by copyright providing that some judgment at least, has been expended in their making; *Macmillan & Co Ltd v K & J Cooper* (1923) 40 TLR 186. Until the changes to the protection of databases resulting from compliance with the EC Directive, it was probably true to say that UK copyright law was amongst the strongest in the world, if not the strongest, in its protection of databases, even though the word "database" did not appear in the Act.

To some extent, the changes to the law throughout the European Community in the protection of databases may be a response to developments in the United States. These developments are likely to have been in the minds of those in the European Commission drafting a harmonising Directive. There was concern that the approach in the United States, discussed below, and some other countries could leave some databases, that required substantial investment in time or money or both in their creation and subsequent modification, without effective protection because they failed to reach a higher standard of originality.

The United States experienced something of a retreat from strong protection of compilations. In particular, the "sweat of the brow" principle, affording copyright protection to works which are the result of labour only, was rejected by the Supreme Court in *Feist Publications Inc* v *Rural Telephone Service Co Inc* (1991) 111 S.Ct. 1282, in which it was held that the "white pages" section in a telephone directory is not protected by copyright because of a lack of creativity, not owing its origin to an act of authorship. In other words, there is need to expend skill and judgment in compiling a copyright work. However, the court accepted that a compilation of facts could be the subject of copyright if the author has to choose which facts to include and in what order to place them. The court also held that copyright could subsist in the "yellow pages" section of a telephone directory because of the presence of original material. There is also the skill and judgment in devising the classification system, the structure of the yellow pages. It is interesting to note that in English cases, concerning the alleged infringement of the copyright in a legal directory containing names and addresses of barristers and firms of solicitors, the subsistence of copyright in the directory was not questioned; see, for example, *Waterlow Directories Ltd* v *Reed Information Services Ltd* [1992] FSR 409.

Copyright and Rights in Databases Regulations 1997

These regulations implement the Directive on the legal protection of databases (OJ 1996 L77/2) and came into force on 1 January 1998 as required. The Directive provides for a two-tier level of protection for databases, being copyright for those that are the author's own intellectual creation and a *sui generis* right, named in the regulations as the database right.

The database right is intended to protect databases that are the result of a substantial investment without necessarily possessing the required new test for originality for a copyright database. It is clear that the database right will also apply to most, if not all databases subject to copyright. In such cases, having both rights could prove useful as the scope of the rights, particularly in terms of infringement, are not identical. An act may infringe the database right without infringing copyright. For example, the database right may be infringed by repeated insubstantial taking. It is not clear whether this infringes copyright. Laddie J cast some doubt on this in *Electronic Techniques (Anglia) Ltd* v *Critchley Components Ltd* [1997] FSR 401.

Both database copyright and database right are without prejudice to the fact that the individual contents of the database may themselves be subject to other rights, in particular copyright. Hence, a database of computer program sub-routines (each requiring skill and judgment in their creation), where the selection or arrangement of those sub-routines required an act of intellectual creation and where its making was the result of a substantial investment will result in the following rights:

- copyright in each of the individual sub-routines,
- copyright in the database as a whole,
- additionally, the database right will apply to the database.

The rights provided apply to both electronic and non-electronic databases. The policy of the Commission of the European Communities is not to distinguish between computer databases and paper databases otherwise this could result in regulatory advantage to those who choose not to make use of information technology.

Copyright provisions

Copyright is applied to databases in a relatively conventional manner. Databases are classified among literary works. They are no longer compilations and this is made clear in section 3 of the Copyright, Designs and Patents Act 1988 which is modified accordingly. However, although copyright for databases mainly follows the other provisions relating to literary works, there are a number of important changes. In particular there is a modified test for originality, a special permitted act and a non-derogation from grant provision.

A new section 3A is inserted into the 1988 Act defining "database" and "originality", following the language of the Directive. A database is defined as a collection of independent works, data or other materials which –

> "(a) are arranged in a systematic or methodical way, and
> (b) are individually accessible by electronic or other means."

A database is original if, and only if, by reason of the selection or arrangement of the contents of the database the database constitutes the author's own intellectual creation. This test derives from that previously used in Germany and was also used in the Directive on the legal protection of computer programs. It was not, however, applied to the test for originality for computer programs under the Copyright, Designs and Patents Act 1988 which remains that for other literary works, based on case law. To that extent the Directive on computer programs was not properly complied with.

Section 21 of the Act now includes a definition of adaptation in relation to a database, being an arrangement or altered version or a translation of it. The Directive makes it clear that neither the database copyright nor the database right apply to computer programs and that the legal protection of computer programs, rental right and lending right and the term of protection of copyright and certain related rights are unaffected by the Directive.

Apart from these changes and the changes to the permitted acts for copyright databases, the other copyright provisions apply to databases as they do to other literary works. For example, the owner has a right to perform the same restricted acts, the same provisions for assignments, licences and presumptions and the same provisions for infringement (including secondary infringement) and offences apply. Importantly, the moral right provisions apply in full whereas, for computer programs, they are severely restricted. The right to be identified as author and the right to object to a derogatory treatment apply to databases but not to computer programs. Any person drafting a licence agreement needs to be aware of this as a great deal of software packages or systems include databases.

Permitted acts

The Directive leaves some discretion to Member States as to the permitted acts to apply with the exception of a "non-derogation from grant" exception, mentioned below. The approach taken by the United

Kingdom is to apply the traditional permitted acts that apply to literary works with the exception of fair dealing for which specific provision is made. Section 29 of the Copyright, Designs and Patents Act 1988 (fair dealing for research or private study) is extended to databases. However, unlike the other works covered by section 29, research for a commercial purpose is expressly excluded from the fair dealing provisions and, where fair dealing with a database is allowed, the source must be indicated, again something which is not required for other literary works in respect of this particular permitted act. Of course, the new fair dealing provision only applies to the copyright in the database *per se* and not to the individual works contained within it.

Section 50D is inserted into the Copyright, Designs and Patents Act 1988 which is essentially a non-derogation from grant provision for lawful users. It allows persons who have a right to use the database or any part of it to do, in exercising that right, anything necessary for the purposes of access to and use of the contents of the database (or of that part of the database if the right is restricted to part only). Any term in an agreement, to the extent that it purports to prohibit or restrict acts carried out under section 50D, is made void under section 296B.

Database right

The database right came into being on 1 January 1998 and is intended to afford protection to databases which, although they may fail to meet the requirements for copyright protection as a database, are commercially valuable, being the result of a substantial investment. The right is not limited to databases not subject to copyright and many databases will enjoy both forms of protection. The database right does not last anything like as long as a copyright but, in many cases, this will not be a serious limitation as future development and modification of the database may trigger a new database right.

Definitions

Regulation 12 of the Copyright and Rights in Databases Regulations 1997 contains the relevant definitions (sometimes by reference to other regulations). It should be noted that "database" has the same meaning as it does for copyright purposes. The other definitions are:

> "extraction", in relation to any contents of a database, means the permanent or temporary transfer of those contents to another medium by

any means or in any form;

"insubstantial", in relation to part of the contents of a database, is to be construed subject to regulation 16(2) which states that the repeated and systematic extraction or re-utilisation of insubstantial parts of the contents of a database may amount to the extraction or re-utilisation of a substantial part of those contents;

"investment" includes any investment, whether of financial, human or technical resources;

"jointly", in relation to a database – a database is made jointly if two or more persons acting together in collaboration take the initiative in obtaining, verifying or presenting the contents of the database and assume the risk of investing in that obtaining, verification or presentation;

"lawful user", in relation to a database, means any person who (whether under a licence to do any of the acts restricted by any database right in the database or otherwise) has a right to use the database;

"maker", in relation to a database, is the person who takes the initiative in making a database and assumes the risk of investing in its making;

"re-utilisation", in relation to any contents of a database, means making those contents available to the public by any means;

"substantial", in relation to any investment, extraction or re-utilisation, means substantial in terms of quantity or quality or a combination of both.

Lending (not for direct or indirect commercial advantage) does not constitute extraction or re-utilisation but this exception does not apply to making available for on the spot reference use which could, therefore fall within extraction or re-utilisation. Exhaustion of rights within the European Economic Area (EEA) applies to copies sold within the EEA by or with the consent of the owner of the database right.

The maker of a database is the first owner of the database right. However, the usual copyright rules apply to databases made by employees and there is an equivalent rule as there is for Crown Copyright.

From the definition of "jointly" it would seem that there is no requirement that the contribution of each is not distinct as there is with joint works of authorship under copyright law.

Subsistence

The database right itself is, under regulation 13, a property right subsisting in a database where there has been a substantial investment in obtaining, verifying or presenting the contents of the database. There are qualification requirements, basically to the effect that, at the material time, the maker (or at least one of them where there are joint makers) is a national of an EEA state or body incorporated in an EEA state, having its central administration or principal place of business in an EEA state or registered office in the EEA and the body's operations linked on an ongoing basis with the economy of an EEA state. The "material time" is time when a database is made or, if extended over a period, a substantial part of that period.

Duration

The term of the database right is 15 years from the end of the calendar year during which its making is completed. However, if it is made available to the public before the end of that period, the right will continue to endure for 15 years from the end of the calendar year during which it was first made available to the public.

Many databases are subject to modification, either as a continuing process or by subsequent releases or updates. Substantial changes to the contents of the database including a substantial change resulting from the accumulation of successive additions, deletions or alterations, which would result in the database being considered a substantial new investment, qualifies the database resulting from that investment for its own term of protection. That is, the database, as modified, will have its own database right. Databases made on or after 1 January 1983 in which database right subsists on commencement qualify for 15 years beginning with 1 January 1998. Thus, if the right begins to subsist on 1 January 1998 it will continue for 15 years, even if it would have otherwise expired after a shorter period.

Infringement

The extraction or re-utilisation of all or a substantial part of the contents of the database without the consent of the owner infringes the database right. Furthermore, the repeated and systematic extraction or re-utlisation of insubstantial parts of the contents of a database may amount to the extraction or re-utlisation of a substantial part of those contents. This form of infringement reflects the harm that could be done to the maker of a database by an accumulation of insubstantial takings. The Directive has a test for infringement by repeated taking of insubstantial parts but which is not mentioned in the regulations. This is where the repeated and systematic extraction and/or re-utilisation imply acts which conflict with the normal exploitation of the database so as to unreasonably prejudice the legitimate interests of its maker.

Exceptions to infringement

Where, under an agreement a person has a right to use a database which has been made available to the public, or any part of it, any term or condition in the agreement is void in so far as it purports to prevent the lawful user from extracting or re-utilising any part of the contents of the database in a way which does not infringe the database right.

There is also an exception for fair dealing by a lawful user for purposes of illustration for teaching or research (except for a commercial purpose) provided the source is indicated. Some further exceptions set out in Schedule 1 to the regulations cover parliamentary and judicial proceedings, Royal Commissions and statutory inquiries, material open to public inspection or on official register, material communicated to Crown in the course of public business, public records and acts done under statutory authority. These mirror the equivalent permitted acts for copyright. However, none of the other permitted acts under copyright law that apply to literary works apply to the database right.

Miscellaneous

There are some presumptions similar to those applying to literary works under copyright law. Thus, where a name purporting to be that of the maker of the database appears on copies of it, it is presumed that the named person is the maker and the database was not made by an employee nor for the Crown, unless the contrary be proved.

The provisions for dealing, rights and remedies (including those of exclusive licensees) that apply to copyright works are declared under regulation 22 to apply also in respect of the database right. There are equivalent provisions for licensing the database right under a licensing scheme as apply to copyright and the jurisdiction of the Copyright Tribunal is enlarged accordingly.

Pre-existing databases can be subject to the database right. Under regulation 26 and subject to regulations 27 and 28 the regulations apply to databases made before or after commencement (1 January 1998). Regulation 27 states that agreements made before commencement are unaffected and no act done before commencement or in pursuance of an agreement made before commencement infringes the database right. Regulation 28 provides that if a database was made on or before 27 March 1996 (the date the Directive was published in the *Official Journal*) and was a copyright database immediately before commencement, that copyright continues for the remainder of its term in accordance with section 12 of the Copyright, Designs and Patents Act 1988 being, in most cases, life plus 70 years. This means that expectations as to protection of databases existing before the new regime was published are not prejudiced. This provision is needed because a database that would have been protected by copyright under the old rules might not be protected now, in particular, because of the new test for originality for copyright databases.

Database structure

When a database is designed, some thought must be given to its structure. Aspects such as what items of information to store in the database, the form in which it will be stored and, in most cases, the amount of space to be allocated to each record must be calculated. A slot into which data is entered is called a field. For example, in a simple database of names, dates of birth and addresses, there will be a name field, a date of birth field and one or more address fields. An entire entry about one individual is a record. 40 characters may be allotted to the name field which will contain letters only. The date of birth field will contain eight positive integer numbers. A now familiar example of the importance of taking great care in designing a database field is the massive problem caused by the "Millennium bug" resulting from the past practice of allocating only sufficient space in a database field to hold two numbers to represent the year in a date.

In a simple database such as the one, described above, the work in designing its structure is relatively trivial. However, in more complex databases, a substantial amount of skill and judgment will be expended in designing the structure of the database. In many cases, the design of the database structure is the most important aspect of the software. If that is not right, the software will be seriously limited. Design of a database also has to take into account practical aspects such as efficiency, speed and storage capacity in addition to future possible development and modification. This may include links to other databases and new programs.

If the structure of a computer program is protected under copyright law as a non-literal element of the program, there seems to be no reason why the structure of databases cannot also be protected, providing sufficient skill, effort and judgment has been used. However, in *Total Information Processing Systems Ltd v Daman Ltd* [1992] FSR 171, it was held that the field and record specifications as expressed in the data division of a COBOL program were not protected because, in this form, the information did not form a substantial part of the computer program as a whole. It is submitted that this approach is wrong and that it would be better to consider the database structure as a form of expression in its own right and not as part of the computer program. Jacob J expressly disapproved of this aspect of the above case in the *Ibcos* case discussed earlier. His view is much to be preferred.

During the work of designing the structure of a database a number of tables and diagrams are likely to be created. Copying the structure of a database could indirectly infringe the copyright subsisting in some of these materials. Note that these materials are not preparatory design material falling to be literary works under section 3(1)(c) as they are not preparatory to the creation of a computer program; they are preparatory to the creation of a database. Although the concept of indirect copying is well established and expressly stated in section 16(3), there has been some doubt about indirect copying of artistic works as it was held that a copy of an artistic work should bear some visual resemblance to it; see *Anacon Corp Ltd v Environmental Research Technology Ltd* [1994] FSR 659, discussed earlier in this chapter at page 48.

It should be noted that the intention behind the Directive on the legal protection of databases was that the structure of a copyright database should be protected and this is stated in recital 15 of the Directive. However, this fact is not mentioned in the Articles in the Directive nor is it mentioned in the regulations implementing the Directive. As regards the structure of databases in which the database right only subsists it would seem that the Directive did not intend to extend protection to the structure of the database as it is silent on this point. However, this is not necessarily conclusive and, even though the selection or arrangement of the contents of a database is not an intellectual creation, this might not hold true in respect of the design of its structure. Unless, of course, "arrangement" is taken to include the design of database field and/or the inter-relationships in relational databases. If this is the case, a database could be a work of copyright by virtue of its structure and not by virtue of its contents. That being so, it is not clear whether taking the contents of the database will

Industrial Property Rights in Computer Software

Industrial Property Rights in Computer Software

Introduction

Apart from copyright, there may be a number of other intellectual property rights subsisting in computer software. For example, software may be part of a patentable invention. Software may also be subject to an obligation of confidence and there may be some trade mark associated with it or even embedded within the software. Where software is installed on an integrated circuit, there may also be a semiconductor topography right, being a right which protects the layout of the circuitry as installed in a computer chip and which is based on a modified version of the design right. Collectively, these rights are referred to as industrial property rights, to distinguish them from copyright and neighbouring rights such as rights in performances. Where software is being licensed (or where the copyright is being assigned) it is important to consider the existence of these industrial property rights as regards the software itself or as regards third party rights that may be affected by the creation, distribution or use of the software subject to the licence agreement.

There follows in this chapter a brief description of these various industrial property rights together with some discussion of how they may affect software licences. The law of breach of confidence is considered first, followed by patent law and design law (including the protection of semiconductor products) and finally, the law relating to business goodwill; that is, trade mark law and the law of passing off.

Law of breach of confidence

This area of law protects, *inter alia*, information relating to trade secrets and commercial activity. The basic requirements are that the information concerned must have a quality of confidence about it (not necessarily a particularly high standard), it must have been imparted in circumstances where there is an obligation of confidence and there must have been or, is likely to be, an unauthorised disclosure or use of the information which is or will be detrimental to the person to whom the information "belongs"; *Coco* v *A N Clark (Engineers) Ltd* [1969] RPC 41. The most important remedy for a breach of confidence is the injunction, especially a *quia timet* injunction to prevent an anticipated unauthorised disclosure or use. However, if the information has been disclosed or used in breach of confidence, damages or an account of profits may be available.

Nature of information protected

The law of confidence protects trade secrets. But that is not limited to details of secret processes or methods of manufacture and can extend to business information that is commercially valuable or sensitive. As Staughton LJ said in *Lansing Linde* v *Kerr* [1991] 1 WLR 251 at 260:

> "[the term trade secret] can thus include not only secret formulae for the manufacture of products but also, in an appropriate case, the names of customers and the goods which they buy. But some may say that not all such information is a trade secret in ordinary parlance. If that view is adopted, the class of information which can justify a restriction is wider, and extends to some confidential information which would not ordinarily be called a trade secret."

In terms of the subject matter of software licences, the type of information that can be protected by the law of confidence includes the idea and design specification for a new computer system, the structure of a computer program or database or a suite comprising programs and databases and information contained within a database (which well might be something no more sophisticated than a list of customers and their buying preferences). Of course, if the software is made available to others, its confidential nature will be lost or prejudiced, unless the information is not available without reverse engineering the software. In this case, it may be possible to impose a duty not to perform the reverse engineering as in *K S Paul (Printing Machinery) Ltd* v *Southern Instruments Ltd* [1964] RPC 118 where the plaintiff hired to the defendant a telephone answering machine. The mechanism was enclosed and hidden from view in a box. There was a term in the hire contract to the effect that the box should not be opened. It was held that the defendant could not use the confidential information he obtained after opening the box and inspecting the mechanism.

Where computer programs are involved, the effects of the permitted act of decompilation under section 50B of the Copyright, Designs and

Patents Act 1988 must be taken into account as must be section 296A which allows lawful users of computer programs to do certain things to gain access to the ideas and principles underlying a computer program. Indeed, the Directive on the legal protection of computer programs states that underlying ideas and principles are not protected by copyright.

It should be noted that the law of confidence is, potentially, much wider than copyright law which requires some form of expression. For confidence to apply there is no such requirement and ideas with no tangible form may be protected.

Obligation of confidence

An obligation of confidence may be express or implied by law. Express obligations of confidence are common in employment contracts or contracts for services provided by self employed consultants. The computer software industry is notable in that there is a great deal of mobility of software designers and programmers between employers and many are self employed, working on a freelance basis or operating through small limited companies. Although an obligation of confidence will be implied in such circumstances, it will generally be weaker than an express obligation, particularly after termination of the contract of employment or contract for services. The position of ex-employees is considered later in this chapter at page 63.

That professional advisers owe an obligation of confidence to their clients goes without saying. In the software industry, a computer professional who has been asked to advise on a computer software system will be under an obligation not to divulge confidential information about his client's business to anyone without the client's permission. The same applies to a software company engaged to develop software for a client. The employees or agents of the software company are bound to come into contact with confidential information in the process of carrying out their work. Whilst a duty of confidence will be implied, it is useful to impose an express duty (which may be mutual) to strengthen, define and focus the obligation, so concentrating the minds of the parties. It will also make an action for breach of contract a useful supplement to an action in breach of confidence should one party be in breach of the obligation. One helpful approach is for the parties to specify beforehand what type of information is confidential and what is not.

Unauthorised use (actual or anticipated)

This requirement does not really add anything. It can be said that any unauthorised use of any confidential information is detrimental to the party to whom the information belongs *per se*. If no harm is suffered or likely to be suffered, then an injunction should still be available unless the defence of public interest is relevant. This might be so where the client of a software company is storing personal information in contravention with the Data Protection Act 1998 and the software company has divulged or intends to divulge this fact to the Data Protection Commissioner. The same might apply to information concerning a price fixing ring; *Initial Services Ltd* v *Putterill* [1968] 1 QB 396.

Ex-employees

The position with ex-employees is a reflection of the difficulty the law has in performing a balancing act between protecting the interests of an employer and the desirability of allowing an ex-employee to put his own skill and experience at the disposal of a new employer or using it on his own behalf. Separating skill and experience from trade secrets or other information that the previous employer is justified in protecting is notoriously difficult. However, some basic rules can be stated, see especially Goulding J in *Faccenda Chicken Ltd* v *Fowler* [1985] 1 All ER 724 (at first instance) where he suggested the following basic rules:

- an employee owes his present employer a duty of fidelity which is contractual in nature and provided for by express or implied terms. A present employee cannot properly disclose information relating to his employer's business to a competitor or otherwise assist a competitor;
- after termination of the employment, the implied duty is more limited and would apply only to genuine trade secrets;
- an employer can, by use of a reasonable covenant in restraint of trade, obtain a promise from an employee that he will not disclose or use confidential information (presumably information of a lesser standard than a trade secret).

Where there is a conflict between the employer's interests and the employee's "right" to use his accumulated skill and knowledge elsewhere, the public interest is likely to favour the employee.

Implied duty to maintain confidence subsequent to employment

If the information concerned is not a trade secret, it will not be protected in the absence of a restrictive covenant unless the ex-employee has deliberately memorised it or copied it out. Of course, the ex-employee will be able to make use of some information relating to the previous employment, especially if it has become part of his own skill and experience. According to Marais J in *Northern Office Micro Computers (Pty) Ltd* v *Rosenstein* [1982] FSR 124 (a South African case involving an alleged infringement of copyright and breach of confidence by an ex-employee computer programmer), an ex-employee is not expected to wipe clean the slate of his mind and forget everything he has learnt about his employer's business. See also *Printers and Finishers Ltd* v *Holloway* [1964] 3 All ER 731 which concerned a process for flock printing.

The position of the ex-employee was considered further in the Court of Appeal by Neill LJ in *Faccenda Chicken Ltd* v *Fowler* [1986] 1 All ER 617. This case concerned alleged wrongful use by the ex-employee of sales information; the sort of information that is now likely to be stored in a computer database (there was no covenant in restraint of trade). Neill LJ said the relevant principles to apply in cases involving confidentiality between master and servant were:

- If there is a contract of employment the employee's obligations were to be determined from that contract.
- In the absence of any express terms, the employee's obligations would be implied.
- Whilst still in employment, there was an implied term imposing a duty of good faith or fidelity on the employee. This duty might vary according to the nature of the contract but would be broken if the employee copied or deliberately memorised a list of customers.
- The implied term imposing an obligation on the employee after the termination of his employment was more restricted than that imposed by the duty of fidelity. It might cover secret processes of manufacture or designs or special methods of construction or other information of a sufficiently high degree of confidentiality to be classed as a trade secret.
- To determine whether information fell within this implied term to prevent its use or disclosure by an ex-employee depended on the circumstances and attention should be given to the following:

(a) the nature of employment, a higher obligation might be imposed where the employee regularly handled confidential material;

(b) the nature of information, it should be an authentic trade secret or at least highly confidential;

(c) whether the employer stressed the confidential nature of the material, and;

(d) whether the information could be easily isolated from other material the employee was free to use; this being useful evidentially rather than being a conclusive test.

Covenants in restraint of trade

A substantial amount of bespoke software is written by companies or partnerships with just a small number of employees. It is not uncommon for one of the directors or partners to have played an important role in developing and writing software. If that person later decides to move on, perhaps setting up his own business independently (again, a common occurrence), a covenant in restraint of trade may be included in the parting arrangements. The person leaving may covenant not to write competing software for a period of time and not to make use of confidential information. The courts take a fairly strict view of covenants in restraint of trade and will enforce them only if they are reasonable and intended to protect the interests of the person taking the benefit of the covenant (covenantee). A covenant will not be enforced if it is designed purely to insulate the covenantee against fair competition or if it would make it very difficult for the person restrained by the covenant (covenantor) to continue to practise his trade or profession.

The reasonableness of a covenant is often determined by looking at the length of time that it will have effect and, where relevant, its geographical scope. A covenant not to write software for insurance brokers in the West Midlands for 12 months may be acceptable but a covenant not to write software of any description will not be acceptable, whatever the duration. In the former case, the covenantor can still practise his profession of writing software as long as it is not for insurance brokers and, even then, that restriction only applies for one year. Furthermore, it is limited geographically. In the latter example, the covenantor is prevented totally from practising his profession.

Drafting covenants in restraint of trade needs special care because of the operation of the *contra proferentum* rule. Any ambiguity will be resolved against the party seeking to rely on the relevant provision.

In *Ibcos Computers Ltd* v *Barclays Mercantile Highland Finance Ltd* [1994] FSR 275, a clause in an agreement made at the end of a computer programmer's employment with the plaintiff imposed a restrictive covenant to the effect that the programmer must not sell similar software or be employed by a company doing so for a period of two years was held not to prevent the programmer from *writing* such software during that period. An invitation to Jacob J to read the clause more widely was refused on the well established principle that such clauses must be construed narrowly. The clause offended in other ways because it was, on its face, world-wide whereas the plaintiff's business was restricted to the United Kingdom. To summarise, Figure 3.1 shows whether information received by an employee is protected after the termination of his contract of employment.

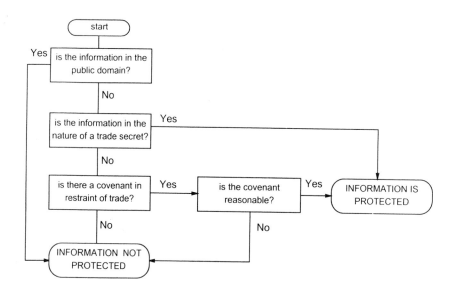

Figure 3.1 Ex-employees and Confidential Information

Patent law

A patent gives a monopoly to work a new invention for up to 20 years. The invention may relate to a new product or a new process. In many respects it is the strongest form of intellectual property but there are a number of safeguards to prevent or control abuse of the rights granted

to the proprietor of the patent. The essential requirements for the grant of a patent are, under section 1(1) of the Patents Act 1977, that the invention must be:

- new;
- involve an inventive step;
- be capable of industrial application; and
- not excluded under section 1(2) and (3) which declare that certain things are not patentable.

Obtaining a patent requires compliance with certain rigorous formalities and examinations. It is a difficult and costly process and, furthermore, litigation tends to be protracted and expensive. Patents are territorial in nature and applications must be made for patents in each of the countries in which protection is sought. There are two conventions that ease this to some extent, the European Patent Convention with 19 Member States and the Patent Co-operation Treaty with over 60 Member States. The United Kingdom is a signatory to both and application for a UK patent or patents in the other countries in the conventions may be made through the UK Patent Office. It is an offence for a resident of the United Kingdom to file or cause to file an application for a patent elsewhere without first giving the Patent Office an opportunity to inspect that application.

The basic procedure for obtaining a patent is that an application is filed with a specification, abstract and claims following which a search is made by the Patent Office for material that may show that the patent is not new or does not involve an inventive step, for example. The date of filing becomes the priority date for the patent unless the priority of an earlier application elsewhere within the preceding 12 months is claimed. Unless the patent application is withdrawn it will be published 18 months from the priority date ("A" publication). The applicant can request earlier publication if he so wishes. There then follows a substantive examination for compliance with the Patents Act 1977 by the Patent Office examiners and, if all is well, the patent will be granted and published again ("B" publication). Figure 3.2 shows the procedure in simplified form and it assumes that there are no amendments, no claim to an earlier priority date and that the examination is satisfactory.

During the application process, amendments may be made providing they do not widen the scope of the patent. The patent specification must, under section 14, disclose the invention sufficiently so that the invention could be performed by a person skilled in the art. Typically, grant will take place between two and four years following

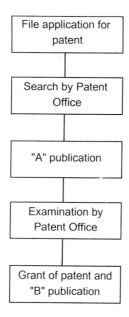

Figure 3.2 Simplified Patent Procedure

filing the application. Initial grant is for four years and thereafter, the patent can be renewed annually until the end of its 20th year. Infringement actions cannot be commenced until after the patent has been granted but damages (or an account of profits) can be recovered for any infringement occurring after the first publication of the patent, usually 18 months after its priority date.

Basic requirements

The basic requirements have been mentioned above as being novelty, inventive step, industrial application. Further the grant of a patent must not be excluded under section 1(2) and (3). Those elements are considered further below.

Novelty

Under section 2 of the Patents Act 1977 an invention is new if it does not form part of the state of the art. The state of the art is defined as all matter (whether a product, a process, information about either, or anything else) which has, at any time before the priority date of the patent, been made available to the public (whether in the United Kingdom or elsewhere) by written or oral description, by use or in any other way. Inventions contained in unpublished patent applications having an earlier priority date are included in the state of the art. If the invention has been so made available to the public, it is said to have been anticipated and a patent cannot be granted for it. An example of where a patent was anticipated was in *Windsurfing International Inc* v *Tabur Marine (Great Britain) Ltd* [1985] RPC 59 where occasional use by a 12-year old at Hayling Island was deemed sufficient to make the invention available to the public. As a consequence the patent for a sailboard was revoked.

Inventive step

It is self-evident that an invention must involve an inventive step. Section 3 defines this as being not obvious to persons skilled in the art, having regard to any matter which forms part of the state of the art by virtue only of section 2 but disregarding matter contained in unpublished patent applications even though they may have an earlier priority date. Sometimes, commercial success may provide a guide as to this. If the invention answers a long felt want and is an immediate commercial success, it is highly likely that it was not obvious at the priority date of the application, otherwise someone would have thought of the invention before. However, this is not a conclusive test and can be misleading, such as where commercial success is attributable to marketing effort.

Industrial application

An industrial application is one which can be made or used in any kind of industry, including agriculture; section 4. However, this is declared not to include the invention of a method of treatment of the human or animal body by surgery or therapy or of diagnosis practised on the human or animal body. This does not prevent patents on drugs. In practice, apart from the above exception, the requirement for an industrial application rarely causes problems. The computer industry is certainly included, subject to the exclusions below.

Exclusions

A number of things are excluded from the grant of a patent. Section 1(2) excludes:

- a discovery, scientific theory or mathematical method;
- a literary, dramatic, musical or artistic work;
- any other aesthetic creation;
- a scheme, rule or method for performing any mental act, playing a game or doing business or a program for a computer;
- the presentation of information.

However, as regards these things, the exception applies only in as much as the application relates to the thing "as such". Applications directed to the technical effect, say, produced by running a computer program or flowing from the use of a discovery, should be acceptable providing the other requirements are met. Of course, some of the exclusions are not controversial as other intellectual property rights provide adequate protection but it is in respect of computer programs that most controversy arises particularly as the computer industry sees patents as a very desirable form of protection notwithstanding that computer programs are protected by copyright (see the following section).

Other exceptions are contained in section 1(3) and are:

- anything which would be generally expected to encourage offensive, immoral or anti-social behaviour;
- any variety of animal or plant;
- any essentially biological (not micro-biological) process for the production of animals or plants.

The second exception has been considered by the European Patent Office's Board of Appeals which granted a patent for a genetically altered mouse designed to develop tumours, *Onco-Mouse/Havard* [1990] EPOR 4 and 501. There is a European Directive on the patentability of biotechnological inventions that will allow the patenting of such inventions subject to a number of safeguards (OJ 1998 C100/17).

Software patents

In view of the exception relating to computer programs in section 1(2), it is surprising that there have been a large number of applications for patents in respect of computer programs. Some have met with success. The logic behind this apparent contradiction is that an application directed to the technical effect produced by a programmed computer is not an application for a patent for a computer program "as such". Thus, the European Patent Office granted a patent for a method of digital image processing controlled by a programmed computer in *Vicom Systems Inc's Patent Application* [1987] 2 EPOR 74. This approach was approved in the Court of Appeal in *Genentech Inc's Patent* [1989] RPC 147 which involved a discovery (another of the excluded materials). If the inventive step resides in the excluded material, that does not prevent the grant of a patent providing that there is some technical effect.

In most cases, patents are refused for inventions having computer programs at their core because in these cases, there is no technical effect outside the computer itself. For example, an application for a patent in respect of a ROM chip containing instructions for a method of calculating square roots based on a new algorithm was refused in *Gale's Application* [1991] RPC 305 and patents have been refused for expert systems and compiler programs. In *Nissan's Application* (unreported) 29 April 1994, heard in the Patent Office, an application for a method of evaluating designs comprising several elements using a programmed computer was refused, being no more than an application in respect of a conventional computer suitably programmed.

Some applications to patent software inventions fail because the "technical effect" is itself among the excluded items. For example, in *Fujitsu Ltd's Application* [1997] RPC 610, which concerned an application in respect of a software technique for manipulating crystalline structures on screen in order to create new compounds, it was held that the application was caught by the exclusions in section 1(2). The application was for a computer program as such, and it also related to a method of performing a mental act as such. In this case, the application was for a computer program as such. The invention used a conventional computer to do what had previously been done using plastic models. The only advance was that using a computer enabled the results to be achieved more quickly. This is just the sort of advantage that is obtained by the application of a computer program and, for this reason, it is arguable that the invention also lacked novelty. The same invention was previously granted a patent in Japan.

The fact that computer programs may be subject to patents (patent law is more liberal in this respect in the United States, Australia and, potentially, in other Member States of the European Patent Convention) must be taken into account when exploiting software, particularly if it is to be distributed outside the United Kingdom. There is always a possibility that it might be found that the software infringes a third party patent and, therefore, any licence agreement or assignment should contain an indemnity clause to cover this eventuality. What should be borne in mind is that, whilst copyright infringement requires some act in relation to the original work, such as copying it, that is not so for some forms of patent infringement. Making, disposing of, offering to dispose of, importing, using or keeping a patented product or doing the same in respect of a product made by a patented process infringes regardless of knowledge of the existence of the patented invention. Although damages are not available against innocent infringers, injunctive relief is always a strong possibility and an account of profits may also be available. Other forms of infringement require knowledge on the part of the infringer.

Design law

"Artistic" designs are protected by the law of copyright as artistic works, particularly works of artistic craftsmanship. For some of these works the term of copyright is effectively reduced to 25 years if they are exploited industrially, for example, if 50 or more articles are made by an industrial process; section 52 of the Copyright, Designs and Patents Act 1988. This does not apply to sculptures and other works primarily of a literary or artistic nature which continue to enjoy the protection of copyright for its full term.

Industrial designs can be classed as "aesthetic" (having eye-appeal – the reason why persons acquire or use articles of a particular design) and functional where the appearance of articles made to the design is not a material factor. Designs having eye-appeal are registrable under the Registered Designs Act 1949 for five years, renewable in further five-year blocks for up to a maximum of 25 years. Functional designs are protected by an unregistered design right (although many registrable designs will also qualify for this form of protection). This gives a protection of 15 years although limited to 10 years maximum of commercial exploitation. The nature of a registered design can be thought of as being similar (though much simpler) to a patent whereas the design right is similar to a copyright.

Design law does not generally have any relevance for software licensing apart from the fact that semiconductor topographies are protected by a variant of the design right and this would be relevant where a program or database had been permanently installed on a silicon chip and was made available in that form. What is protected are the patterns in the chip which represent the electronic circuitry which in turn represent the program or data.

Registered designs

A design may be registered under the Registered Designs Act 1949 if, under section 1, the design:

- relates to features of shape, configuration, pattern or ornament;
- is new, that is, not previously registered or published in the United Kingdom;
- has features which appeal to and are judged by the eye;
- has features which are applied to an article by an industrial process.

There are a number of exceptions. A design is not registrable if, or to the extent that, it is a method or principle of construction or relates to features of shape or configuration which are dictated by the function or the appearance of another article with which an article made to the design is intended to form an integral part ("must-fit" and "must-match" exceptions). The eye-appeal requirement is satisfied if aesthetic considerations are a material factor in the reason for acquiring or using articles made to the design.

A design is registered at the Design Registry following a simple application procedure requiring the submission of details as to the proprietor, a description of the article to which the design is to be applied, an address for service, representations of the design and a novelty statement, together with the application fee. It is an inexpensive and, regrettably, under-utilised system of monopoly protection for designs.

The proprietor of the design has exclusive rights in relation to articles to which the design has been applied, for example, making or importing articles for sale or hire or for trade or business purposes or to sell, hire or offer or expose for sale or hire articles made to the design. There are arrangements for international protection, for example, with parts of the West Indies and some African countries. Registration in the United Kingdom automatically gives protection in some of these countries whilst for others local re-registration is required. Around two-thirds of design registrations result from applications from proprietors outside the United Kingdom.

Software designs, such as typefaces, are not registrable as they are not usually applied to an article. (Typefaces in "hot metal" are not usually registered even if new as each letter and other character would have to be registered separately unless protection was sought only for some common element such as a new design of serif.) However, registered design law is useful for new designs of computer hardware such as a new design of the appearance of a notebook computer or mouse or computer printer.

Design right

This right only applies to shape or configuration and not to pattern or ornament. The right is, in many respects, very similar to a copyright and it is provided for under Part III of the Copyright, Designs and Patents Act 1988. Under section 213, the right applies to the design of any aspect of the shape or configuration (whether internal or external) of the whole or part of an article. The design must be original. A design is not original if it is commonplace in the design field in question at the time of its creation. The question of originality was discussed in *C & H Engineering* v *Klucznick & Sons Ltd* [1992] FSR 421 where it was said that, first, the design must be original in the copyright sense (originating from the author) and then the question of whether it was commonplace at the time of its creation must be considered. In the end a test not far short of the novelty requirement for a registered design is arrived at. In *Ocular Sciences Ltd* v *Aspect Vision Care Ltd* [1997] RPC 289, it was accepted that a good working definition of commonplace is "trite, trivial, common-or-garden, hackneyed or of the type which would excite no peculiar attention in those in the relevant art".

There are exceptions to the subsistence of the right which broadly equate to those for registered designs. Some of the exceptions are identical but others have a different scope. There are similar "must-fit" and "must-match" exceptions. Surface decoration is also expressly excluded. An important point is that the design right does not apply to designs created prior to 1 August 1989. For these designs protection is available through copyright in drawings for a curtailed period (until 1 August 1999 unless the copyright expires otherwise before that date).

As with copyright, there are qualification requirements. This may be by reference to the designer, the commissioner or employer or the first marketing of articles made to the design. The rules as to ownership are somewhat different to those for copyright as the person who commissions a self-employed designer to create a design will automatically be the first owner of the design. There is also provision for the owner to be the person who first markets articles made to the design within the European Community if the design qualifies by reference to that person and not by any other means.

The owner of a design right has the exclusive right to reproduce the design for commercial purposes. Anyone who does this without the permission of the owner, infringes the right. There are also secondary infringements associated with dealing with infringing articles. Remedies are as for copyright infringement. If an act infringes copyright, the design right is suppressed, leaving an action in copyright.

Semiconductor topographies

The Design Right (Semiconductor Topographies) Regulations 1989 provide a model for the protection of semiconductor topographies based on the design right, following regulations dating from 1987 which gave a *sui generis* protection. The topography of a semiconductor is protected and is, under regulation 2(1), a design which is either the pattern in or upon a layer of a semiconductor product or the arrangement of the patterns in or upon the layers of a semiconductor product in relation to one another. Included are patterns in or upon a layer of material used in the manufacture of a semiconductor product. A semiconductor product is an article the purpose, or one of the purposes, of which is the performance of an electronic function and which consists of two or more layers, at least one of which is composed of semiconducting material and in or upon one or more of which is fixed a pattern appertaining to that or another function.

As with conventional designs subject to the design right, the semiconductor topography must be original and not commonplace in the design field in question at the time of its creation. The qualification requirements are very similar to those for "normal" designs with some minor differences and there are reciprocal arrangements for protection with EC countries and other countries such as the United States, Switzerland and Japan.

The owner's rights are as for conventional designs and infringement (primary and secondary) is similarly defined but there are some permitted acts including reproduction of the design privately for non-commercial aims. Section 226(1A)(b) of the Copyright, Designs and Patents Act 1988 allows reproduction for the purpose of analysing or evaluating the design or analysing, evaluating or teaching the concepts, processes, systems or techniques embodied in it. This may permit reverse analysis of existing semiconductors for the purpose of developing new products. This is reinforced by regulation 8(4) which states that it is not an infringement of the semiconductor design right to create another original topography as a result of such analysis or evaluation or to reproduce that other topography other than by making articles containing it. In some respects, this is similar to the permitted act of decompilation in relation to computer programs.

The duration of the semiconductor design right is as with conventional designs. However, whereas licences are available as of right for the conventional design right during the last five years they are not in respect of semiconductor topographies. Nevertheless, such licences may result from a report by the Monopolies and Mergers Commission as with other designs (this possibility applies also to some other intellectual property rights). Remedies for infringement are as for the conventional design right, that is, as for copyright infringement.

Business goodwill

Trade mark law and the law of passing off are very important in terms of marketing products or services and commercial goodwill. The value of some marks and names is almost incalculable. When developing software to license or choosing a business name for a software company, care must be taken not to infringe a trade mark or to use a name or get-up that may result in a passing off action. It is possible to embed trade marks in the software itself so that, for example, a trade mark is displayed on a screen when the software is loaded into a computer. Trade marks and names may also be relevant because software companies often require that licensees attach the company's name (which may be a registered trade mark) on back-up copies together with an appropriate copyright notice. This area of law may also be important in terms of advertising software, particularly in respect of comparative advertising and in the choice of Internet domain names.

Trade marks

The purpose of trade mark law is to protect marks that indicate a connection between a trader and his goods or services and to distinguish them from the goods or services of other traders. Registration is effected in one or more classes of goods or services, there being 34 classes for goods and eight classes for services. Registration is for 10-year periods, renewable in 10-year blocks. A trade mark registration may be renewed *ad infinitum*, providing it is still in use (non-use for five or more years is one of the reasons why a registration may be revoked).

For software, registration is usually in class 9 which includes data processing equipment and computers. This would be appropriate for ready-made software. For a company in the business of writing specialised bespoke software, a registration under class 42 which includes computer programming would be appropriate to cover the service of writing computer programs though registration under class 9 could also be useful for marks to be applied to the finished software.

Under the Trade Marks Act 1994, which came into force on 31 October 1994, the definition of a trade mark is generously wide. It is, by section 1(1), any sign capable of being represented graphically which is capable of distinguishing goods or services of one undertaking from those of other undertakings. The section then goes on to say that a trade mark may, in particular, consist of words (including personal names), designs, letters, numerals or the shape of goods or their packaging. Thus, it is entirely possible that a mark generated whilst running a computer program and displayed on a screen could be registered as a trade mark. It could even be a moving mark such a sign that rotates or a logo that transforms its shape, providing that a static representation will give sufficient protection to the mark in all its phases. Such marks should be registrable providing that they are "capable of distinguishing". In the past this phrase has been fairly liberally interpreted as meaning that the mark will become distinctive in use and that it will afford an indication of origin without trespassing on the legitimate freedom of other traders; *Torq-Set Trade Mark* [1959] RPC 344.

There are a large number of grounds for refusing to register a mark, apart from the basic statement of what a mark is. Thus, registration will be refused if the mark is, *inter alia*, descriptive, in general use, deceptive, the same or similar to another mark or a specially protected emblem. In *Foundation Trade Mark* [1994] RPC 41, decided under the old Trade Marks Act 1938 Act, it was held that applications software and systems software were goods of the same description and an application to register the mark FOUNDATION for systems software was refused because of an earlier registration by another company in respect of applications software. It is likely that the decision would be the same under the 1994 Act.

By section 9, the proprietor of a registered mark has exclusive rights in the mark which are infringed by use in the United Kingdom without his consent. Section 10 details the particular acts. Using an identical mark for identical goods or services infringes without proof of confusion on the part of the public. However, a likelihood of confusion on the part of the public is required if the use complained of is in respect of an identical mark for similar goods or services or a similar mark for either identical or similar goods or services. Trade marks having a reputation in the United Kingdom can be infringed where they are used on non-similar goods or services. However, the use must be such, without due cause, as to take unfair advantage of the trade mark or be detrimental to its distinctive character or repute.

The use of the infringing sign must be in the course of trade and includes fixing the offending sign to goods or packaging, offering or exposing goods for sale, importing or exporting goods under the sign and using the sign on business papers or in advertising.

Under the Trade Marks Act 1938, comparative advertising infringed. Thus, in *Compaq Computer Corp* v *Dell Computer Corp Ltd* [1992] FSR 93 it was held that, by using the "Compaq" name (a registered trade mark) in comparative advertising, the defendant had, arguably, infringed the mark. However, the present legislation, the Trade Marks Act 1994, permits comparative advertising as long as it is in accordance with honest practices in industrial or commercial matters and does not, without due cause, take unfair advantage of or is detrimental to the distinctive character or repute of the trade mark.

The Trade Marks Act 1994 contains clear provisions dealing with assignment and licensing of registered marks, a significant improvement over the 1938 Act which did not allow registration of a mark if it appeared that this would lead to trafficking in the mark (as is common in character merchandising); see the House of Lord's criticism of this old provision in *Holly Hobbie Trade Mark* [1984] FSR 199.

If the licence so provides, exclusive licensees can have the same rights and remedies as a proprietor and can sue for infringement on this basis. In other cases, and this includes non-exclusive licences and sub-licences, unless the licence provides otherwise, the licensee is entitled to call upon the proprietor to sue for any infringement which affects the interests of the licensee. If the proprietor refuses to do so or fails to do so within two months, the licensee may bring proceedings in his own name as if he were the proprietor; section 30. For other than interlocutory relief, the proprietor must be joined in the action (either as co-plaintiff or defendant) unless the court gives leave for the licensee to proceed on his own. An important point is that licences must be registered under section 25 otherwise the licensee will not be allowed to commence proceedings against infringers. Registration is also desirable otherwise the licence will not bind a third party who acquires a conflicting interest in ignorance of the licence and will prevent the recovery of damages and an account of profits unless, normally, the licence is registered within six months of it being granted. Certain other transactions, such as assignments and mortgages, also must be registered.

Licensed software may include or incorporate a trade mark which is part of the subject matter of the licence. For example, this could be where a software developer having his own trade mark grants an exclusive licence to a software publisher who then distributes copies of the software on the basis of non-exclusive licences. The software licence may include a term granting a licence to the publisher allowing him to use the mark to advertise and sell the software. It may be useful for the publisher to have the right to sue for infringement of the trade mark. The licence should, therefore, deal with this and have provision for joining the software developer, paying his expenses and indemnifying him against legal costs and sharing any damages obtained.

Unauthorised use of a registered trade mark with intention to obtain a gain or cause a loss is a criminal offence carrying a maximum term of imprisonment on conviction on indictment of 10 years and/or a fine; section 92. Software pirates beware! The maximum penalty under copyright law is two years.

The Trade Marks Act 1994 introduced into trade mark law a remedy for groundless threats of infringement proceedings. If such an action is brought, the trade mark proprietor would have to prove that the act he complained of does, indeed, infringe the trade mark. Certain things can be threatened, such as applying the trade mark to goods, importing goods to which the mark has been applied or supplying services under the mark. Other things, which could infringe a registered trade mark, such as selling or offering for sale goods to which the mark has been applied or using the mark on business papers, are within this remedy. Any person aggrieved by the threats can bring an action. Although it would appear that this remedy is designed to protect retailers, distributors and the like from groundless threats it can allow a person responsible, for example, for applying the mark to goods, to bring an action. He could be "any person aggrieved" because his retailers have received a threat of court action and refuse to sell any of his goods in the future.

In *Prince plc* v *Prince Sports Group Inc* [1998] FSR 21, the plaintiff (an English company) registered "prince.com" as its Internet domain name. The defendant was an American company with "Prince" as its trade mark which had been registered in the United Kingdom. The defendant's lawyers sent a letter to the plaintiff complaining of its use of the domain name and claiming that the plaintiff was infringing the defendant's trade mark. Infringement proceedings were threatened unless the plaintiff assigned the domain name to the defendant. The court granted a declaration that the threats were unjustified and an injunction against continuance of the threats. As the threat was general in nature, the defendant could not take advantage of the exceptions to a threats action.

Groundless threats actions are also available in respect of patents, registered designs and the design right. They are not, however, available in relation to copyright nor, of course, breach of confidence or passing off.

Passing off

The law of passing off gives remedies where one trader uses a name or get-up belonging to another trader, having a goodwill in the name or get-up, in relation to goods or services such that the buying public will be deceived and think that those goods or services originate from or are provided by that other trader. It is also passing off if the buying public are not so deceived but the use of the other trader's name or get-up imputes some quality attributable to that other trader's goods. The second form is described as extended passing off and is actionable because the practice may tend to erode the goodwill associated with the name of get-up; for example, where names such as Spanish Champagne, Elderflower Champagne or Keeling's Old English Advocaat are used by persons other than the French Champagne producers or Dutch Advocaat makers.

In many respects, the law of passing off can be seen as a common law equivalent to trade mark law although of earlier origin. Indeed, trade mark law came about because of the perceived deficiencies of the law of passing off. However, passing off is still a very popular form of action and it protects non-registered names and marks and has, in the past, shown itself to be of considerably wider application than trade mark law although the 1994 Act should extend trade mark law into fields previously only occupied by passing off. The Trade Marks Act 1994, like its predecessors, expressly recognises the law of passing off and is without prejudice to it; section 2.

The leading case on passing off is *Erven Warnink Besloten Vennootschap* v *J Townend & Sons (Hull) Ltd* [1979] AC 731 where Lord Diplock defined passing off as requiring a misrepresentation made by a trader in the course of trade to prospective customers of his or ultimate consumers of goods or services supplied by him which is calculated to injure the business or goodwill of another trader and which causes actual damage to the business or goodwill of the trader by whom the action is brought. Put more simply, essentially what is required is business goodwill belonging to the plaintiff which is being or will be harmed by the misrepresentation made by the defendant.

In *International Business Machines Corp* v *Phoenix International (Computers) Ltd* [1994] RPC 251, the plaintiff alleged that the use of terms such as "IBM" and "IBM manufactured" in relation to circuit boards made by the defendant using components made by the plaintiff was passing off. In an interlocutory hearing the judge refused to strike out a number of defences including one claiming that there had been no misrepresentation and that the plaintiff had acquiesced in the defendant's use of the terms.

Passing off may be a possibility where an unregistered name is used with the intention to deceive (there are a lot of unregistered names used for computer software) or where some other reference is made to another trader's name such as in the phrase "IBM Compatible" or "IBM approved".

Using a name which belongs to, or is otherwise associated with, another person as a domain name on the Internet is likely to be passing off. There have been a number of examples where passing off has been found in such cases. For example, in *Marks & Spencer plc* v *One in a Million Ltd* [1998] FSR 265 well known commercial organisations brought an action against the defendant which was a dealer in Internet domain names. It registered a number of domain names including "bt.org", "sainsbury.com" and "marksandspencer.co.uk". Injunctions were granted ordering the defendant to transfer the domain names to the plaintiffs.

Trade libel

A tort related to passing off is malicious falsehood, often referred to as trade libel. This would be relevant where, for example, one trader wrongfully suggests that the goods of another trader are sub-standard or defective. It would also be trade libel to wrongfully suggest that another software company's products infringe a third party intellectual property right or are subject to a patent that should be revoked for invalidity. Another example of malicious falsehood is where an announcement is made to the effect that the plaintiff has ceased trading; see *Ratcliffe* v *Evans* [1892] 2 QB 524. Care must be taken in any advertising literature to avoid committing this tort.

Summary

Software licensing requires an awareness that rights other than copyright may be involved and an understanding of the basic principles of those rights. Of course, copyright is the primary right that will be involved in the vast majority of cases but, as has been noted, the law of breach of confidence may be invoked in actions involving software licences and some software may be part of a patented invention. The licence agreement must address the various issues raised by these other rights. Appropriate warranties and indemnities are obviously important. In some cases, it may be important that the licensee does not disclose the software to others.

Trade mark law should not be forgotten. Wherever possible software should be licensed under a trade mark and provision be made for licensing the trade mark as well as the software where appropriate. Care must be taken with advertising software and in respect of claims relating to compatibility with or the performance of other software or hardware products.

Chapter 4

The Legal Environment of Software Licensing

The Legal Environment of Software Licensing

Introduction

This chapter is concerned with the legal framework within which software licences exist and which places constraints on the terms or conditions within them. Naturally, the basic rules of contract law apply but it is in their application to the technical aspects of licence agreements that confusion may arise. In addition, other areas of law are critically important such as copyright law, the law of breach of confidence and competition law. The general law of tort is also relevant and this is dealt with in the following chapter which looks at the liability for loss or damage caused by defective software.

Before looking at software licences in detail, it is important to dwell on the main subject-matter of the licence and the legal nature of software licences; for example, are they in the nature of sale of goods contracts or service contracts or neither? These issues are fundamental to the determination of the applicability and effect of legal constraints upon the terms contained within software licences. Another important question is the standard of quality to be attained by the supplier of software and whether the client or customer can alter the software in order to correct any errors that are present at the time of delivery or at a later time. As well as looking at the legal provisions that normally apply, the effect of any terms that attempt to modify or exclude those provisions is a critical aspect of software licensing. In many cases, the parties to the licence will be commercial organisations and the law on consumer protection will not apply or will apply only on the periphery.

Potentially, competition law could have serious impacts upon software licences. The owner of the software may be in a very good position if that software has become the *de facto* industry standard. He may be sorely tempted to apply premium prices to his product or limit supply or unduly interfere with the licensee's use of the software. He may buy up competing products or be the sole source of information or data.

Computer software generally is not subject to patent rights (it can be in rare cases, see Chapter 3, p 70) and, therefore, is not subject to the safeguards contained in patent law designed to prevent abuse of a monopoly position. However, competition law has shown itself willing to step in and, to some extent, control the exploitation of software. A good example is the use of antitrust law in the United States against software suppliers and the work of the European Commission constraining anti-competitive software exploitation with respect to operating systems software. It is sensible to be aware of this when drafting licence agreements so that care may be taken to avoid terms that could be seen as anti-competitive. In many cases, European Community competition law will be relevant as will United States antitrust law, because the exploitation of software is often set on a global stage. First, the subject matter of software licences will be examined.

Subject matter of the licence agreement

The use of computer software normally involves an act restricted by copyright law or is subject to the law of breach of confidence. Loading a computer program into a computer produces a copy of the program or parts of the program and this will also apply to other forms of software such as databases or documents stored in a computer or on a magnetic disk. Therefore, the copyright owner's licence is required otherwise, unless the act concerned is permitted by copyright law, there will be an infringement of that copyright. A computer program and other forms of software may be confidential and their use will require the permission of the owner of the information because an obligation of confidence is expressly or impliedly imposed on the client or customer.

The main subject matter of most software licences is the grant of a right to perform one or more of the acts restricted by copyright. It is a licence to use the software. However, the licence agreement almost certainly will provide for other rights and obligations. In particular, services may be provided such as installation and testing of software, training the client's staff to operate and use the software, and the continued maintenance of the software. Goods too may be provided, such as computer equipment, magnetic disks and documentation. Although the licence to perform acts restricted by copyright might be seen as the essence of the agreement, it is much more complex than that and apart from the provision of services and goods, the agreement will have to deal with a number of other issues, some of which will be concerned with apportioning risk. As the copyright licence is such an important element of the agreement, it is briefly considered next.

What is a copyright licence?

Fundamentally, a licence is a permission to perform some act that otherwise would be unlawful. To use a computer program or other items of software without the licence of the copyright owner is an infringement of the copyright. Therefore, some form of permission must be granted and this usually takes the form of a licence agreement, although an assignment of the copyright might be effected instead in appropriate cases. A licence may be exclusive, sole or non-exclusive. With an exclusive licence, the licensee is given the right to perform specified acts to the exclusion of all others including the owner of the right. The basis of a sole licence is that the licensor and a single licensee may perform the specified acts in relation to the software whereas a non-exclusive licence grants the relevant rights to the licensee but the same rights may be granted to any number of other licensees. Under copyright law, the sole licence has no special place and is treated simply as if it were a non-exclusive licence.

In terms of the rights under copyright law that exist in software, licences may be whole or partial, as noted in Chapter 2. That is to say, the entire bundle of rights under copyright law may be involved or only one or more of the various rights may be granted to the licensee. For example, the licence may permit the licensee to use the software but not to rent or lend copies to the public.

Copyright licences will usually be express. Terms may be implied by law. Even an entire licence may be implied where this is consistent with the intention of the parties; see *Blair* v *Osborne & Tomkins* [1971] 2 WLR 503. Terms may be implied by statute or common law. Examples of terms implied by statute are those implied by the Sale of Goods Act 1979 or the Supply of Goods and Services Act 1982. Similar terms might be implied by common law or to give the licence business efficacy. This may be particularly appropriate where a licence agreement is silent about the ownership of the copyright in any printed output or whether the licence can be assigned to a third party.

Compulsory licences, granted to a third party regardless of the wishes of the owner of the right, after formal application by the would-be licensee, are a possibility in some areas of intellectual property law such as patents though they are not generally available for copyright works. Licences as of right may be appropriate in some cases, particularly where the owner of the relevant right is abusing the right in some way, such as by restricting access to the work involved. A licence as of right is one which any person can take as of right, subject to the payment of a fee or royalty. Such licences may be declared to be available by the appropriate Secretary of State following a report by the Monopolies and Mergers Commission. Section 144 of the Copyright, Designs and Patents Act 1988 has provisions for licences as of right for copyright works. The author is not aware of licences being made available as of right in respect of computer software.

Legal nature of software licences

A difficult and still not entirely resolved question is to determine the precise legal nature of an agreement to acquire and use software in terms of its classification as a sale of goods contract or a service contract (that is, a contract for services as opposed to a contract of service). If it is a sale of goods contract, it will be subject to the Sale of Goods Act 1979 whereas, if it is deemed to be a service contract, it will be governed by the Supply of Goods and Services Act 1982. This simple two category classification is not exhaustive and some types of software may fail to fall into either category. Important factors in classifying software licences are whether the software is being specifically produced for a particular client at that client's request (bespoke software), whether it is ready-made software (off-the-shelf software) and whether it is provided along with computer hardware (bundled software). An example of the latter is where a person buys a computer with operating systems and applications software pre-loaded onto the computer's hard disk.

Bespoke software

In *The Salvage Association* v *CAP Financial Services Ltd* [1995] FSR 654 before the Official Referee, the plaintiff, the client, wished to computerise its accounting system and invited tenders for this work. The defendant, a software company, submitted a proposal which was accepted and the defendant was awarded a contract for a feasibility study for £30,000. Following this, a second contract was awarded to the defendant for the development and implementation of the software that had been specified as a result of the first contract.

The Official Referee considered that the contracts were, in essence, service contracts and, as such, subject to the implied terms under Part II of the Supply of Goods and Services Act 1982. He went on to imply a term under section 13 of the Act which states that where a supplier is acting in the course of business, there is an implied term that the supplier will carry out the service with reasonable skill and care. Under section 12 of the Act, a service contract is one where a person (the supplier) agrees to carry out a service though this does not include a contract of service. The contract will remain a service contract whether or not goods are also transferred or hired under the contract. There is no definition of "service" in the Act and it is entirely reasonable to assume that its provisions are capable of extending to agreements to write bespoke software.

The other terms implied by Part II of the Supply of Goods and Service Act 1982 are that the service shall be carried out in a reasonable time (section 14) and that the client will pay a reasonable charge; section 15. These provisions apply only where the contract does not fix or provide for the fixing of the time for completion and the payment to be made and there is not a previous course of dealing from which they can be fixed. In the vast majority of cases, these matters will be provided for by the agreement. However, they may be relevant where the supplier has, at the client's request, undertaken additional work and there is no mechanism in the contract for working out the additional payment and the revised delivery date. Of course, it is always better to provide for such eventualities, for example, by including a schedule of rates in the contract. The time and effort required in writing or adapting software is notoriously difficult to predict and the licence should include terms for extension to the time for delivery and for liquidated damages in the event of late delivery.

A software licence may lay down the standard of workmanship required and the implied term of reasonable care and skill is only a safety net in the absence of specific standards. In any case, sections 13 to 15 of the Supply of Goods and Services Act 1982 essentially do no more than restate the common law. Indeed, such terms were being implied into commercial contracts over 100 years ago, a good example being *The Moorcock* [1886-90] All ER Rep 530 where a term was implied into a contract to the effect that a wharfinger should ensure, so far as was reasonably possible, that the river bottom alongside his jetty was in such a condition so as not to damage any vessel moored there.

Terms may be implied by virtue of legislation or by common law. In the case of the latter such terms will only be implied if necessary to give effect to the presumed intention of the parties to the contract. In *Trollope & Colls Ltd* v *North West Metropolitan Regional Hospital Board* [1973] 1 WLR 601, Lord Pearson said:

> "An unexpressed term can be implied if and only if the court finds that the parties must have intended that the term should form part of their contract:

it is not enough for the court to find that such a term would have been adopted by the parties as reasonable men if it had been suggested to them: it must have been a term that went without saying, a term necessary to give business efficacy to the contract, a term which although tacit, formed part of the contract which the parties made for themselves."

One question that arises is what the standard is in terms of writing computer software. It is obviously an objective test, determined by comparison with the level of skill and care to be expected from a reasonably experienced software company. An incompetent programmer writing software may fail to reach this standard even though he may try his very best. That is not to say that software, when delivered, must be error free. It is in the nature of software, and in particular, a computer program, that it is likely to contain errors and the courts have accepted this. In *Saphena Computing* v *Allied Collection Agencies* [1995] FSR 616 (actually decided in 1989), it was held by the Court of Appeal that a computer program might be reasonably fit for its purpose and yet still contain errors. The logic behind this approach is a welcome acceptance of reality because a computer program of any complexity is almost certain to contain errors even if written by the most able and experienced programmers. Many of the errors may not be detected for a considerable length of time because they may only be triggered by a rare combination of input data. As far as other forms of software are concerned, such as databases, text and images, it is much simpler to check for errors. Programs present challenges of a much greater magnitude and it is almost impossible to exhaustively test every combination of data and every path through a suite of numerous computer programs.

A software house will discharge its duty to use reasonable care and skill by employing suitably qualified staff and making sure that work carried out by lesser experienced programmers is adequately supervised and checked. If it is decided to engage a sub-contractor to perform part of the software house's obligations under the contract, the software house has a duty to select a reasonably competent sub-contractor and the software house will remain responsible contractually for the sub-contractor's work; *Stewart* v *Reavell's Garage* [1952] 2 QB 545.

Off-the-shelf software

A great deal of software is available "off-the-shelf". Examples include popular word processors, spreadsheets, graphics packages and computer games. Whilst the categorisation of contracts to write new software as service contracts is uncontentious, it is much more difficult to classify ready-made, off-the-shelf software. This also applies where the contract is for the supply of hardware as well as software or for hardware that incorporates software.

In the case of off-the-shelf software, some commentators argue that the contract is, essentially, a sale of goods contract and governed by the Sale of Goods Act 1979, see Smith, "Software Contracts" in Reed, C (ed), *Computer Law*, Blackstone, 3rd ed (1996) at 55 *et seq*. Certainly, there is the appearance of a sale of goods contract. For example, the person wishing to acquire the software might go into a "computer shop" and ask for a particular software package. He is then handed a sealed box containing disks and manuals in return for a payment. However, the essential nature of a sale of goods contract is given in section 2(1) of the Sale of Goods Act 1979 as a contract in which the title to goods passes in return for a money consideration called the price. The title to the disks, manuals and other documentation, box and wrapper may pass but the title to the copyright in the computer programs does not. In any case, copyright is not a "good" for the purposes of the Act. The purchaser obtains a licence to use the software and this is the main purpose of the contract.

Above all other considerations, a person acquiring software wants the permission of the copyright owner to use the software. For example, in the case of word processing software, the person acquiring it wants to use the software to produce letters, reports and other documents. The fact that tangible items are also provided is of secondary importance. The disks are merely the carrier, the medium by which the programs, dictionary, thesaurus and associated computer files are stored. The documentation is of some interest in that it will provide instructions as to the installation and use of the software (although such information is frequently contained within the files stored on disk in addition to or instead of being written down on paper); it is ancillary to the use of the programs and other computer files. The subject-matter of the contract is essentially the service of providing a copy of the programs and other files to enable the user to create, store, format and print written works. As more software becomes available "on-line", this fact will become even more self-evident.

In *Ashley* v *Sutton London Borough Council* (unreported) 8 December 1994, Queen's Bench Divisional Court, Ashley had supplied books on mail order describing a strategy for winning at fixed odds gambling with a guarantee to refund the purchase price if not satisfied. He was charged with making statements that were false as to the nature of the services provided in the course of a trade or business contrary to section 14 of the Trade Descriptions Act 1968. He appealed against his conviction in the magistrates' court to the Queen's Bench Divisional Court by way of case stated. Counsel for Ashley contended that he had supplied books which were goods and not services and, as a result, he was not guilty under section 14. However, Scott Baker J held that although goods were supplied as well as services (the service of providing information), the essential nature of the contract was the provision of information; that is, the provision of a service. Persons acquiring the book wanted the information contained within the book which was merely the carrier of that information, as evidenced by its high purchase price. The contract was, therefore, a contract for services and the appeal was dismissed. The same principle applies to software, *a fortiori*. Software is information and the price of a software package reflects that it is the right to use the software that is important rather than the tangible items supplied.

Another factor is that, to be able to use a computer program, the acquirer will need a licence as loading a program into a computer's volatile memory is an act restricted by the copyright subsisting in the program because, by section 17(6) of the Copyright, Designs and Patents Act 1988, copying includes making copies that are transient. The licence is the fundamental mechanism which is, itself, inconsistent with a sale of goods contract, the latter being by section 2(1) of the Sale of Goods Act 1979, as noted earlier, a contract in which the seller transfers or agrees to transfer the property in goods to the buyer for a money consideration called the price. The Sale and Supply of Goods Act 1994 has amended the Sale of Goods Act 1979 but has not changed the meaning of "goods" which include all personal chattels other than things in action and money. A copyright is, of course, a thing in action.

Even if it is accepted that the purchase of a book is a sale of goods contract only and no service is performed by the author, there is still a distinction between the purchase of a book and a contract for the acquisition of off-the-shelf software such that the latter is not, or not exclusively, a sale of goods contract. In a contract for the sale of a book tangible goods incorporating intellectual property rights are acquired by the buyer. The buyer obtains goods in the form of paper, cover and printers ink and a copy of a work in which copyright subsists. However, there is one fundamental and crucial difference between the sale of a book and the acquisition of off-the-shelf software. The purchaser of a book does not perform any of the acts restricted by copyright by simply reading the book or even lending it to a friend. A copyright licence is not required to read a book. In the case of software, a licence under copyright law is required to use the software because using the software will result in copies of the software being made and, even if those copies are transient only, without the copyright owner's permission there will be an infringement of copyright. Hence the importance of the licence. The essence of the contract is the right to use the software. The fact that goods may be delivered with the software may be dealt with by considering the contract to be, in effect, two separate contracts, one being a licence to use the software, the other being a sale of goods contract in respect of the physical items such as magnetic disks, manuals and so forth. This reflects the fact that two forms of property are involved, the copyright (the acquirer obtains a right under the copyright) and the tangible items (the acquirer usually obtaining the title to these items).

In a Scots case, *Beta Computers (Europe) Ltd* v *Adobe Systems (Europe) Ltd* [1996] FSR 367 it was held that a contract to acquire off-the-shelf software was a contract *sui generis*, that is, it did not fit into any of the traditional classifications of contracts. The judge rightly stressed that it was not a sale of goods contract as that would subordinate the main purpose of the arrangement, being granting the right to use the software, to the tangible items delivered such as disks and manuals. Beta had supplied Adobe with computer software produced by a third party, Informix Software Inc which owned the intellectual property rights in the software concerned. It had been ordered by Adobe over the telephone and was a standard upgrade package suitable for Adobe's computer. The software was delivered with a "shrink-wrap" licence and the package bore the words:

> "Opening the Informix S.I. Software package indicates your acceptance of these terms and conditions."

Adobe attempted to return the software, not having used it but this was rejected by Beta which then sued for payment of the price. It was held that the time such a contract is made is when the conditions imposed by the owner of the intellectual property rights subsisting in the software were accepted by the purchaser of the software. Lord Penrose considered the Copyright, Designs and Patents Act 1988 in relation to computer programs and concluded that the supply of the medium on which the program is stored must be accompanied by a licence to use it which was either express or implied. He said that an essential feature of the supply of software is that the supplier undertakes to make available to the purchaser both the medium and the right of access and use of the software.

The approach of Lord Penrose is pragmatic though it is difficult to reconcile with the English doctrine of privity of contract. In the United States, the 7th Circuit Court of Appeals, held that a shrink-wrap licence was enforceable. It accepted that the terms of the licence did not have to be exposed on the outside of box and it was sufficient if there was a notice to the effect that there was a licence agreement inside. Furthermore, and consistent with Lord Penrose's judgment, the purchaser of the software would be entitled to a full refund if, after reading the licence, he did not agree with the terms and conditions (*The Times*, "Interface Supplement", 10 July 1996, p 6).

Bundled software

Frequently, the acquisition of hardware also involves copyright materials. For example, a person buying a computer will commonly be supplied with computer software. Operating systems software such as "MS-DOS" or "Windows" is generally supplied with computers, frequently "pre-loaded", and applications software may also be "bundled" with the computer. The distinction between operating systems software and applications software is important.

Where a computer is sold with operating systems software, the essence of the contract is the sale of the hardware. The buyer wants to acquire a computer. However, a computer must have operating systems software to be usable. One way to view such a transaction is to consider it to be a sale of goods contract coupled with a licence to use the operating system software. If there is a defect in that software, the computer will not operate at all or will operate unreliably. Because operating systems software is so basic to the operation of a computer and its ability to run applications software such as word processing, spreadsheets or databases, a defect in an operating systems program can be equated to a defect in the computer itself. The computer itself is defective as a result and the buyer would expect to have remedies under the Sale of Goods Act 1979, as amended, as a result.

Sale of goods law has been changed by the Sale and Supply of Goods Act 1994 which came into force on 3 January 1995. The changes may be relevant to contracts for sale or supply of computer software bundled with computer hardware. Previously, section 14(2) of the Sale of Goods Act 1979 implied a condition that goods sold in the course of business were of merchantable quality. This was defined by section

14(6) in terms of fitness for the purpose or purposes for which goods of the relevant kind were normally sold. Also, by section 61(1) of the 1979 Act, quality in relation to goods included their state or condition. The precise meaning of merchantable quality was not an easy matter to determine and the buyer's right to reject was, accordingly, uncertain in many cases. In particular, the presence of minor defects did not necessarily render a good unmerchantable as in *Millars of Falkirk Ltd* v *Turpie* [1976] SLT 66 where an oil leak from the power steering unit of a new car did not make the car unmerchantable. Thus, the buyer was not entitled to reject the car: the breach, such as it was, was not a breach of condition (or, in Scotland, a material breach). The issue of whether goods ought to be durable also caused problems. For example, in *Bernstein* v *Pamson Motors* [1987] 2 All ER 220, an engine seizure in a car no more than three weeks old and having covered only 140 miles did not render the car unmerchantable although the Court of Appeal, in *Rogers* v *Parish (Scarborough) Ltd* [1987] QB 933, redressed the balance somewhat in favour of the buyer.

The Sale and Supply of Goods Act 1994 substitutes a new section 14(2) in the Sale of Goods Act 1979 and added new subsections (2A) and (2B). The overall effect is to replace the implied condition of merchantable quality with a new term that the goods should be of satisfactory quality. Section 14(2A) states that goods are of satisfactory quality if they meet the standard that a reasonable person would regard as satisfactory. As before, account is to be taken of the description of the goods, the price (if relevant) and all other relevant circumstances. However, in a departure from the previous law, section 14(2B) defines some of the aspects of the quality of the goods to be taken into account in appropriate cases being:

(a) fitness for all the purposes for which goods of the kind in question are commonly supplied (this is a simple restatement of the prior law),
(b) appearance and finish,
(c) freedom from minor defects,
(d) safety, and
(e) durability.

The implied term as to quality of goods is a condition in England and Wales and Northern Ireland. It is simply a term in Scotland where the possible remedies available depend upon whether the breach is a material one; if it is a material breach, the buyer may reject the goods. A material breach is broadly equivalent to a breach of condition in England, Wales and Northern Ireland.

Other important changes are made to the Sale of Goods Act 1979. In non-consumer sales, defined in accordance with section 12 of the Unfair Contract Terms Act 1977 (or, in Scotland, section 25(1) of the 1977 Act), the buyer loses the right to reject for breach of any of the conditions in sections 13, 14 and 15 of the Sale of Goods Act 1979 if the breach is so slight that it would be unreasonable for the buyer so to reject. The implied condition is transformed into a warranty. The burden of proof is on the seller both in respect of the nature of the breach and whether the sale is a non-consumer sale.

There are some other changes to the provisions in the Sale of Goods Act 1979 dealing with delivery of the wrong quantity, the buyer's right to examine the goods and acceptance. Thus, in relation to non-consumer sales, section 30 is amended to take away the buyer's right to reject where the wrong quantity is delivered but the shortfall or excess is so slight that it would be unreasonable for the buyer to reject (the burden of proof being on the seller). Where the sale is a sale by sample, the buyer is given a reasonable time to compare the goods with the sample. The buyer is, as before, not deemed to have accepted the goods until he has had a reasonable opportunity to examine the goods for conformity with the contract (or, in a sale by sample, of comparing the bulk with the sample) but now, under section 35(3), in a consumer sale, the buyer cannot lose this safeguard by agreement, waiver or otherwise. A welcome amendment is that, by section 35(6), if the buyer has asked for or agreed to repairs to defective goods, or if the goods have been delivered to another under a sub-sale or other disposition, this does not necessarily mean that the buyer has accepted the goods. An important new provision, section 35A, deals with the buyer's rights of partial rejection. Unless a contrary intention appears in, or is to be implied from, the contract, where the buyer has the right to reject the goods because of some breach of the seller's obligations that entitles the buyer to reject all or some of the goods, the buyer may accept some of the goods without losing the right to reject the rest.

It is clear that items of computer hardware are goods within the meaning assigned by section 61(1) of the Sale of Goods Act 1979 even if they contain software (such as the bootstrap, start-up or operating system programs stored on computer chips or hard disk inside a computer) and the provisions of that Act will apply if the goods are defective even if the defect is attributable to a defect in the software. In *Toby Constructions Products Pty Ltd* v *Computer Bar Sales Pty Ltd* [1983] ALR 684, hardware was sold complete with operating systems software. The hardware cost A\$ 12,230 and the price of the software was A\$ 2,160. The New South Wales court held that this was a sale of goods contract and the implied terms of merchantable quality, compliance with description and fitness for purpose applied. If the equipment did not work because of a defect in the software, this would still fall within the statute. This case was approved in *St Albans City & District Council v International Computers Ltd* [1995] FSR 686, (at first instance), in which the defendant had supplied hardware and software. The plaintiff suffered a loss because of a defect in the software. The judge held, *inter alia*, that the contract was probably a sale of goods contract. In fact, because he found breaches of an express term in the licence and a term implied under the Supply of Goods and Services Act 1982, he did not have to decide this point and his reasoning was unconvincing on this point. However, in the Court of Appeal (*St Albans City & District Council v International Computers Ltd* [1997] FSR 251), Sir Ian Glidewell accepted that the contract was not a sale of goods contract as the program was not sold but licensed.

The new provisions as to quality simply make it easier for a buyer to reject an item of hardware that exhibits minor defects or is lacking in durability. Prior to the changes to the Sale of Goods Act 1979, the presence of minor defects and a lack of durability did not inexorably lead to a conclusion that there had been a breach of section 14(2) of the Sale of Goods Act 1979. For example, in *Micron Computer Systems Ltd v Wang (UK) Ltd* (unreported) Queen's Bench Division, 9 May 1990, it was held that failure of a hard disk was a perfectly normal teething problem and did not give the buyer the right to reject the computer as it was still of merchantable quality assuming, of course, that the seller repaired the disk or replaced it with a new one. Now, it is more likely that the buyer would be able to reject the goods under the modified requirement of quality, especially as expectations in terms of the reliability of computer equipment have risen.

To summarise, the right to reject defective computer hardware (including bundled software) is now subject to the following provisions:

- the strengthened quality provisions under section 14(2). Particularly important for hardware contracts are the aspects of quality relating to freedom from minor defects, safety and durability. Minor defects could, potentially, be attributable to software errors;
- in non-consumer sales, the possibility that a defect that would otherwise give rise to a breach of condition will be treated as a breach of warranty if the breach is slight; section 15A. For example, a minor flaw in the plastic casing of a keyboard that has no material effect on its performance may be treated as a

breach of warranty only (it is arguable whether such a minor defect would be a breach of section 14(2) in any case). The same approach might be taken in respect of defective software which causes the computer to "crash" occasionally though infrequently (although it is notoriously difficult to identify the source of such a problem) – many computers are prone to this;

- that the buyer agrees to or asks for repairs to be carried out to the goods does not necessarily lead to a conclusion that the goods have been accepted. For example, if a computer has a faulty disk drive or defective software, the buyer may allow the seller to replace the drive or reinstall the software in the hope that the defect will be cured. If the new disk drive as fitted is defective or the software still does not operate properly, the buyer may still be able to reject the computer and claim back the price.

Under the new provisions as to quality, if a computer has an intermittent but troublesome fault, such as the occasional failure of the operating system to load, requiring that the computer is switched off and on again, that is likely to mean that the computer is not of satisfactory quality, similarly if the hard disk on a computer fails after one month. Alternatively, the computer might crash frequently causing loss of data. Where the seller is selling in the course of a business, any of these defects will be a breach of new section 14(2) and give the buyer the right to reject the goods and, where appropriate, to claim damages. The view of merchantable quality taken in *Micron* v *Wang* must now be seen as too narrow although the test of what is usual in goods of the same type should still be useful in assessing whether a particular item is of satisfactory quality. The classification of software contracts is shown in Figure 4.1.

Legal controls over software licences

The law relating to software licences has been obscure and subject to much controversy. This has been so not only in relation to whether items of software are goods but also in terms of the legal controls over such licences. For conventional sale of goods and supply of services contracts, the law has been well settled for some time. Terms were implied by common law and by statute to provide some measure of "consumer protection". Nevertheless, exclusion clauses remained a problem. Initially, the courts developed ways of overcoming badly

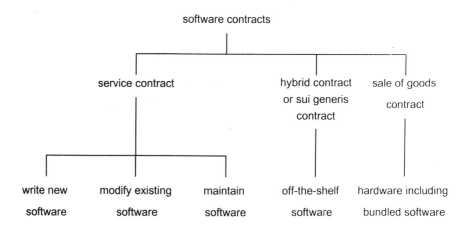

Figure 4.1 Nature of Software Contracts

drafted exclusion clauses by use of the *contra proferentem* rule (ambiguities to be construed in the way least favourable to the party seeking to rely on the clause) and, eventually, the doctrine of fundamental breach evolved to curb the worst excesses of exclusion clauses. Eventually, the Unfair Contract Terms Act 1977 provided an adequate mechanism for controlling exclusion clauses which has proved to be reasonably predictable in its application. However, the relevance of this legislation to software licences has been strongly doubted but recent case law demonstrates how effective it can be in this context. Changes made to the Copyright, Designs and Patents Act 1988 also have a bearing on the validity of some terms in software licences.

Implied terms

Software that is specifically written for a client will be subject to the implied terms in the Supply of Goods and Services Act 1982. Further terms may be contained in the licence agreement imposing a higher standard. In *The Salvage Association* v *CAP Financial Services Ltd*

[1995] FSR 654, the software licence contained a term to the effect that the software developer would assign suitably qualified staff to perform the work involved in writing the software. This was not the case and most of the staff assigned were unfamiliar with the ORACLE fourth-generation language used to write the software. The Official Referee held that there was a breach of this term. He also implied a term under section 13 of the Supply of Goods and Services Act 1982 (that the provider of a service should use reasonable care and skill) and held that there was also a breach of this term. The standard to be achieved is that of the reasonably competent software company.

If operations system software is sold with hardware it is likely that the Sale of Goods Act 1979 applies as discussed above and the question is then one of whether there has been a breach of the implied terms, especially those under section 13 or 14 (description, quality and fitness for purpose). In *Saphena Computing* v *Allied Collection Agencies* [1995] FSR 616 the Court of Appeal suggested that the law on fitness for purpose in terms of computer software was the same whether the contract was one for goods or services.

Unfair Contract Terms Act 1977

Given the difficulties associated with developing reliable and satisfactory software, it is not surprising that software companies may be tempted to exclude or limit their liability for failure to deliver software free from defects by the agreed date for delivery and in respect of any defects in the software. Section 2 of the Unfair Contract Terms Act 1977 deals with contractual terms of notices that purport to exclude or restrict liability for negligence. Section 3 controls terms that attempt to exclude or restrict liability for breach of contract (including misperformance or non-performance) but only applies where one party deals as a consumer or on the other's written standard terms. Section 4 applies where a person who deals as a consumer is contractually bound to indemnify another for a breach by that other person for negligence or breach of contract. In some cases, the application of sections 2 to 4 are based on a requirement of reasonableness, the test for which is given in section 11. Schedule 2 to the Act contains guidelines for the application of the reasonableness test but is expressed as being relevant to section 6 or 7 of the Act which deal with liability for breach of the implied terms under the Sale of Goods Act 1979, the Supply of Goods (Implied Terms) Act 1973 and other contracts under which the title to goods passes.

In the context of the subject matter of this book, sections 2 to 4 of the Unfair Contract Terms Act 1977 are the most important. However, at first sight, it seems easy to exclude liability for breach of contract or for negligence as paragraph 1(c) of Schedule 1 to the Act states that the provisions in section 2 to 4 of the Act do not extend to any contract:

> "so far as it relates to the creation or transfer of any right or interest in any patent, trade mark, copyright, registered design, technical or commercial information or other intellectual property right ..."

Of particular importance is whether section 2, concerning the exclusion or limitation of liability for negligence (including negligence in respect of an obligation arising from a contract) and section 3 (contractual liability for breach or in relation to performance) can be excluded in a software contract. If these sections apply, a software company would only be able to exclude or limit liability subject to the requirement for reasonableness, except in the case of negligence leading to death or personal injury, where liability cannot be excluded or restricted at all.

In *The Salvage Association* v *CAP Financial Services Ltd* [1995] FSR 654, the Official Referee held that the nugatory effect of paragraph 1 only concerned those provisions in a contract that dealt with the creation or transfer of a right or interest in the relevant intellectual property and did not extend to the other terms of a service contract simply because the service will result in a product that is subject to intellectual property rights. Thus, terms that are concerned with aspects of the contract other than those relating to the creation or transfer of an intellectual property right are still subject to sections 2 to 4 of the Unfair Contract Terms Act 1977. In the case under consideration, the terms subject to judicial scrutiny were concerned with aspects such as the competence and performance of the defendant's staff, the quality of the product and liability for breach of contract and negligence. There were two contracts, the first being a feasibility study for the proposed software and the second was for the development, testing and implementation of the software. Both contracts had clauses limiting liability to £25,000. The Official Referee considered the reasonableness of the defendant's limitation clauses. This was important in the context of section 2(2) (liability for loss or damage other than death or personal injury arising from negligence) for both contracts and, for the first contract only, in the context of section 3 (liability arising in contract) as the first contract was made on the defendant's written standard terms.

In respect of the reasonableness test expressed in section 11 of the Unfair Contract Terms Act 1977, the burden of proof is on the defendant to show that a term satisfies the test. Section 11(4) states that regard shall be had to the resources available to the person seeking to restrict liability to a specified sum and to the possibility of that person covering himself by insurance. Although the Schedule 2 guidelines are not expressed as being applicable to sections 2 and 3 of the Act, the Official Referee accepted the suggestion of Potter J in *Flamar Interocean Ltd* v *Denmac Ltd (The Flamar Pride)* [1990] 1 Lloyds Rep 434 that it would be sensible to take the guidelines into account in such cases. He referred also to the judgment of Lord Griffiths in *Smith* v *Eric S Bush* [1990] 1 AC 831 identifying four matters that should always be considered, being:

(1) the relative bargaining power of the parties;
(2) whether it was reasonably practicable to obtain advice from an alternative source;
(3) the difficulty and dangerousness of the task to be undertaken, that is, the risk; and
(4) the practical consequences of the court's decision, the ability of the parties to bear the losses involved and the availability of insurance.

The parties were of equal bargaining power but it would have been almost impossible for the plaintiff to insure to cover the liability excluded by the defendant. Insurance was a crucial factor as the defendant had already recognised the inadequacy of the £25,000 figure in its standard form contracts and it had been raised to £1,000,000 at around the time of the first contract. The defendant had not been able to explain convincingly why the higher figure had not been used in its contracts with the plaintiff. It may have simply been a mistake or oversight. The defendant could, and had, obtained insurance for negligent performance at a reasonable premium. Therefore, it was held that the terms limiting liability to £25,000 were unreasonable. The plaintiff was awarded a total of £662,962 damages comprising £291,388 (the sums already paid to the defendant), £231,866 for items of wasted expenditure (computer time, wasted computer stationery, payments to consultants and for testing) and £139,672 for wasted management time.

The approach taken in the above case has been confirmed in the Court of Appeal in *St Albans City & District Council* v *International Computers Ltd* [1997] FSR 251. The plaintiff was a local authority responsible for setting the level of and collecting the community charge (poll tax). The plaintiff invited tenders for the supply and delivery of hardware and software to keep a register of charge payers and produce bills, etc. The contract was awarded to the defendant, a major international computer company. Because of an error in the software, the total population figure was overstated by 2,966 and as a result, the plaintiff set the community charge too low. It also suffered loss because of precepts and grants that were calculated on the basis of the population figure. The total loss suffered was £1,314,846. The contract had been made on the defendant's standard written terms.

At first instance, the judge decided that the defendant was under an obligation to provide reliable software and that it had to be reasonably fit for its purpose and that the defendant was in breach of this obligation. There was a term in the contract limiting liability for defects to £100,000 but this was held to be unreasonable under the Unfair Contract Terms Act 1977 (on the basis of sections 3, 6 or 7) and based on the reasonableness test in section 11 and the guidelines in Schedule 2. In particular, the defendant had failed to discharge its burden of proof that the term was reasonable in the circumstances. The judge awarded the full amount claimed of £1.3 million in spite of the fact that the plaintiff could recoup its losses by increasing the charge in the following year (which is what it did). The Court of Appeal confirmed that the limitation clause was unenforceable. However, it was held that the plaintiff could not recover losses in relation to payments by chargepayers as they were under an obligation to pay (otherwise they would get a bonus). The appeal was allowed in part in that the award of damages was reduced to £685,000.

The question as to whether a term is reasonable is not answered in a vacuum. It depends on the particular circumstances. A particular term limiting liability may be reasonable in some circumstances but not others. Section 11(1) of the Unfair Contract Terms Act 1977 states that the term must be:

> "fair and reasonable ... having regard to the circumstances which were, or ought reasonably to have been, known to or in the contemplation of the parties when the contract was made."

Even a standard disclaimer on a standard form used by solicitors and which derived from an initiative from the Law Society could, in some circumstances, be unreasonable; *First National Commercial Bank plc v Loxleys* (unreported) *The Times*, 14 November 1996, Court of Appeal. The wise software developer will re-evaluate any terms in the licence agreement which limit liability for breach of contract or negligence in the light of the circumstances prevailing each time he makes a contract with a new client.

Time-bombs

It is not unknown for software developers to build "time-bombs" into their programs. These are activated after a period of time and prevent or hinder further use of the program. The reason some software developers use time-bombs is not usually out of some malicious or twisted sense of humour but is to protect their interests. It can help to prevent unlicensed use of software or encourage the acquisition of upgrades by the client. A typical scenario is for the time-bomb to lay dormant for, say, a couple of years and then it is triggered to partially disable the program. The licensee then has to contact the software developer for a new code number to be entered into the software to make it fully functional again. If this is not done, eventually the software becomes completely unusable. An example of such a time-bomb was subject to litigation in *Amac Computer Systems* v *Systems Union Ltd* (unreported) 1 May 1997, Court of Appeal. In refusing leave to appeal from the decision of the Bristol County Court, Hobhouse LJ said that:

> "... it may be that there are now market or legal constraints on the supply of software containing such devices, certainly without the consent of the purchaser."

Unfortunately, the plaintiff was not legally represented and the original particulars of claim were inappropriate to the facts of the case. Had the plaintiff been better advised from the outset, the outcome may well have been different. Nevertheless, it raises some interesting points.

If the licensee has not agreed to the time-bomb, it is possible that an offence has been committed under section 3 of the Computer Misuse Act 1990 which is discussed later in this chapter at page 110. Also, the licensee should have remedies for breach of contract. If the software is bought off-the-shelf, the licensee may be able to sue the software developer, on the basis of the licence agreement, and the supplier. The cause of action against the supplier could be on the basis of a breach of a sale of goods contract if we are prepared to accept that there is a collateral contract to the licence agreement or, possibly, on the basis of negligence for failing to point out the existence of the time-bomb or for negligently holding out that the software was "fit for its purpose".

Where the licence agreement provides for the inclusion of time-bombs in the software the situation is somewhat different and it is a matter of whether the relevant term in the agreement is valid.

Probably the best form of attack is the Unfair Contract Terms Act 1977 in that such a term fails to pass the test of reasonableness as required by section 3. Factors which may assist in determining whether contractual provision for time-bombs is reasonable are:

- the existence of other, equivalent software, without a time-bomb;
- how common they are in that type of software;
- the relative bargaining strength of the parties;
- whether the existence of the relevant term in the agreement has been brought to the attention of the licensee; and
- whether it is reasonable to expect a licensee to comply with the conditions to obtain a new code word to "reset the clock".

Of course, the burden of proof to show that the term in the licence concerning the existence of a time-bomb is reasonable in the circumstance lies with the licensor in such a case. It is suggested that it will be very difficult to discharge that burden successfully. Another legal doctrine that may be applicable is non-derogation from grant. This is described later in this chapter at page 111.

There may be one difficulty with section 3 of the Unfair Contract Terms Act 1977 in the context of a term such as the following:

> "The licensee agrees that the software has a time device embedded within it which will prevent further use of the software on a date two years from the installation of the software. One month prior to this, a warning message will be displayed when using the software. The licensee agrees to contact the licensor for a new code word which may be used to reset the time device for another two years. At the same time, the licensor will inform the licensee of any subsequent upgrades to the software, if any, and to give the licensee the opportunity to obtain a copy of such upgrades at a discount of 10% on the then current list price. The parties agree to repeat this process until such time as the licence is terminated in accordance with its terms."

The problem is that, when dressed up in this form, this does not look like a contract term which excludes or restricts liability for breach of contract. It looks more like a term which is of mutual benefit to the parties. Of course, it is the substance and not the form which is important in considering whether terms are caught by the Unfair Contract Terms Act 1977 but the above example indicates that it may be possible to avoid the application of the Act to the use of time-bombs in software.

As Hobhouse LJ stated, market constraints may be an important factor to deter software developers from using time-bombs. Persons acquiring software should be very wary of software that contains time-bombs, especially in the lead up to the year 2000. They should check the licence agreement to ensure that there is no mention of them and, in the case of bespoke software, insist on a warranty to the effect that the software is free from such devices.

Void terms under the Copyright, Designs and Patents Act 1988

The EC Directive on the legal protection of computer programs extended the range of express permitted acts available in the case of computer programs (although it was debatable whether the permitted act of fair dealing and the potential use of implied terms would not have had the same effect in practice). Lawful users of computer programs are permitted to make necessary back-up copies of computer programs and to decompile computer programs if necessary to achieve interoperability by sections 50A and 50B respectively. By section 296A(1) where a person has the use of a computer program under an agreement, any term or condition in the agreement shall be void in so far as it purports to prohibit or restrict the making of any back-up copy of the program which it is necessary for him to have for the purposes of the agreed use or where the conditions in section 50B(2) are met, the decompiling of the program. Furthermore, any term or condition shall be void in so far as it purports to prohibit or restrict the use of any device or means to observe, study or test the functioning of the program in order to understand the ideas and principles which underlie any element of the program.

Those drafting licence agreements must take care not to include terms caught by section 296A. One way to deal with this is to allow the licensee to make back-up copies or to decompile the computer program in accordance with sections 50A and 50B only and to prohibit all other forms of copying and decompilation unless otherwise expressly granted by the licence agreement, bearing in mind that simply using the program will involve the making of transient copies at the very least. It must also be remembered that the provisions in sections 50A and 50B do not apply to items of software other than computer programs and, in respect of these (with the exception of databases, for which see later), the normal fair dealing provisions and the use of implied terms may be applicable. For example, a court may imply a term to the effect that a licensee can make a back-up copy of a licensed database.

The permitted act in section 50C, copying and adapting necessary for lawful use, appears to be vulnerable to being prohibited or restricted by a term in a licence agreement. However, this must be balanced with the doctrine of non-derogation from grant and any restriction could not be used to interfere with the use of the program envisaged by the parties as ascertained by construing the contract. Competition law may also control such terms.

Databases

The Copyright and Rights in Databases Regulations 1997 made specific provision for copyright databases and introduced a new database right. For copyright databases, section 50D of the Copyright, Designs and Patents Act 1988 allows a person having a right to use a database, or part of it, to do anything, which would otherwise infringe copyright, necessary to access and use the contents of the database, or part of it. This right cannot be taken away or restricted by any term or condition in an agreement, and any such term or condition is void under section 296B. The permitted act of fair dealing for research or private study has been modified to exclude commercial research and to require an indication of the source. Apart from these changes, the other permitted acts that apply to literary works generally also apply to databases.

In respect of the database right, where a database has been made available to the public, and a person has a right to use the database under an agreement, any term or condition in the agreement which purports to prevent that person extracting or re-utilising insubstantial parts of the contents of the database is made void under regulation 19(2) of the Copyright and Rights in Databases Regulations 1997. The same applies to the situation where the person has a right to use part of a database only in relation to that part.

The impact of the permitted acts for computer programs and databases is different to that for other works. In other cases, permitted acts are vulnerable to an agreement which excludes or restricts them. This is not so in relation to the special permitted acts for computer programs and databases, except, it would appear, under section 50C. Thus, it is possible in a licence agreement to prohibit copying by printing of any part of a novel in digital form for any purposes including private study. It is not possible, however, to prevent copying or adapting the computer program accompanying the novel in order to decompile it to discover the program's interfaces so that a new program can be written such that it can operate with that program or some other program. Apart from the rights granted in the normal run of things by the licence, a licensor will not want to allow any copying or other use beyond that he is required to permit under the 1988 Act and 1997 Regulations. A form of words that may be used in a licence agreement to achieve this could be:

> "Except as provided for elsewhere in this agreement, the licensee may not copy, adapt, modify, decompile, transmit, download, or otherwise reproduce, alter or make available the licensed software except as provided by sections 50A, 50B and 50D of the Copyright, Designs and Patents Act 1988 and regulation 19 of the Copyright and Rights in Databases Regulations 1997."

Other legislation relevant to software licences

Many other areas of legislation could impinge upon the commercial exploitation of software, examples being breach of confidence, the laws of defamation, obscenity, blasphemy and blackmail. It is important that, where appropriate, these matters are considered in full and dealt with. Where the agreement involves the assignment of copyright rather than a licence, the assignee will need to satisfy himself that the assignor has the right to transfer the copyright and that he will enjoy the copyright unencumbered by third parties claiming to have rights in it. Sections 2 and 3 of the Law of Property (Miscellaneous Provisions) Act 1994 provides a useful mechanism for doing this simply by using the form of words "with full title guarantee" as in

> "[The assignor] hereby assigns the entire copyright and any other rights subsisting in [description of work], whether now or in the future, with full title guarantee to [the assignee]."

There are two particular statutes that could have special significance in terms of software licences that are likely to be relevant in many cases, so much so that terms dealing with them ought to be contained in standard licence agreements: the Data Protection Act 1998 and the Computer Misuse Act 1990.

Data Protection Act 1998

The Data Protection Act 1998 imposes obligations on persons (data controllers) who decide the purposes for which personal data are processed. Personal data are data which relate to a living individual who can be identified from those data or from those data and other information in the possession of the data controller. The 1998 Act replaces the Data Protection Act 1984 and implements the European Directive on the protection of individuals with regard to the processing of personal data and on the free movement of such data (OJ 1995 L281/3).

Although the 1998 Act follows a similar mechanism to the 1984 Act in that data controllers must notify the Data Protection Registrar (now re-named the Data Protection Commissioner) of their processing activity, it is more stringent and has more implications for software licences where the software includes, for example, a database of information about individuals. The new law even applies to structured manual files, although these do not normally require to be notified.

Enforcement of the Act is through two routes. First, there is a system of notices, including an information notice (whereby the Commissioner seeks information about processing activity) and an enforcement notice, where the Commissioner considers that there has been or is a contravention of the data protection principles (see below). The second way in which data protection law is enforced is through a number of criminal penalties. For example, failing to notify is a criminal offence as is failing to notify changes in registrable particulars. Obtaining or procuring the disclosure of personal data without the consent of the data controller is also an offence.

At the heart of data protection law are the data protection principles. They are contained in Schedule 1 to the Act which also contains provisions interpreting the principles. The principles are as follows:

1. Personal data shall be processed fairly and lawfully and, in particular, shall not be processed unless –
   (a) at least one of the conditions in Schedule 2 is met, and
   (b) in the case of sensitive personal data, at least one of the conditions in Schedule 3 is also met.
2. Personal data shall be obtained only for one or more specified and lawful purposes, and shall not be further processed in any manner incompatible with that purpose or purposes.
3. Personal data shall be adequate, relevant and not excessive in relation to the purpose or purposes for which they are processed.
4. Personal data shall be accurate and, where necessary, kept up to date.

5. Personal data processed for any purpose or purposes shall not be kept for longer than is necessary for that purpose or those purposes.

6. Personal data shall be processed in accordance with the rights of data subjects under the Act.

7. Appropriate technical and organisational measures shall be taken against unauthorised or unlawful processing of personal data and against accidental loss or destruction of, or damage to, personal data.

8. Personal data shall not be transferred to a country or territory outside the European Economic Area unless that country or territory ensures an adequate level of protection for the rights and freedoms of data subjects in relation to the processing of personal data.

Schedules 2 and 3 set out conditions where data may be processed. For example, Schedule 2 allows processing, *inter alia*, with the data subject's consent or if necessary for the legitimate purposes of the data controller. There are several more conditions and the scope of most of them is tightly limited. Data subjects' rights include a right of access to data, a right to object to processing likely to cause damage or distress or processed for the purposes of direct marketing, a right to compensation and, also, in most cases, a right to be informed of the processing of personal data relating to them.

Whilst it is not appropriate here to describe the detailed workings of this important and complex piece of legislation, it is vital that some of its provisions are considered when drafting licence agreements in cases involving personal data. Some of the issues include:

- data processors are persons who process personal data on behalf of the data controller – computer bureau and companies providing facilities management services in respect of a client's IT function will be processors and, as such, are required to carry out such processing under a contract which is made or evidenced in writing to the effect that the processor is only to act on the data controller's instructions and complies with the seventh data protection principle (this feature is considered more fully in Chapter 10 on facilities management; see p 228);
- programmers working on the development of, or modification to, the client's software may access or use a database containing personal data belonging to the client – it is important to ensure that the client's notification with the Data Protection Commissioner allows such persons to access the

personal data and a warranty in the licence agreement may be advisable or even a copy of the relevant register entry in a Schedule to the licence agreement;

- programmers working for a software developer should be made aware of data protection law, otherwise there is a risk that they might commit criminal offences (the developer and senior officers may also be liable vicariously) or precipitate an enforcement notice – a client may want a term in the licence imposing a duty on the software developer only to use staff or consultants who are reliable and who will respect the security of any personal data they have access to.

Computer Misuse Act 1990

This Act contains three offences designed to impose criminal penalties on forms of computer misuse. Especially important is the computer hacking offence (unauthorised access to a computer or computer material). This had been seen as a particular threat but the Act also filled a few of the gaps that had been perceived in the criminal law as applied to computer fraud, destruction of computer programs and data and computer viruses. The offences under the Act are:

- unauthorised access to computer material (programs or data); section 1;
- unauthorised access with intent to commit or facilitate the commission of further offences (the "ulterior intent" offence); section 2. For example, unauthorised access with the intention to obtain property by deception, carry out blackmail or even murder;
- unauthorised modification of computer material; section 3. This covers the alteration, erasure or addition of computer programs or data.

In terms of software licensing, particularly where a program is being specially written for a client on-site, the question of authorisation is a key one and it is important that the agreement provides either for a schedule of programs or data to which the software company has access to or a means of obtaining that information and authority from the client. Section 17(5) of the Act states that access of any kind is unauthorised if the person making access is not himself entitled to control such access and he does not have the consent for such access from the person entitled to control access. Although implied authorisation should apply in many circumstances, it is better to have express authorisation. This is particularly so in respect of modification made to programs and data. For example, a programmer working for the software company could change an existing batch program file to assist in running the new software. Before doing this, the programmer should be satisfied that the client is aware of this and has given permission for the change. Apart from being good practice it will avoid any embarrassment caused by misunderstandings. The software company should ensure that its own staff are aware of the provisions of the Computer Misuse Act 1990.

The software company should make every endeavour to ensure that it does not introduce computer viruses on the client's computers or media. Whilst this is good practice, it does no harm to mention it in a licence agreement as this will help to focus attention on the danger. A set routine could be required such as the software company exposing every computer disk to be used on the client's computers to a virus checker with the possibility of imposing contractual liability for damage resulting from a failure to take this simple precaution. The software company, if it is working on the client's computers might require that the client, if he does not already do so, carries out periodic virus checks on his own equipment.

Error correction

It is extremely likely that software, when completed, will contain errors ("bugs"). Most software systems have thousands of lines of program code and an almost infinite number of alternative routes through it. It is almost impossible to test conclusively. The source code for the control system for a Canadian nuclear power station took 35 person years to check and some serious errors were discovered (*The Times*, 20 March 1992). What is worrying is that there may be more errors as yet undetected. The position regarding the enforcement of copyright so as to prevent error correction has already been alluded to in Chapter 2; see page 36.

By analogy, the principle of non-derogation from grant may be applicable to computer software just as it is to articles that will need replacement parts. A company developing software for a client should not be able to insist that the client must not correct errors himself or use the services of a third party maintenance company. In *Digital Equipment Corp* v *LCE Computer Maintenance Ltd* (unreported) 22 May 1992, High Court, the plaintiff alleged infringement of copyright by the defendant who was in the business of providing independent maintenance for clients using the plaintiff's computers. The defendant was using the plaintiff's diagnostic software for this purpose. It was held, *inter alia*, that the defendant had an arguable defence based on the principle of non-derogation from grant. The defendant claimed that, having bought a copy of the diagnostic software, it should be entitled to use it to provide maintenance services for others without the need for a further licence or permission.

In practice, there is no general duty on the software developer to provide a copy of the source code to the client and, without that, error correction will be far more difficult to perform. In real terms, the crux of the matter is whether the client is given a copy of the source code. The importance of error correction must not be underestimated. In terms of negotiating software licences it is usually the most important aspect and, often, other provisions can pale into insignificance in comparison. However, delivery of source code will not be subject to negotiation in all cases as some software developers steadfastly refuse to make it available to clients. If source code is not delivered, then it is essential that there is a satisfactory arrangement for on-going maintenance. Even then, if the item of software is substantial and important to the client's operations, a copy of the source code and design materials should be subject to an escrow agreement, whereby the source code and other materials are placed in the possession of a third party who will release those items to the client should the software developer go out of business or be unable or unwilling to continue to maintain the software.

Even with off-the-shelf software, the question of error correction is important. The source code will not be available and the acquirer will be totally reliant on the software company (which may be a foreign company). However, it is worth investigating the company's track record in terms of providing upgrades (which will hopefully cure any existing defects in addition to providing new features) and any support (customer service) offered. Most companies offer a telephone hotline. In some cases it is almost impossible to get through. In most cases, off-the-shelf software has been thoroughly tested and any errors tend to be minor, though there are exceptions.

Competition law

EC competition law recognises the existence of intellectual property rights. Article 222 of the Treaty of Rome states that nothing in the

Treaty shall prejudice the rules in Member States governing the system of property ownership. However, the manner in which those rights are exercised may well be controlled. EC competition law is only relevant if and to the extent that trade between Member States is affected or likely to be affected. EC competition law derives from the Treaty of Rome (EC) and there are three provisions of note:

- Article 30 and the freedom of movement of goods;
- Article 85(1) prohibiting restrictive trade agreements;
- Article 86 prohibiting abuses of dominant trading positions.

There is a *de minimis* rule and small undertakings will not be affected by Article 85(1) where the effect on the market is insignificant; *Volk* v *Vervaecke* [1969] CMLR 273. Guidance from the Commission suggests the following situations will be outside Article 85(1):

- where the goods or services do not represent more than 5% of the total market for such goods or services in the area of the common market affected by the agreement; and
- the aggregate annual turnover of the participating undertakings is not more than 300 million ECU (approximately £200m at the time of writing).

Article 30 may be relevant in cases of parallel importing and the doctrine of exhaustion of rights applies. However, this is without prejudice to the rental and lending. A licensor of off-the-shelf software may be unable to prevent subsequent assignment of the licence but he will be able to prevent the rental of the software to the public (this is the same as under section 18 of the Copyright, Designs and Patents Act 1988 where copies of computer programs have been issued to the public). However, Article 30 is couched in terms of quantitative restrictions on goods, *not services*.

Article 85(1) is particularly concerned with terms in licence agreements. If terms offend, they will be void, although Article 85(2) states that the agreement shall be void (more usually, however, it may be a matter of whether the term is severable – if so only that term is affected). A licence is a vertical agreement, with the licensor usually in a stronger position than the licensee and, consequently, he may be tempted to impose onerous terms on the latter including a prohibition on error correction by the client or a third party. Article 85(3) allows the making of block exemptions from Article 85(1) and there have been some such exemptions, for example, in relation to patent and/or know-how licences under the Technology Transfer Regulation. There is no equivalent for software licences but it may be that lessons can be learnt from these block exemptions. These, and the experience of their application, can assist in deciding what terms in software licences might be caught by Article 85(1) and what terms might escape.

Forrester suggests that the following terms may be acceptable (Forrester, I.S., "Software licensing in the light of current EC competition law" [1992] 1 ECLR 5):

- minimum royalty clauses;
- post-term use prohibitions (for example, prohibiting use of the software after expiry or termination of the licence agreement);
- terms prohibiting sub-licensing;
- terms imposing a duty to defend the copyright (and to assist in any ensuing legal action);
- terms requiring the grant back of any rights in any improvements made by the licensee on a non-exclusive basis.

The following terms may be caught by Article 85(1):

- terms tying the acquisition of the software to the purchase of other items, such as hardware;
- terms requiring the grant back of exclusive rights in improvements;
- terms imposing absolute territorial restrictions.

In some cases, the above types of terms which have parallels in the Technology Transfer Regulation will not be particularly relevant to software licences. However, care should be taken to prevent having any of those that may be contrary to Article 85(1). Terms prohibiting decompilation would probably have been within the remit of Article 85(1) but for the comprehensive provision now incorporated into copyright law. Terms preventing error correction could be controlled if they are deemed likely to distort competition. This they will certainly do as they prevent or restrict free competition in the provision of software maintenance services. Sometimes, the licensor will insist that the software is to be used on a designated machine or a limited number of designated machines. It is common to restrict the installation of software to one computer only. This should not cause any problems except where the licensor has also provided hardware and use of the software is limited to that hardware. That could be seen as a tie-in clause such that the software may not be obtained separately (Powell, "Drafting software licences in light of EEC competition rules" [1993] 9 CLSR 254).

Article 86 typically deals with a situation where a dominant trader abuses his position. A software company might do this by refusing to disclose details of its software interfaces to other software companies (although they should be able to glean this information by decompiling the appropriate software) or by selectively refusing to grant licences. For example, if a company makes hardware and associated software but refuses to grant licences in respect of the software to a competitor making alternative hardware. IBM were investigated by the Commission because it was refusing to release interface details concerning its mainframe computers to competitors who wished to interface their own products with IBM's. In *Digital Equipment Corp* v *LCE Computer Maintenance Ltd* (unreported) 22 May 1992, High Court, mentioned above, it was held also that the defendant had an arguable defence under Article 86 because, by restricting the defendant to using the plaintiff's software on one computer only, the plaintiff was unduly restricting the market in the maintenance of the plaintiff's computers.

Articles 30, 85 and 86 are of direct effect and can be applied by the national courts. It is clear that they can be used as a sword or as a shield.

Chapter 5

Liability for Defective Software

Liability for Defective Software

Introduction

The potential liability for defective software can be enormous. A programming error can leave the software company responsible for it with a large bill which it may not be insured against. International Computers Ltd found itself being sued for a client's £1.3 million loss caused by a software error in *St Albans City & District Council* v *International Computers Ltd* [1995] FSR 686 discussed in the previous chapter; see page 101. At first instance, the judge awarded the full amount but this was reduced on appeal to £685,000. But liability for defective software is not restricted to the other party to a contract and liability can arise in respect of third parties who are injured or suffer loss because of the defect. Computers are now being used in many situations where death or injury can result from a defect. For example, an alleged programming error was discovered in a computer controlled system for treating cancer patients with doses of radiation in a Staffordshire hospital after several years of use (*Computing*, 13 February 1992, p 4, reputedly a settlement of £2m was agreed, *Computing*, 1 May 1997, p 18). The London Ambulance computer system collapsed in 1992. To this must now be added the potentially immense bill for errors caused by the Millennium bug. The introduction of the single European currency is also likely to cause problems due to the complex manner in which currency conversions will have to be made. At the time of writing, it is claimed that only a small proportion of financial software packages are EMU compliant.

Computers are being used increasingly to give advice. That advice may be in the form of treatment for a patient or as to what shares to invest in. The consequences of defects in the software coupled with the fact that it is almost impossible to test software completely should concentrate the mind on liability issues. For example, what if a suite of programs controlling a nuclear power station are defective? What if a bank's main computer fails, losing details of several days of transactions? What if a patient is crippled for life as a result of a defect in diagnostic decision-support software? What if an air traffic control system suffers a catastrophic failure at a busy time?

It is clear that the questions of when and how liability can attach to someone are of the utmost importance and must be given full consideration by anyone developing, distributing and using computer software. In the previous chapter, the effectiveness of exclusion clauses and their applicability were discussed. This chapter concentrates on the ways in which liability for defects can arise and the nature of that liability. Four main areas are covered. Contract law is mentioned only briefly as it is more relevant to the previous chapter. The law of negligence is described in the context of computer software as is product liability under the Consumer Protection Act 1987. Finally, the law relating to negligent misstatement is considered in the context of expert systems or decision-support systems which are being used to provide advice, either to the client or to be used by the client to advise another person though the principles are not restricted to this particular type of system.

Contractual liability

Consider the situation where a consulting engineer has obtained a licence to use software to assist in the design of building structures. He is engaged by a client and uses the software to design the steel frame for a warehouse. There is a fault in the final design and the warehouse collapses resulting in considerable financial loss to the client and a number of injuries to employees of the client and third parties who were in the vicinity of the warehouse at the time.

The client will be able to sue the engineer for breach of contract and, possibly, also negligence. The engineer's contractual liability will be based primarily on section 13 of the Supply of Goods and Services Act 1982, the duty to exercise reasonable care and skill in providing the service of designing the steel frame for the building. Of course, the contract may impose a higher standard by express terms. Whether reasonable care and skill was used is an objective test and the standard of the reasonably competent consulting engineer would be called into play. In this case, the test would require a consideration of whether it was reasonable to choose the software used, what testing and verification of the results would be expected and would the reasonably competent engineer have used it for the particular task. The position of the engineer vis-à-vis the software is analogous to that of a main contractor engaging a sub-contractor. A main contractor will not escape contractual liability if the sub-contractor carries out his work badly and remains liable for defective work carried out by the sub-contractor. Thus, the engineer must ensure, as best he can, that the software is reliable and the results produced accurate. To this end, he should not take the computer output at face value and should find ways of verifying it, for example, by the use of "rules of thumb". One thing the engineer should do, of course, is check the terms of the licence agreement for the software to see what restrictions there are in relation to the licensor's liability for defects and to assess to what extent these match his own potential liability.

Insurance is an important factor. The engineer will almost certainly have professional indemnity insurance. He should check the terms of the insurance to make sure that his potential risk is fully covered. It could prove embarrassing if the insurer refuses to cover a claim because it considers that the engineer has not been negligent; that the mistake was due to an error in the software and the engineer was not negligent in spotting it, yet the engineer finds himself liable for the client's loss under the contract.

The engineer will not be contractually liable to the employees of the client personally, nor to any third parties because there is no contractual relationship between them. He could be liable, however, under the law of negligence.

Law of negligence

A client suffering loss will usually sue on the basis of breach of contract. However, an action in negligence is not out of the question in such cases, particularly in the alternative. It should be remembered that the tests for whether damages are recoverable in contract and in tort are slightly different. A further factor is that the duty in tort may be greater than that imposed by the contract; *Holt* v *Payne Skillington* (unreported) *The Times*, 22 December 1995, Court of Appeal.

Third parties will rely on the law of negligence, to seek satisfaction for their loss or injury. In the example above, a third party injured by the building collapse would sue in negligence. Generally, for a claim in negligence to succeed, there must, first of all, be a duty of care owed to the injured person. This is based on the "neighbour" principle, first expounded by Lord Atkin in *Donoghue* v *Stevenson* [1932] AC 562 to the effect that a duty of care is owed to one's neighbours being those who, with reasonable foresight, would be affected by the relevant act or omission. It might seem reasonable to limit this to those whose identity is known to the defendant. However, it is reasonably foreseeable that, if a building one has designed falls down, persons in the building and in its immediate vicinity, would be likely to be injured. In *Clay* v *Crump* [1964] 1 QB 533, it was held that an architect owed a duty of care to the building contractor's employees to make a careful inspection of a wall he had been engaged to examine and which later fell down injuring the employees.

Breach of the duty of care will occur even if the design fault is attributable to a defect in the software if the engineer was negligent in his choice of software, the way it was used or because he did not check the output sufficiently well.

As regards an action by a third party against the client, the position is less satisfactory. A person is not generally vicariously liable in negligence for the acts or omissions of an apparently competent sub-contractor; *D & F Estates Ltd* v *Church Commissioners for England* [1989] AC 177. Generally, the tort of negligence does not provide remedies for loss that is purely economic in nature (subject to the narrow exception in *Hedley-Byrne* v *Heller*, discussed later). There must be some physical damage caused by the defect.

In terms of the liability under the law of negligence of the software company producing the defective software, the position is uncertain because the "neighbour" principle becomes stretched for want of proximity and because the software company has little control over how the software is used. It may reduce the possibility of attracting liability still further by making it clear to persons using the software what its limitations are and advising that the output is checked. However, liability may still attach to the company producing the software if the software is of the type designed to provide advice or to assist in decision making; see page 134.

Millennium bug

For some time now, there has been serious concern about the disruption to computer equipment caused by the "Millennium bug" or the Year 2000 problem, resulting from the past practice of only using two digits to represent the year of a date. Vast sums of money have already been spent or committed to re-writing computer software to eliminate problems likely to result from this by changing all date references to allow four digits for the year. This is not an easy task. It requires that all dates stored in databases must be changed, for example, by changing the field design in the database and resetting all the existing dates in the database. Worse still, every occurrence of a date in a computer program must be located and modified. Sometimes dates are used in calculations, such as determining whether a particular vehicle or aeroplane is due for servicing or periodic checking. This can be very time consuming, particularly as all manner of variable names may have been used, some of them not particularly obvious. It is not just a matter of re-writing software stored on magnetic disk either. Some software affected may reside on silicon chips and these must be replaced. The use of silicon chips is now immense and cars, washing machines and cookers are just some examples of equipment containing them. On 1 January 2000 your washing machine might decide it needs to rinse its load for nearly 100 years. Of course, this might be annoying and expensive to overcome but computer technology is now used in a great deal of "safety critical equipment", such as radiography machines, life support systems and air, road and rail control systems. It is almost beyond doubt that some systems will fail because of the Millennium bug.

If a computer systems fails because of the Millennium bug, this will raise issues of liability for that failure. Suing on a contract might be possible and/or bringing an action for negligence. However, one major difficulty stands in the way. The test for breach of duty is, in both cases, based upon the reasonably competent software developer unless, of course, there is a contract with an express warranty that the software is "Millennium-proof". Going back some years (and not necessarily that many years) most computer programmers used two digits only for the year. This is a consequence of the severe restrictions and high cost of computer memory. If a lot of dates were used in a software system, the saving could be substantial. Having got used to using two digits as a convention, this practice seemed to have stuck with programmers for longer than it should. It is likely that most programmers who gave consideration to the matter thought a fix or magic bullet would be found before it became a problem or that the software would be obsolete by 2000.

If the software is of fairly old pedigree or includes old sub-routines, it is unlikely that the software developer will be found to be in breach of contract or breach of the duty of care for tortious liability. With more recent software, it really depends on the timing of when the potential for major problems resulting from the use of two digits for the year became known amongst reasonably competent programmers. The problem has certainly been widely known from about early 1996, possibly earlier than that. If software written since that time uses two digits then it is highly likely that there has been a breach of duty unless there is some good reason for it. This might be where the programmer has modified exiting software which uses two digits, pending a full scale exercise to change the software to operate with four digits.

If new software is commissioned now, it is vital that a warranty that the software is Year 2000 compliant is inserted into any licence agreement. Provision should also be made for extensive testing and for the software developer to demonstrate that it does comply. Failure to do this may leave the client vulnerable to a claim if a third party, including an employee suffers injury or loss as a result of any date error. However, this is not necessarily the complete answer as any date error may be caused by other software such as operating systems software or an existing database accessed by the software. In some cases it may be very difficult to establish the source of the error. It could even be the combined result from several items of software.

Other forms of liability might ensue. For example, a date error might result in an employee being injured. Apart from any exposure to a negligence claim, there may be issues of health and safety which impose criminal liability. Directors and managers of companies and even the company itself could find themselves prosecuted for offences under the Health and Safety at Work etc Act 1974. It may also be used by an employee on the basis of breach of statutory duty. For example, section 2 of that Act places a general duty on employers, as far as possible, to ensure the health, safety and welfare at work of their employees. Other duties are imposed such as in relation to persons who are not employees on the premises and even on the employees themselves. A number of other statutes impose duties that could result in civil and criminal liability resulting from defective software in appropriate circumstances. Examples include the Medicines Act 1968, the Food Safety Act 1990 and the Environmental Protection Act 1990 (*Computing*, 7 May 1998, p.74). The British Computer Society publishes a guide – *The Year 2000 – A Practical Guide for Professionals and Business Managers*. The Consumer Protection Act 1987 provides for civil liability on a producer or importer of defective equipment which causes damage and is discussed in the next section. Whilst these statutes are likely to be relevant where a person suffers injury as a result of a date error, they also apply to other forms of defects in software.

It is not only the Millennium bug which is causing current concern. Financial software will soon have to cope with the Euro and European Monetary Union. Here, personal injury is highly unlikely but there may be an action based on contract or on negligent misstatement, for which see page 134.

Product liability

Part I of the Consumer Protection Act 1987 introduced product liability law, as such, into the United Kingdom and implemented EC Directive 85/374/EEC. It imposes a form of strict liability (though there are some defences) on the producer or importer of a defective product. A product is defective when it does not meet the level of safety such as persons generally are entitled to expect. However, the definition of "product" in section 1(2) is such that it appears not to apply to computer software. "Product" means any goods or electricity and includes a product which is comprised in another product, whether by virtue of being a component part of raw material or otherwise. The supplier of a product made up from component parts or raw material is not to be treated as a producer of those components or raw materials by reason only of his supply of that product. "Goods" are defined in section 45(1) as including substances, growing crops and things comprised in land by virtue of being attached to it and any ship, aircraft or vehicle. From these definitions, it would appear that, apart from electricity, products must be tangible items. Information is not within the meaning of product and neither is a computer program. However, the tangible items on which the information of program is stored and other materials supplied such as documentation would fall to be products for the purposes of the Act.

There is no difficulty in classifying computer hardware as a product. The position as regards software bundled with the hardware is more difficult. However, if some physical damage is caused by an item of computer hardware, even if attributable to a fault in the software contained within it, a claim under the product liability provisions could be a possibility. The product is defective after all. It does not matter what the source of the defect is. Product liability law imposes liability on a producer to a person who has suffered damage caused wholly or partly by a defect in a product, or to a dependant or relative of such a person. That liability cannot be limited or excluded by any contract term or notice or any other provision; section 7. However, as regards damage to property, the property must be of the type ordinarily intended for private use, occupation or consumption and intended for such use by the person suffering the loss or damage, by section 5(3), and there is a limit of £275 before damages can be claimed for property loss or damage but there is no such limit as regards death or personal injury.

By section 2, there will always be someone to sue as a person who holds himself out to be the producer, for example, by attaching his trade mark to the product, is deemed to be the producer as is the importer from outside the EC. The supplier of a product will be liable for a defective product if he is requested to identify the producer and fails to do so in a reasonable time. The only time that there may be no defendant to an action is if the producer no longer exists, for example, in the case of a company that has been wound up.

Part II of the Consumer Protection Act 1987 also provides, by section 10, criminal penalties for supplying, offering or agreeing to supply or exposes or possesses for supply any goods which fail to comply with the general safety requirement (goods that are not reasonably safe having regard to the circumstances which includes published safety standards). This is highly relevant in the supply of computer hardware which, being electrically powered, must comply with the relevant safety regulations.

Expert systems and advice-giving systems

Computers are being used increasingly to provide advice at a high level of expertise. The dangers inherent are obvious, especially as the person using the system may not have sufficient depth of knowledge to satisfy himself as to the veracity of the advice provided. Just as in the past, when printed material tended to be accepted as being correct in preference to hand-written material, computer output is often taken at face value without any attempt to check or confirm it. Such is human nature. Because of the advice-giving role now being taken by computer systems, in some cases analogous to a consultation with an expert, the law relating to medical negligence is an apt platform upon which to examine the legal implications for advice which turns out to be wrong. The principles discussed should be applicable in most cases where computer software, intended to produce advice or other information to assist decision-makers, is licensed. It may be used by a decision-maker direct or by a professional who is advising a client. First the nature of such systems is discussed.

What is an expert system?

The phrase "expert system" has been used to describe computer systems which are capable of performing at or near to the level of an expert. These systems may be recognised by their manner of construction or by their performance. Structurally, expert systems usually comprise a knowledge-base, an inference engine and an interface with the user. The knowledge-base contains the raw material of the expert system; the rules and facts representing the expertise, an important part of which will be heuristic and this is particularly so with respect to expert systems in medicine. A large amount of a specialist's knowledge is informal and experiential in nature and this heuristic knowledge is what sets the specialist apart from the general practitioner. The inference engine is a computer program which attempts to resolve the user's enquiries by interacting with the knowledge-base. The interface with the user serves two purposes; first, to make the system easy to use and, secondly, and very importantly, to provide an explanation and justification for the results, advice and suggestions obtained from using the system.

The performance of an expert system is the most fundamental test for whether a computer system falls into this classification. The system should contain an explicit representation of empirical knowledge (including informal heuristic knowledge); be designed for use by persons having at least a basic knowledge of the subject area and be capable of providing explanations of the reasoning used and justifications for the results obtained. The inclusion of heuristic knowledge is a key point in the performance of expert systems. A great deal of medical knowledge is heuristic in nature; for example, an experienced doctor might use a rule in diagnosis such as "if symptoms A and B are observed then C is plausible but certainly not D."

Expert systems promise the wider availability of specialist expertise. Potentially, a general practitioner can have the skill and experience of specialist consultants at his fingertips. The most famous early medical expert system is MYCIN which was to assist in the diagnosis of blood infections and to suggest treatments. A number of other systems are now in regular use in some hospitals. This may be a very good thing and may lead to the earlier diagnosis of diseases and ailments bringing benefits to the patient in terms of quicker, appropriate treatment or earlier referral to a consultant or the selection of the most effective tests to be performed. There are, however, some serious drawbacks which may have important legal consequences if the advice or diagnosis obtained by a general practitioner using an expert system is defective and the patient suffers injury or pain as a result. The defect may arise in a number of ways such as a fault in the expert system itself or the misinterpretation by the general practitioner of the results; for example, he may have misunderstood the scope or limitations of the system he is using. In the future, liability could even attach for failing to use an appropriate, available and widely used expert system.

Basic principles of professional negligence

A doctor must exercise reasonable care and the test used is an objective one. In *Bolam* v *Friern Hospital Management Committee* [1957] 1 All ER 118 it was said that the standard of the ordinary skilled man exercising and professing to have the special skill involved was the standard to be applied in testing for reasonable care. However, the courts will not readily imply a term or extend the doctor's duty to the effect that the treatment or operation will be successful; *Eyre* v *Measday* [1986] 1 All ER 488. Sometimes, medical opinion will be divided as to the most appropriate form of treatment; there will be two schools of thought.

Where there exist two bodies of competent medical opinion, for a finding of negligence, it is not sufficient to show that one body of opinion considers the decision as to treatment wrong if another body of opinion, equally competent, would have considered the decision reasonable in the circumstances. In *Maynard* v *West Midlands Regional Health Authority* [1985] 1 All ER 635, the court recognised that differences of opinion existed within the medical profession and even though the court may prefer one body of opinion over another, that was not a sufficient basis, *per se*, to found an action in negligence. Inexperience of the area of expertise involved is no defence. In *Jones* v *Manchester Corporation* [1952] 2 QB 852, it was said that inexperience is a reason for seeking more experienced advice, it is not a shield against liability. In the difficult case of *Wilsher* v *Essex Area Health Authority* [1986] 3 All ER 801, Glidewell LJ, in recognising the desirability of applying an objective standard, suggested that the required standard of care is likely to be reached if, where appropriate, an inexperienced doctor seeks the advice of his more experienced colleagues. This is not without difficulties because it may be expecting too much of an inexperienced doctor to be able to identify situations when the advice of more senior colleagues should be sought.

One thing that is clear is that advice or treatment that is wrong in retrospect is not conclusive of negligence. In *Whitehouse* v *Jordan* [1981] 1 All ER 267, the defendant was a senior registrar in a hospital who had been in charge of the delivery of a baby. The delivery by Caesarean operation followed a high risk pregnancy after the mother had been in labour for 22 hours. The head of the department, a consultant professor of obstetrics, had made case notes suggesting the use of forceps to aid delivery. The defendant decided to use forceps and pulled on them four or five times but then, fearing for the safety of mother and child, he carried out the Caesarean operation which he did so competently. The baby was born severely brain damaged. It was claimed that this resulted from a lack of professional skill and care by the defendant pulling too long and too hard on the forceps. The House of Lords held that an error in clinical judgment did not necessarily lead to a finding of negligence. Lord Fraser said at 281:

> "[t]he true position is that an error of judgment may, or may not, be negligent; it depends on the nature of the error. If it is one that would not have been made by a reasonably competent professional man professing to have the standard and type of skill that the defendant held himself out as having, and acting with ordinary care, then it is negligent."

A problem which undoubtedly will arise in the context of expert systems is whether a general practitioner using a medical expert system is to be tested on the basis of an ordinary skilled general practitioner or by reference to the specialisation appropriate to the knowledge represented in the expert system. If the expert system is intended to be used to diagnose skin complaints, would the general practitioner using the system have to meet the standard of the ordinary skilled dermatologist? If so, this could be a very onerous standard to reach. An alternative and more controversial possibility is that the very act of consulting an expert system could be equivalent, by analogy, to seeking the advice of more skilled and experienced practitioners.

In determining whether harm is foreseeable, the wisdom of hindsight is excluded. For example, in *Roe v Minister of Health* [1954] 2 QB 66, the plaintiffs underwent minor surgery and were given a spinal anaesthetic by a consultant anaesthetist. The anaesthetic was contained in sealed glass ampoules which had been stored in a solution of phenol. Before using the anaesthetic, the ampoules were washed and visually inspected for cracks to make sure that none of the phenol had penetrated the ampoules. The plaintiffs developed paraplegia as a result of the anaesthetic being contaminated with phenol and it was later discovered that glass ampoules could contain microscopic flaws, undetectable by visual examination. The action in negligence failed because, at the time of the plaintiffs' treatment, this danger was not generally appreciated. Whether harm is foreseeable depends on contemporary medical knowledge.

At the present time, a doctor, in common with other professionals, if he is to reduce the possibility of negligence claims, is obliged to update his knowledge continually but he is not required to read every article appearing in a learned journal. For example, in *Crawford* v *Charing Cross Hospital* (unreported) *The Times*, 8 December 1953, an anaesthetist was not deemed to be negligent although the practice he used was shown to be unsatisfactory in an article in the *Lancet* six months earlier. It is only when a new technique becomes accepted as part of "common practice" that failure to adopt the technique or change present methods will be suggestive of a lack of reasonable care. In some respects, the increasing availability of expert systems in the future will widen the contemporary knowledge base conceptually. This is because expert systems do not deal solely with formal knowledge and techniques but also contain in their knowledge bases heuristic or experiential knowledge. This will have implications in the future both for practitioners who use expert systems and, especially, those who do not.

There must be a causal link between the negligence and the injury or damage suffered by the patient. For example, in *Hotson* v *East Berkshire Health Authority* [1987] 1 AC 750, a 13-year old boy injured his hip in a fall and his injuries were incorrectly diagnosed by the health authority. But, because the boy's subsequent chances of permanent disability were, on the balance of probabilities, caused by the fall and, even correct diagnosis and treatment would not have prevented this, the health authority was not liable. The plaintiff failed on the issue of causation even though the faulty diagnosis increased the likelihood of permanent disability. But see the earlier Court of Appeal decision in *Wilsher* v *Essex Area Health Authority* [1986] 3 All ER 801 where, on the issue of causation, it was suggested that a medical practitioner could be liable if his negligent conduct was merely one of several possible risk factors even though the contribution of the practitioner's breach of duty could not be ascertained.

Finally, on the question of the patient's consent, a doctor is not obliged to inform the patient of all the possible risks inherent in the form of treatment recommended if the particular risk is very small and withholding such information is accepted practice; *Sidaway* v *Bethlem Royal Hospital Governors* [1984] 1 QB 493, affirmed in the House of Lords [1985] AC 871. However, there may be circumstances in which there is a substantial risk of grave consequences and the need for the patient's consent is so obvious that he ought to be informed, notwithstanding any practice to the contrary accepted as proper by a responsible body of medical opinion. In the House of Lords, Lord Bridge of Harwich said that if a patient, of apparently sound mind, specifically asks about the risks, the doctor's duty would be to answer truthfully and to such an extent as the patient requires. This is particularly so in respect of innovative techniques and such techniques should be adopted with caution. A court would take into account evidence of trials of the technique and the attendant dangers. Even the attitude of the patient towards the use of novel or risky treatment could be important. As the use of expert systems in medical diagnosis is clearly still innovative, it would seem that a general practitioner should only use an expert system which has been thoroughly tried and tested and must have the patient's consent to its use in assisting with the diagnosis of the patient's condition providing, of course, that the patient is conscious and in a position to give his consent.

Relationships appropriate to expert systems

Figure 5.1 illustrates a typical scheme of relationships relating to an expert system to be used in medical diagnosis. Other arrangements may exist, such as where the specialist experts are directly employed by the expert system software company or the latter may use its own expert system shell. The scheme chosen is not unusual and should help

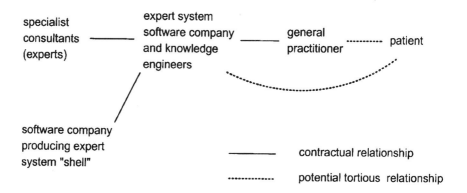

Figure 5.1 Expert System Relationships

to clarify the issues involved. In the scenario indicated in the diagram, a general practitioner has obtained an expert system, to be used to assist in the diagnosis of back pains. The general practitioner has obtained the system under a licence agreement which contains terms dealing with, *inter alia*, the contractual and tortious liability of the expert system software company for defects in the system and the terms under which the system may be used. In the example shown, the expert system software company has developed the expert system using its own knowledge engineers who have worked with independent specialist consultants to collect and formalise their knowledge before entering it into the knowledge-base of the expert system. Once this has been done, the knowledge engineers and the specialist consultants are likely to do further work in refining and validating the expert system. An expert system shell has been acquired from an independent software company under a licence agreement which allows the subsequent marketing of expert systems built using that shell (by way of "run-time" licences).

In terms of the legal relationships, the doctor obviously owes a tortious duty to take reasonable care in respect of his patient. If the doctor has been consulted privately, there will also be a contractual relationship between the doctor and patient. The doctor has a contractual relationship with the expert system software company which has contracts with the specialist consultants and the expert system shell company. As a claim in tort is independent of any contractual arrangement, the patient may find, depending on the circumstances, that he can bring a claim in negligence against the expert system software company. A limitation may be the lack of a nexus along the lines of the "neighbour" principle, but as discussed later, this may not be the hurdle it appears at first sight.

Scenario

To set the scene for the following discussion, suppose that a patient with a slipped disc has gone along to his general practitioner, complaining of back pains. The doctor has used an expert system to assist in his diagnosis and the patient does not object to this. A mistaken diagnosis results and the patient is recommended treatment which is inappropriate. Eventually, the patient's spine is permanently damaged, he is confined to a wheelchair and has had to give up his employment. Suppose it is shown that, if the correct diagnosis had been made by the general practitioner, the patient would have been referred to a specialist who could have prevented the permanent injury to the patient's spine. Who does the patient sue?

At first sight, the patient would be inclined to sue the doctor on the basis of medical negligence. If there is a contract between the doctor and patient it may be preferable to sue on the contract depending on any express terms and any terms which may be implied by the courts. However, concentrating on negligence, the identity of the potential defendant depends to some extent on the nature of the defective advice and the source of that defective advice in a causal sense. First, the situation when the expert system itself is shown to be unsatisfactory is considered; that is, where the defective advice flows from the expert system.

Faulty expert system

Obviously the expert system software company is a likely defendant in a negligence lawsuit, but the general practitioner still may not escape liability; for example, if he did not go to reasonable lengths to satisfy himself that the system was suitable and worked satisfactorily. That is, if the general practitioner was negligent in his choice of expert system or in his decision to use the system in a particular situation. After all, the patient would not know what the scope and limitations of the expert system are and it would be reasonable to expect him to rely on the doctor for this.

Doctor's liability

In a contractual relationship between a doctor and a patient, the doctor may be liable for defective advice given by a consultant to whom the patient has been referred. A contractor who sub-contracts part of his work under the contract is under a duty to select his sub-contractor carefully and merely seeking the other party's agreement to the sub-contractor does not lessen the contractor's liability; see *Stewart* v *Reavell's Garage* [1952] 2 QB 545. A contractor is liable for defective work carried out by a sub-contractor however carefully the contractor has been in selecting the sub-contractor. In this respect, the contractual duty to appoint a suitable sub-contractor (for example, the contractual duty of a doctor to refer the patient to a suitable specialist consultant, where there is a contract between doctor and patient) is stronger than is the case in tort. The corollary is that, in the case of contractual liability, the choice of an expert system can be equated to the choice of a specialist and the legal position should be the same.

If, as will often be the case, there is no contract as such between the doctor and the patient, the latter will have to rely on the tort of negligence. If the doctor delegates to a specialist, the doctor will not be liable for the specialist's negligence if that specialist was an apparently competent independent person; see *AMF (International) Ltd* v *Magnet Bowling Ltd* [1968] 2 All ER 789. Of course, if the specialist has himself been negligent, the patient may be able to bring an action in tort against him directly. The only situations where the doctor is personally liable for the specialist's negligence is when the doctor was negligent in choosing a suitable specialist or, if the specialist has made an error, the doctor is negligent in not warning his patient of the specialist's error, for example, if the specialist prescribed penicillin having failed to notice from the patient's records that he is allergic to penicillin and the patient's general practitioner does not spot this elementary error.

Using an expert system is, in some respects, analogous to using a specialist or a sub-contractor. Therefore, it would appear that the doctor using a medical expert system must take reasonable care in selecting the system and must not take the results obtained from using the system at face value. He should verify the results as best he can; this is one reason why it is so important that expert systems can justify the advice they produce. Additionally, the doctor should satisfy himself that he is capable of understanding the system and its limitations and that the system is working properly. This begs the question as to what amount of testing a general practitioner should be expected to carry out on an expert system that he intends to use in practice. The answer is complicated by the fact that the general practitioner probably will not have the depth of specialist knowledge contained in the knowledge-base and, *a fortiori*, probably will not have the ability to satisfy himself that the inference engine and user interface are appropriate to the knowledge-base and do not contain programming errors. Also, as many expert systems have an almost unlimited number of potential routes through them, absolute testing is a practical impossibility. The fact is that testing an expert system will be outside the scope of the general practitioner's skills and he can do no better than rely on independent tests carried out by some third party such as a professional body. It will certainly be dangerous for a general practitioner to use an expert system for the purpose of advising patients unless he has good independent evidence of the satisfactory performance of the system and, because of the very nature of expert systems, the doctor would be unlikely to reach the standard of reasonable care if he relied on his own testing exclusively.

Software company's liability

It has been shown that a doctor threatened with a negligence suit after using an expert system cannot afford to breathe easily if the system itself is found to be defective. However, the doctor may be covered by his professional indemnity insurance or he may have a counterclaim in contract against the expert system software company, subject to any exclusion clauses and controls over those clauses (an insurance company might pursue this claim). A defective system might leave the expert system software company directly liable to the patient in tort if sufficient proximity on the basis of the neighbour principle can be found between the patient and company. The latter might argue that, as it has no control over the subsequent use of the system and certainly will not know of the identity of the patients, there is insufficient proximity or nexus between the company and individual patients. However, in *Hedley Byrne & Co Ltd* v *Heller & Partners Ltd* [1964] AC 465, the House of Lords contemplated that the defendant bank giving information as to the liquidity of one of its customers to another bank could be liable to a client of that other bank even though the defendant did not know the identity of the client. The fact that the defendant bank must have appreciated that the information would be shown to a third party was sufficient to satisfy the neighbour test and a special relationship was capable of existing between the defendant bank giving the information and the plaintiff, the client of the other bank. It could be said that the relationship might exist where one person holds himself out as an expert and gives advice which is intended to be taken seriously and acted upon.

A licence agreement for an expert system will almost certainly contain provisions excluding or limiting the liability of the expert system software company for defective advice and any claims arising from the performance of the system. In fact, in *Hedley Byrne*, the defendant bank was not liable because its reply to a request for information was headed "WITHOUT RESPONSIBILITY" and the plaintiff had seen this disclaimer. *Hedley Byrne* is a case about negligent misstatement and this has consequences for the suppliers of expert systems. Incorrect information given by a bank is conceptually similar to defective advice derived from an expert system.

If the company supplying the expert system is potentially liable to ultimate patients injured as a result of defects in that system, can the expert system software company avoid this liability simply by adding to their software a disclaimer in the manner of the defendant in *Hedley Byrne*? Will this be effective against third parties? As noted in the previous chapter, the full force of the Unfair Contracts Terms Act 1977 will be brought to bear on terms or notices attempting to exclude or restrict liability for loss or damage caused by defective software. Section 2 of that Act states that business liability for death or personal injury resulting from negligence cannot be restricted at all. In the case of other loss or damage resulting from negligence, liability can only be excluded or restricted in as much as the term or notice purporting to do so satisfies the requirement of reasonableness, having regard to the circumstances known to, or which ought to have been known to, the parties. The advantage of *Hedley Byrne* type negligence is that it is possible to recover damages for purely economic loss, such as where an expert system is used to advise on potentially profitable financial investments.

It appears that it is possible to attach a *Hedley Byrne* type of liability for defective advice given by an expert system, irrespective of any disclaimer. This is sensible as, in the future, expert systems will be obtained for the advice they can generate and that advice will be intended to be taken seriously. One difficulty the courts may have in determining whether there has been negligence is what standard of care should be applied. In the case of a medical expert system, it would seem sensible to expect the system to perform at the level of an appropriate competent practitioner. But this may be too high a standard as it will be unlikely that the system can be used directly by the patient himself and will require some input and interpretation from the general practitioner.

Liability of others

If the defects in the expert system can be traced back to the experts or the expert system shell company, it is unlikely that the patient will have sufficient proximity to be able to sue either. The patient may still have a claim against the expert system software company on the basis that it was negligent in selecting suitable experts or an appropriate expert system shell or that it should have spotted errors in the system; in other words, on the basis that the expert system software company has assumed a responsibility for the quality of the system and the quality of the advice it produces. Of course, as between the expert system software company, the experts and the expert system shell company, there are likely to be contractual provisions dealing with indemnities and apportionment of damages arising from legal actions taken against any of them. Therefore, if the defect relates to the expert system shell, the patient may sue the expert system software company who will seek redress from the company which provided the shell on the basis of an indemnity clause in the licence agreement between them. One problem for the expert system software company is how to verify the knowledge as expounded by the experts? Perhaps it ought to employ other experts to check the knowledge-base.

Another factor making any action by the patient against the experts is that their participation in the advice given by the doctor will not be known by the patient. In *Abbott* v *Strong* (unreported) *The Times*, 9 July 1998, Ferris J said that:

> "... it was not comprehensible that a person X, who made a statement or gave advice to another, Y, for the purpose of assisting Y to make representations to a third party, Z, was to be regarded as owing a duty of care to Z when the participation of X in the preparation of Y's statement was unknown to Z."

Expert system not faulty

Prima facie, the general practitioner will be liable if the expert system is shown to perform as it should do and, within the constraints of its area of knowledge, it is capable of providing suitable advice if it is used correctly. It would appear that the doctor using the system has been negligent although it must be noted that a wrong diagnosis does not inevitably mean that there has been negligence; it depends on whether the objective standard of care has been reached. Questions relevant here will be whether an ordinary skilled doctor would choose to use an expert system or the particular system used in the circumstances, whether the ordinary skilled doctor would enter the same information into the system, carry out the same tests on the patient, query the advice resulting from the use of the system, etc. The doctor using a medical expert system must therefore ensure that he knows how to use the system properly, when the system may be used, when it should not be used, what other information and tests are appropriate to the diagnosis of the patient's condition, whether the advice from the system can be taken at face value or whether it needs qualifying in some way. If the doctor can show this standard of care then he will not have been negligent, even if the advice or diagnosis is shown to be wrong retrospectively. However, if it can be shown that the mistake probably would not have been made if the expert system had not been used, the doctor could find himself in a very uncomfortable position.

The expert system software company need not think it is free from tortious liability even if the system works perfectly well. It may be deemed to have been negligent vis-à-vis the patient if it failed to indicate to the doctor using the system what the limitations and the scope of the system are, what level of knowledge is needed to use the system and in what circumstances the system may be used. Alternatively, the mistaken advice may relate to a fault in the documentation for the expert system. The liability of the expert system software company will be subject to the same qualifications as mentioned above as regards its liability for defects in the expert system.

Liability for failing to use an expert system

A doctor, no more than any other professional, cannot escape from the legal issues and implications of expert systems simply by turning his back on them and refusing to use them. As we have seen, a professional of any sort who is in the business of advising clients is under a duty of care to his clients to use reasonable care in formulating and/or applying that advice. That duty of care is measured by the ordinary skilled man in that particular profession and there is a limited obligation for a professional to keep his expertise up to date. Say a new drug is discovered which cures a debilitating disease which had, hitherto, been incurable and, furthermore, this new drug is readily available, has no significant side effects and is widely prescribed. If a doctor does not prescribe this drug to a patient suffering from the disease it would be clear that he has been negligent unless he has some substantial reason for not doing so.

Looking ahead, if medical expert systems become readily available and are shown to perform satisfactorily and are beneficial in terms of more accurate or earlier diagnosis of illnesses what would be the position of a doctor who refused to use such a system? He may be guilty of negligence if it can be demonstrated that a particular patient, who has suffered as a result of a wrong diagnosis, would have had his condition correctly diagnosed if an expert system had been used. It is unlikely that an extreme approach will be adopted such as that existing in the United States where the mere fact that some improvement is available is sufficient to found a claim in negligence. For example, in *The T J Hooper* 60 F. 2d 737 (2d Cir. 1932), it was held that two tugs were unseaworthy because they were not equipped with radio receivers although this was not common practice at the time. The court held that this was not crucial; the fact that the benefits of radar were known about was clear evidence of negligence. It is submitted that in the United Kingdom, apart from knowledge that the improvement is beneficial, that improvement would have to fall into common practice before failure to use it would give rise to a claim in negligence (if the other ingredients were present such as consequential loss).

It is possible that failure to use a medical expert system will be sufficient to ground an action in negligence if the patient suffers injury or loss as a result of that failure if, and only if, it becomes common practice for expert systems to be used in medical practice. This may be some time away at the moment, but given the pace of development in the computer industry and the massive investment in expert systems, decision-support systems and knowledge-based systems, the time when a practising doctor needs to keep abreast of developments in expert systems may not be too far away.

If expert systems in medicine are developed to a level at which they can improve the performance of medical practitioners, particularly at the crucial stage of preliminary diagnosis, it would be foolish not to use them. Although attaching liability for non-use has its attractions in that it may help to promote the use of a new tool which can be of general benefit, the legal problems arising from "computer-aided mistakes" must be addressed and provided for. The doctor using an expert system is particularly vulnerable to negligence claims arising from defective advice, even if the system itself is shown to operate satisfactorily, and he may find that he has no come-back against the company supplying the system which may not be liable due to a lack of proximity and because it has no control over how the system is used.

Summary

Because expert systems promise so much in terms of the improvement of professional performance generally and in helping to raise standards of health care specifically, it would be a pity if their development and use were to be stifled because of difficulties in identifying and allocating legal liabilities. Certainly, thorough investigation and testing of systems should be undertaken before they are used in practice to assist in the treatment of patients. Perhaps the equivalent of a British Standards Institution for expert systems is required which would give a seal of approval to those systems which satisfy stringent testing. Professional bodies and academic institutions could fulfil a useful role in this respect in addition to providing training in the use of expert systems. A medical practitioner would then have a good defence to a claim in negligence if he used an expert system which had undergone independent and rigorous testing and the practitioner had received sufficient training in the use of the system and had reached a satisfactory level of competence in his understanding of the system and its limitations. Of course, if this approach is used, instances of the mistreatment of patients associated with the application of an expert system would be rare.

It is clear that software companies cannot exclude liability for death or personal injury resulting from defective software. As regards other forms of loss or damage, liability can only be excluded or restricted in as much as the term purporting to do so meets the requirement of reasonableness. In this context, the insurance factor can be crucially important. Software companies should investigate the cost of obtaining insurance against defects attributable to their negligence and they should contemplate providing a reasonable level of insurance cover for the client, compatible with the payment of a reasonable premium in terms of the licence fee and the risks involved. Terms dealing with liability for defects should reflect this cover and should also spell out the scope of the insurance and exclude liability for any other form of loss, for example, if the software is not used in accordance with the software company's instructions. It should be noted that, at the time of writing, insurers are increasingly unwilling to insure in respect of claims arising from the Millennium bug.

Potential clients also need to consider insurance. It may be that the client would be happier with a higher level of cover than that offered by the software company. If this is so, the client should investigate the cost of obtaining additional cover and either ask the software company to arrange it or arrange it itself. From the software developer's viewpoint, it may be wise to offer a reasonable level of cover, in the circumstances, and then to invite the client to ask for greater cover to be arranged by the software developer for which the client must reimburse the developer. This element of "negotiation" could help demonstrate that the terms restricting cover was reasonable. However, on the other hand, it could indicate that the software developer himself thinks it is too low. Of course, it is far better to make appropriate and adequate provision for insurance than to rely on a court's construction of an exclusion or limitation clause as being reasonable or not, as the case might be.

Persons using software, such as professional advisors also need to be aware of their potential liability resulting from their choice of or use of software. They also need to check their insurance position.

Chapter 6

Drafting Software Contracts

Drafting Software Contracts

Introduction

The consequences of a badly thought out and drafted software licence can be very serious. For example, it could result in the licensor being exposed to large claims for defects in the software or the client ending up with software that does not perform adequately and is little better than useless without satisfactory recourse to a remedy. These two points, software performance and liability for defects are at the heart of any software licence but there are also a myriad of other issues that must be addressed. Questions relating to future modification of and enhancement to the software, error correction, payment, time for delivery and mechanisms for the failure of either party to perform any of its obligations in whole or in part must be dealt with in a manner that is conducive to the smooth running of the contract. Where the development of software is concerned (or, indeed, modifying existing software), the golden rule is that something will go wrong. A good balanced agreement will help in overcoming problems as they arise whilst minimising the risk of the parties falling out and adopting a confrontational position. At the end of the day, the agreement can be seen as a document that serves two purposes. First, it sets out what each party will do. Secondly, it apportions the risks between the parties. This it should do in a manner that is fair and equitable and workable within the legal framework.

Standard form contracts are available (for example, as supplied by the Institute of Purchasing and Supply at Easton House, Easton on the Hill, Stamford, Lincolnshire, PE9 3NZ) and will be suitable in a good proportion of cases, with or without amendment. However, a standard terms agreement approach will rarely fit the bill where the software to be developed under the agreement is substantial or complex. For example, the licensor may be required to write new programs and supply other programs and items of software that have been licensed to the licensor. To take a simple example, a software company may have been commissioned to develop a database system for a client. The company might decide to write the necessary programs and design the structure of the database using an existing software package. The client will be supplied with these materials but may also need a "run-time licence" to use the software. This is a licence to the client from the owner of the copyright in the development package which is required because certain modules of that package must be included in the finished system. The position becomes more complex where other third party materials are provided, such as an existing database. The software company may grant a licence to the client in respect of the software company's own copyright materials together with a sub-licence (or an assignment of the benefit of a licence) in respect of third party materials included in the overall software package.

Where the software to be delivered to the client requires substantial and difficult work or is unusual, in many ways it is better to design an agreement from scratch using a basic structure or checklist. Some common standard terms (boiler plate terms) may be used and incorporated into the agreement with great care in order to reduce the overall time and effort required but a number of terms must be drafted or modified with the particular circumstances in mind. One eye must be kept on the ultimate goals of clarity, consistency and coherency. The agreement as a whole must fit together, like constructing a jigsaw, everything must be in its proper place and fit together to form a logical and workable whole. One implication of writing each agreement separately in this way is that it avoids the control imposed by section 3 of the Unfair Contract Terms Act 1977 in non-consumer contracts where one party deals on the other's written standard terms.

Battle of the forms

In some cases there may be no scope for writing a licence agreement. It will simply be imposed on the person acquiring the software on a take it or leave it basis. In other cases, the software company will have a standard form contract but may be prepared to negotiate modifications to it. Sometimes, the client and software company will send each other their own standard contract forms. There may be a quotation with one set of terms and an order with another set. The question becomes which set of terms governs the contract. This is referred to as the battle of the forms and occurs where one party (or both) attempts to impose its own terms regardless of the normal principles of contract law. It appears that the terms are those of the party who fired the last shot. In *Butler Machine Tool Co v Ex-Cell-O Corp* [1979] 1 All ER 965 the seller sent an offer on a standard form which included a price variation term. The buyer sent its acceptance together with its own standard terms and a tear-off acceptance slip which the seller returned. It was held that the contract was formed on buyer's terms. See also the Scots case of *Uniroyal Ltd* v *Miller & Co Ltd* [1985] SLT 101 where the buyer made an offer using its standard terms, the seller purported to accept on its standard terms and the buyer accepted the goods. It was held that the contract was formed on seller's terms as the seller's purported acceptance was deemed to be a counter-offer which was then accepted by the buyer.

It is far better to negotiate on the basis of a single form of contract which can then reflect both parties' concerns and which reasonably apportions risk. Negotiating a software licence is the subject matter of Chapter 9.

Scenario

It is dangerous to try to over-generalise when it comes to describing the detail of an agreement for the development and installation of software. Therefore, a hypothetical scenario has been devised which will form the basis of the discussion and the examples provided in the remainder of this chapter. This scenario also forms the basis of the example agreement contained in Appendix 1. The scenario and the parties mentioned in it are hypothetical, although the discussion draws on the author's practical experience of software licences.

Verisopht Ltd is a software company specialising in developing and licensing computer software for mail order retailers. It usually finds that, because each retailer has different manual systems in place and differing requirements that it has to write tailor-made systems for each of its clients although Verisopht often re-uses some of the sub-routines and development techniques in writing other software. Verisopht has a library of standard routines that it tends to use again and again, for example, a routine to produce a status report on the database. Depending on the client's requirements, Verisopht usually includes in the software it produces a database of postal addresses based on postcodes which is licensed to Verisopht by Matalini Data Services Ltd. The licence from Matalini allows Verisopht to grant sub-licences to Verisopht's licensees, the "end-users". Verisopht writes the software, including computer programs, using a fourth generation development software package called Cassandra. To run Verisopht's software requires a run-time licence in relation of Cassandra from Kenwigs Software plc, the company that own the rights in Cassandra.

Squeers Ltd is a mail order retailer that sells its products by catalogue. It accepts telephone orders based on credit card transactions or through its agents who collect weekly payments from buyers. Typically, agents each have a number of customers who are usually neighbours and relatives and they receive a commission on the orders they pass on to Squeers. The software that Squeers requires, to be called Dispatch, will have to be able to do the following, *inter alia*:

- allow Squeers' telephone sales staff to verify a caller's address using his or her postcode as a basis;
- automatically verify the credit-worthiness of a person placing a telephone order by means of the Dispatch software interacting with a subscription credit reference on-line database provided by Cheeryble Credit Assessors Ltd. (CCA). Squeers already has access to this database by annual subscription;
- maintain a database of individual customers (both those dealing direct by telephone and those placing orders through agents) including details of each order, payments made and payments due, goods despatched, etc;
- maintain a database of agents and sales made through them, including payments made and payments due, commission, etc;
- produce various reports and accounts in relation to customers and agents, individually and collectively;
- develop profiles of customers and agents in relation to their buying and payment habits;
- automatically produce samples from the database for targeted mailshots;
- interact with other software used by Squeers, including their creditors and debtors software, Carey, (which was developed by Squeers own data processing staff in-house) and a data management tool for producing charts from databases, Graphit, which is used by Squeers under licence from Grudden Corp Inc.

Figure 6.1 shows the relationships between the various items of software.

Verisopht will supply object code programs only and, therefore, provision will be made for an escrow arrangement by which a copy of the source code of the programs and all necessary preparatory materials required to maintain the software will be deposited with CES Ltd, a company that provides an escrow service. Verisopht will pay an initial fee to CES and, subsequently, an annual fee will be paid to CES by Squeers. CES will release the materials to Squeers in the event that Verisopht become unable to continue to support the software, for example, if Verisopht becomes insolvent or is in breach of its software maintenance obligations.

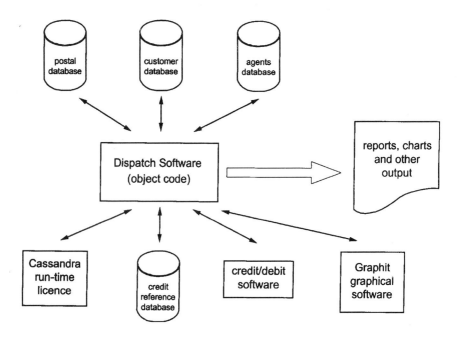

Figure 6.1 Overall Software Requirement

Table 6.1 shows the software items required by Squeers, from whom the items are provided, the owners of the copyright in the items and the rights to be granted to Squeers. The first three items form the basis of the subject matter of the licence agreement between Verisopht and Squeers.

Software	Supplied by	Copyright owner	Right granted to Squeers
Dispatch programs and databases	Verisopht	Verisopht	Exclusive licence
Postal address database	Verisopht	Matalini	Sub-licence
Cassandra run-time modules	Verisopht	Kenwigs	Non-exclusive licence (benefit of)
Credit reference database	CCA	CCA	Non-exclusive licence
Carey credit/debt system	Squeers	Squeers	n/a
Graphit	Squeers	Grudden	Non-exclusive licence

Table 6.1 Squeers' Overall Software Requirement

Basic principles

Before any attempt can be made at drafting the agreement, important preparatory work must have been carried out which should involve both prospective parties. The general nature of the agreement cannot be grasped until reasonably detailed specifications have been drawn up outlining the function of the software and how it will perform that function (functional and operational specifications). The list of operations to be carried out by the software in the above scenario gives some indication of the points that need to be raised initially. For example, what operations are required of the software; what databases or other forms of information will it require and produce; what other software will it interact with; what equipment will the software be installed on? Answers to these and similar questions must be provided. Another important issue which is commonly overlooked is to look into the future and decide how the software should be able to respond to changes in computer equipment, operating systems software, etc. Also, what changes may become necessary to the software as a result of these and other changes such as the future development or diversification of the client's business operations. For example, in our scenario, will Squeers decide to open high street shops in the future and will the role of its agents diminish? Will Squeers obtain other software in the future that will be required to interact with its proposed system, Dispatch? Is it important that Squeers can take over responsibility for the maintenance and enhancement of the Dispatch software?

Once the initial specification has been agreed, consideration can be given to the licence agreement itself. Work will continue on fleshing out the specification and this may result in some fine tuning of the agreement later. A useful starting point is to prepare a set of definitions to be incorporated into the agreement, usually at the very beginning. Definitions are important not only as a word-saving provision but also in determining the precise meaning of some of the words and phrases used in the agreement where the meaning is not obvious. For example, the word "software" should be defined to prevent any misunderstanding. In some cases, the agreement will contain schedules to provide the detail. This is useful where to incorporate a full description in the main text would be unduly disruptive of the flow and render the agreement as a whole less clear. If many separate items of software are to be provided it would be useful to list these individually in a schedule. The same may apply to the payments to be made by the licensee and the timing of those payments.

There follows an example definitions clause (which includes the basic statement as to the nature of the agreement, being a licence agreement):

> Verisopht Ltd, having its registered office at 123 New Street, Westhampton (hereinafter called "Licensor"), hereby grants Squeers Ltd, having its registered office at 77 Sunset Strip, Easton-on-Sea (hereinafter called "Licensee"), an exclusive licence to use the Dispatch Software package as described in the specification annexed to this agreement (hereinafter referred to as "Dispatch Software") and all other rights hereinafter described all in accordance with this agreement.

> For the purposes of this agreement the following definitions have effect:

> "software" includes computer programs, data files, databases, data and other related information stored on computer media or otherwise and any associated printed documentation;

> "hardware" includes computers, terminals, printers, input and output devices, modems and cabling;

> "currency error" means any error in storing, retrieving, calculating, manipulating or converting currency or sums of money but not including any normal rounding operation, any error resulting in whole or in part from software other than the Dispatch Software or any hardware or input error;

> "date error" means any error in storing, retrieving, calculating or manipulating dates but not including any error resulting in whole or in part from software other than the Dispatch Software or any hardware or input error;

> "input error" means any error in data or information submitted to the Dispatch Software in software form or entered via a keyboard or other input device by any person using the Dispatch Software and includes erroneous data or information originating from any person other than the person entering it or submitting it to the Dispatch Software;

> "date of acceptance" is the date at which the Licensee signifies acceptance of the Dispatch Software or the date of deemed acceptance whichever is the earlier and "acceptance" may be actual or deemed acceptance in accordance with this agreement;

> "Postal Database" means the database of postal addresses supplied by Matalini Data Services Ltd, version 2.1 or such later version as may become available at the discretion of the Licensor;

> "Cassandra" means the Cassandra fourth generation development software package supplied by Kenwigs Software plc, version 4.5 or such later version as may become available at the discretion of the Licensor, to be used to develop the Dispatch Software;

"CCA" means the subscription credit reference database service provided to the Licensee under a separate agreement between the Licensee and Cheeryble Credit Assessors Ltd;

"CES" means CES Ltd, which provides source code escrow services.

The agreement is an exclusive licence in respect of the Dispatch software even though other licences are involved, being a sub-licence for the postal database and the benefit of a non-exclusive licence for the run-time modules of Cassandra required by the Dispatch software.

Obligations of the parties

It is useful to concentrate initially on the obligations of the parties. In our scenario, Verisopht will develop, install and test by a given date its programs and databases together with the delivery of the necessary copies and permissions in respect of the third party database and Cassandra run-time licence. Squeers will provide the necessary facilities (for example, access to its offices and equipment and access to CCA's database and its own programs), provide data to assist in the testing of the software and make the payments as they become due. From this basic framework, a number of what-if questions suggest themselves. For example, what happens if Verisopht is late in delivering the software? What if it does not work properly? What if Squeers suffers a loss because of a defect in the software? What if Squeers is late making payments under the agreement? What if Squeers does not provide facilities or data when requested to do so? And so on.

After determining the obligations of each party, a general framework for the agreement can then be developed and the use of a good checklist will be helpful here. A suggested checklist is given at the end of this chapter. First the obligations of the software company and the client are considered below.

Obligations of the software company

Apart from all other things provided by the software company, the most fundamental will be the granting of the necessary licence or licences in respect of the copyright subsisting in the various items of software to be delivered. (Alternatively, some or all of the rights under copyright law may be assigned to the client.) To use software, for example, by loading it into a computer, will involve an act restricted by copyright and, therefore, the software company must grant the relevant rights compatible with the use of the software intended by the parties. Issues to be dealt with here are the scope and extent of the licence and its duration. For example, is the licence a single user licence or is it for a specified number of users or is it a site licence or a licence to use the software throughout the client's organisation? Is the licence to be exclusive or non-exclusive? What acts may be performed in relation to the software? May the client transfer the software or any part of it to a third party? If the software includes items provided by third parties, such as a run-time licence or a third party database, the grant by the software company must include the relevant licences in respect of these items also. The software company will probably have used some particular sub-routines or "mini-programs" that it will wish to incorporate into other programs which it will write for other clients in the future and will wish to reserve the right to do this.

> The Licensor grants to the Licensee an exclusive, non-transferable, licence in respect of the Dispatch Software to be used throughout the Licensee's organisation. The licence will endure for the term of the copyright subsisting in the Dispatch Software programs and databases created by the Licensor unless terminated earlier in accordance with this agreement. The Licensor agrees to grant to the Licensee a non-exclusive sub-licence in respect of the Postal Database and the benefit of a non-exclusive run-time licence in respect of Cassandra. The Licensor reserves the right to use modules contained in the programs in programs or software other than the Dispatch Software.

The duration of the main licence may be for a lesser period than the term of the copyright. It really depends on the nature of the software and the use to which it is put. For example, it may be more appropriate to grant a licence for one year coupled with the possibility of renewal (perhaps automatic) on the basis of some formula to determine the new fee payable. This may tie in with the maintenance of the software. There may also be provision for termination, say by giving three months' notice to take effect at the end of the licence year by analogy to a periodic lease. However, in many cases, the licensee will want to be satisfied that the licence will endure for a much longer period especially if the use of the software is likely to have a major effect on his business operations. If the licence is for the term of the copyright, it is likely to endure for a considerable time, bearing in mind that the software is likely to be modified and added to over the years, creating fresh copyrights, a possibility recognised by Jacob J in

Ibcos Computers Ltd v *Barclays Highland Mercantile Finance Ltd* [1994] FSR 275.

The software company will be expected to install software complying with the specification at or before the agreed time for delivery. As we have seen in the previous chapter, this work will be deemed to be the provision of a service within the Supply of Goods and Services Act 1982 and subject to the implied term in section 13 that reasonable care and skill will be exercised in the performance of that service. It does no harm to make this explicit in the agreement. In some cases, the software company will also have to procure copies of software items from other sources and obtain the relevant licences on behalf of the client. The software company will need to know how many computers (or file servers) the software is to be installed upon and how many copies of the software on disks are to be delivered to the client. A question of utmost importance is whether the client is to obtain the source code of any of the programs included in the software. To a large extent, this will depend upon whether the software company or the client is to carry out error correction and further maintenance to and enhancement of the software. If a copy of the source code is not supplied to the client, it is usual for the software company to deliver a copy of the source code and other materials that are required to maintain the software to an escrow agent who will hold the same to be delivered to the client should the software company be no longer able to maintain the software.

The possibility of date error problems resulting from the "Millennium bug" has concentrated minds in the software industry and predictions of large scale disruption to computer facilities and potential disasters have been widespread. Naturally, a client will want to satisfy himself that his new software will contain no date errors. The same can be said in relation to currency errors, particularly with the coming of European Monetary Union and the Euro. The client may want specific and demanding testing to be carried out to demonstrate that the software is free from such errors.

Other things provided by the software company to the client may include documentation (such as user manuals and, in some cases, installation instructions and maintenance manuals) and a specified amount of training of the client's staff.

> The Licensor agrees to deliver and install the Dispatch Software, Postal Database and run-time version of Cassandra on the Licensee's main computer no later than six calendar months following receipt of a written order to carry out the work from the Licensee. Within a further two months, the Licensor undertakes to test the operation of the Dispatch

Software and to demonstrate its compliance with the specification, including demonstrating that it is free from date errors and currency errors. The Licensor also undertakes to deliver to the Licensee no later than the date of acceptance of the Dispatch Software by the Licensee one copy of the Dispatch Software, Postal Database and run-time version of Cassandra on magnetic disk together with 12 copies of the user manual.

The Licensor undertakes to deliver to CES within three months of the date of acceptance of the Dispatch Software one copy of the source code for the programs contained in the Dispatch Software together with the design materials for said programs and to pay the initial deposit fee to CES.

The Licensor agrees to provide training in the use of the Dispatch Software to three of the Licensee's employees for a period of not more than four days to be completed within one month of the date of acceptance of the Dispatch Software.

The above dates and periods may be varied only in accordance with this agreement.

Most software contains errors, even after it has been in use for a considerable period of time. With newly developed software it is almost certain that several errors will be present, some of which could be serious, regardless how thorough the testing and software trials have been. As recognised by the Court of Appeal in *Saphena Computing* v *Allied Collection Agencies* [1995] FSR 616, software is not a commodity that is handed over once and for all and it may contain errors yet still be reasonably fit for its purpose. In the absence of express provision, the software company has an implied duty to correct errors for a period of time after delivery. It is essential that proper provision should be made for error correction for a period of time following acceptance by the client (acceptance usually will be based on the software passing tests outlined in the specification, see later). The software company will want to make sure that the acceptance tests contained in the specification are not too rigorous so as to allow the client to refuse to accept the software because it contains some trivial error that may take some time to correct.

The Licensor undertakes to maintain the Dispatch Software and correct any errors therein following written notice of such errors from the Licensee for a period of 12 months commencing from the date of acceptance. The Licensor undertakes to make every effort to commence work on correcting such errors within 24 hours of receipt of notification and will make every endeavour to correct the error and install the modified software on the Licensee's main computer within a reasonable time. The Licensor reserves the right to charge if it is discovered that there is no error in the Dispatch Software of the kind notified by the Licensee or if the error is due in whole or in part to any act, omission or input error of the Licensee, its employees, servants or agents or is attributable to the hardware or to software other than the Dispatch Software.

It may be that the licensee will require a faster error correction service than this and there is no reason why it should not be provided. However, the licensor can expect to pay dearly for this service and even then, it will be difficult to provide a mechanism that requires that any error is corrected in a minimum time. Some errors may take some time to evaluate and correct and may have "knock-on" effects, requiring substantial re-writing of parts of the software and re-testing. Whilst requiring fast response and correction of errors within a reasonable time, the client may want some form of compensation if the software is inoperable for a lengthy period. It all depends on the nature of the function to be performed by the software. If it means that a mailshot is delayed by a couple of days, that is probably not very serious. But it would be otherwise if the error resulted in a delay in sending out invoices with the effect that the due date for payment was set back to the following month or if the client failed to meet the deadline for a tender submission. It should be borne in mind that the greater the commitment to fast error correction, the more expensive this service will become and if the software company is required to pay compensation for software that has been out of commission for more than just a few hours it will almost certainly build that in to the overall licence fee even if it is insured against (such insurance could prove expensive). Note that the software company will want to be able to charge when the "error" does not, in fact, exist or is outside the company's control such as where it is due to some other person's default. For example, an employee of the licensee might use the software in a manner contrary to the instruction manual or might enter inaccurate data. Alternatively, the error may be caused by faulty third party software, for example, in our scenario, there may be some mistakes in the postal address database.

Other terms concerning the licensor's obligations include a duty to keep the client informed. This may be linked to progress meetings to be held at set intervals. It is usual for such an agreement also to contain rules as to how notices are to be served on each party, for example, notices to be in writing, signed by a director of the company (or partner of a firm) and sent by recorded delivery to a specified address for service. There will also be terms dealing with confidentiality and staff poaching. Examples of such terms can be seen in the full agreement contained in the Appendix to this book.

Obligations of the client

The primary obligation of the client, certainly as far as the software company will be concerned, will be to pay for the software. However, the client's obligations do not stop there. It will have to provide facilities (for example, access to its computer equipment, office space, office furniture, etc.) as well as assistance, data and information to enable the software company to perform its obligations.

The payment mechanism may take a number of different forms. It may be based on a single lump sum payment, stage payments or an annual licence fee. The timing of lump sum or stage payments will be governed, at least to some extent, by the acceptance of the software by the client, another obligation that the client has: to accept software that complies with the specification. Sometimes, especially where the software company has agreed to maintain the software following acceptance for a period of time, the client will retain some of the payment until satisfactory completion of the maintenance period subject to there being no known errors in the software (of course, errors may still arise in the future, showing the need to provide for error correction in the longer term).

> The Licensee undertakes to pay to the Licensor the sums stated in Schedule 1 within one calendar month of receipt of invoices to be submitted by the Licensor after the occurrence of the events stated in Schedule 1 less a retention of 10 per cent of the sums due. Half of the retention monies so retained by the Licensee shall become due following acceptance of the Dispatch Software, the remainder becoming due upon satisfactory completion of the period of maintenance subject to there being no outstanding errors in the Dispatch Software previously notified by the Licensee awaiting correction by the Licensor. Interest shall accrue in respect of late payment in accordance with Schedule 1.

Note the provision for late payment. Other payment mechanisms include payment for time and materials used by the software company based on a schedule of rates or prices. There may be provision for the addition of a percentage or fixed sum to cover overheads and profit or these items might be built into the rates and prices. These methods are more appropriate where the work is particularly complex or where it covers new ground and it is almost impossible for the software company, no matter how experienced, to pre-estimate the costs. From the software company's point of view, there is little or no incentive to keep costs down and pursue efficiency but the advantage is that it should not make a loss (unless it has miscalculated the rates and prices submitted). However, most commercial organisations like to think that they can make a greater profit by improving their performance standards. That incentive too is lacking in a time and materials contract. If a software company declines to supply a firm quotation or tender it can mean that it is not sufficiently experienced or competent. Alternatively, it knows because of its experience, that it is not possible to quote a realistic firm price at this stage.

Placing a contract on the basis of a schedule of rates or cost plus could be one way to engage a software company to participate in a high risk venture. On the other hand, it might be better to consider engaging an experienced company to carry out a feasibility study first. However, that is not to say that time and materials contracts do not have their place. They are most appropriate in respect of the provision of an unspecified amount of work such as with an annual maintenance agreement where only the work actually done is paid for. Another situation where a time and materials agreement is useful is where unspecified quantities of equipment and materials are to be supplied on an "as and when required" basis. A schedule may also be useful in a conventional firm price contract to be used to calculate the cost of any additional work carried out at the request of the client or delays attributable to the client's default.

The items and facilities to be provided by the client may be listed in a schedule or simply stated in the main text of the agreement, depending on their complexity.

> The Licensee shall provide the Licensor with all facilities, assistance and information reasonably required by the Licensor for the installation and testing of the Dispatch Software. In particular, the Licensee shall provide appropriate access to its main computer for installation and testing following 24 hours written notice given by the Licensor and the Licensee shall provide appropriate test data to enable the Licensee to test the Dispatch Software thoroughly. The Licensee shall ensure that details of and an explanation of the operating system of its main computer will be available to the Licensor and that access to the CCA database will be afforded to the Licensor as and when required.

> Whilst on the Licensee's premises, the Licensee shall make available to the employees and agents of the Licensor reasonable access to photocopying, telephone, facsimile machines as reasonably required for the performance of this agreement. The Licensee shall be responsible for keeping a record of the use of such equipment and the Licensor agrees to pay for its use thereof at cost.

> The Licensee agrees to provide access to its canteen and rest-room facilities to the employees and agents of the Licensor whilst they are on the Licensee's premises, such employees and agents to pay for any food or drink provided to them by the Licensee.

Acceptance of the software can give rise to difficulties. The client may want to delay acceptance as long as it can because part or all of the payment due under the agreement may be tied to this event. At this stage the software may still contain some known minor errors that the software company is still working on and there may be one or two small routines to be completed. The concept of substantial completion may be used although this can cause further difficulties unless it is adequately defined.

> The Licensee agrees to attend acceptance testing of the Dispatch Software following a minimum of 48 hours written notice of such and to accept the Dispatch Software upon its satisfactory completion of the acceptance tests stated in the specification notwithstanding that there may remain some minor work to be carried out by the Licensor providing that the Dispatch Software is in a state such that it may be used to perform all of its main functions adequately and reliably. The Licensor undertakes to complete all outstanding work within the following calendar month. If the Licensee fails or refuses to attend properly notified acceptance testing operations it shall be deemed to have accepted the Dispatch Software unless it submits in writing good reason why it is not acceptable within seven days following notification of testing. In any event, if the Licensee commences using the Dispatch Software in relation to its business activities, the Licensee shall be deemed immediately and unconditionally to have accepted the Dispatch Software if the Licensee has not previously accepted it.

> The Licensee shall at its own expense immediately before acceptance testing back up all its own software including any software belonging to any third party stored or situated on its main computer. During testing for date errors the Licensee agrees to stop all other work on the main computer and to suspend the use of all software on the main computer. If the Licensee fails to take these necessary precautions the Licensor can accept no responsibility for any damage, modification or erasure of any of the Licensee's software caused directly or indirectly by testing the Dispatch Software for date errors in accordance with the specification. The Licensee also agrees at its own expense to test the operation of its own software (and arrange for the testing of any third party's software) during or immediately after the testing for date errors in the Dispatch Software and to inform the Licensor immediately if any problems are discovered. If the Licensee fails to perform any of its duties under this clause, the Licensor at its entire discretion may elect not to check the Dispatch Software for date errors and will not be liable for any damage or loss resulting directly or indirectly from any such date errors.

The manner in which the first of the above terms is drafted is to prevent the client from prevaricating in order to delay the evil day when payment (or a substantial portion of the payment) becomes due. In the event that the software is not yet acceptable, the client simply has to attend the acceptance testing and point out that it either fails to reach the specified standard or is not yet capable of being used to perform its main functions properly. Care must be taken to avoid "deemed acceptance" provisions that take effect at an early stage or on the basis of some minor event. This could make it difficult for the client to rescind the contract at a later date if it becomes apparent that the software is never going to be satisfactory. In *Simpson Nash Wharton* v *Barco Graphics Ltd* (unreported) 1 July 1991, Queen's Bench Division, the software company argued that the client had, by using or attempting to use the software, accepted it by the time it purported to rescind the contract on the basis of the software company's misrepresentation about the performance of the software. However, this was rejected by the court.

The second term is required because testing for date compliance will normally require that the computer's date is changed. This could have unexpected and potentially disastrous consequences if some of the Licensee's other software contains date errors. The purpose of backing up all the software first is that it should be possible to recover the situation. If the Licensee does not cooperate, the Licensor will want to retain a discretion not to check for date errors in case it brings the main computer to a standstill or interferes with other software in use.

Whilst not attempting to interfere with the client's use of the software, the software company will be careful to limit what the client can do with the software (being careful not to be accused of non-derogation from grant and also being aware of the effects of the Copyright, Designs and Patents Act 1988). For example, the software company may have decided, as in our scenario, to carry out error correction and future modification itself. It may also be concerned that the software should not be transferred to other companies (with the possibility that the software company is thereby deprived of a potential client) and that it should not be used by the client to provide services to other companies for the same reason.

> The Licensee undertakes to use the Dispatch Software only in accordance with this agreement for its own business purposes and otherwise not to copy, modify, disclose or transmit it and not to decompile or disassemble the programs without prejudice to sections 50A, 50B and 50D of the Copyright, Designs and Patents Act 1988 and regulation 19 of the Copyright and Rights in Databases Regulations 1997.

> Furthermore, the Licensee agrees that it will not transfer the Dispatch Software or any part thereof to any other person or organisation nor will it sell, rent, lend or otherwise distribute or dispose of copies of the Dispatch Software or any part thereof nor use it or any part thereof to provide

services to other persons or organisations without the prior written consent of the Licensor signed by a Director of the Licensor.

The Licensee agrees to monitor the use of the Dispatch Software and to take reasonable precautions to ensure that copies of it or any part thereof are not sold, rented, loaned, disclosed or transmitted or otherwise made available to any other person or organisation. Any copies of the Dispatch Software made under this agreement are to be clearly labelled as back-up copies and an appropriate copyright notice denoting the Licensor as owner of the copyright is to be attached. Such copies are to be stored in a secure place.

The last paragraph simply places a duty of care on the client to try to prevent copies finding their way to others, for example, by the actions of their own staff (who might be tempted to "sell" copies on the black market or take copies with them to a new employer).

If the source code and other materials are to be deposited with an escrow agent, the usual method is for the software company (licensor) to deposit the materials with the escrow agent and pay an initial deposit fee. The client (licensee) will then pay the further fees as they become due. Usually, this will entail paying a modest annual fee to the escrow agent and, in the event that the software company can no longer maintain the software, a release fee. The remainder of the provisions relating to escrow are mentioned here.

The Licensee agrees to pay the annual escrow fee to the CES escrow service in return for CES holding a copy of the source code of the Dispatch Software programs and associated preparatory materials. In the event that:

(a) the Licensor is unable to continue to maintain the Dispatch Software as a result of entering into liquidation (whether compulsory or voluntary) other than for purposes of solvent reconstruction or amalgamation or if the Licensor has a receiver appointed over all or any part of its assets or undertaking or if the Licensor ceases to be able to pay its debts within the meaning of section 123 of the Insolvency Act 1986, or

(b) is in breach of its error correction or other maintenance obligations within 10 days of receipt of a written notice from the Licensee stating the breach and requesting it be remedied forthwith, or

(c) the Licensor assigns the copyright subsisting in the Dispatch Software and fails within 10 days to obtain equivalent undertakings from the assignee in respect of the escrow arrangement,

CES will upon written request from the Licensee together with evidence that any of the above events have occurred and the necessary release fee deliver to the Licensee a copy of the above mentioned source code and other materials in accordance with the conditions of escrow.

In the event that the Licensee fails to pay the annual escrow fee to CES within four weeks of receiving a final written demand from CES for payment, the escrow arrangement shall come to an end forthwith and all deposited source code and other materials shall be returned to the Licensor.

An escrow service is available from the National Computing Centre Oxford House, Oxford Road, Manchester M1 7ED. Making use of the service will entail entering into an unusual "tripartite" agreement which, in reality can be viewed as two separate agreements.

Other terms dealing with the licensee's obligations will include a reciprocal duty to keep the software company (licensor) informed. Also, there are likely to be terms equivalent to those for the software company in respect of confidentiality and staff poaching. Examples can be seen in the full agreement contained in the Appendix to this book.

Aspects related to the performance of the contract

The main obligations of the parties have been described above. However, during the performance of the contract, there are bound to be unforeseen problems and delays, whether attributable to the default of one or both parties or otherwise. To prevent later arguments it is far better to include express provision for dealing with such things in the agreement. If the software company is late in delivering acceptable software then, if this is its own fault, it should bear the risk and the best way of dealing with this is to include a term awarding liquidated damages for late delivery to the client. Liquidated damages should be a genuine pre-estimate of the damage that the client will suffer due to late delivery (they must not be expressed as a penalty as this would be unenforceable). The software company could be at fault for late delivery because it has not assigned sufficient resources to the task or because its employees are not up to the required standard and lack experience or because the task proved more difficult than the software company anticipated because it failed to appreciate the amount and complexity of the work involved.

> Should the Licensor fail to deliver, install and test the Dispatch Software to the acceptance of the Licensee within eight months from the date of receipt of the Licensee's written order or such later date as provided for by an extension of time in accordance with this agreement, the Licensor shall pay to the Licensee the sum of £1,250 per week by way of liquidated damages. Periods of less than one week shall not be taken into account in calculating liquidated damages.

The figure inserted should be the loss that the client anticipates it will suffer as a result of the late delivery. This may be the profit expected from new business resulting from use of the software. The client may wish to reserve the right to terminate the contract should the delay be more than a specified time. For example:

> Should the Licensee fail to deliver, install and test the Dispatch Software to the acceptance of the Licensee after six months following the period of eight months from the date of receipt of the Licensee's written order or such later date as provided for by an extension of time in accordance with this agreement, the Licensee may at its discretion treat the failure as a breach of condition (or, in Scotland a material breach) and terminate the agreement forthwith notwithstanding its claim for damages under the agreement.

If the late delivery is due to some default of the client, then it is only fair that the client should bear the responsibility for this. For example, the client may have been late in allowing access to its main computer because it was undergoing a lengthy and time-consuming refit at the time. Delays due to the client's default have two consequences. First, the actual time for delivery should be extended otherwise, under the agreement, the software company could be liable for liquidated damages. Secondly, the software company may have been put to additional costs. For example, this could be because its employees have been idle for a period of time and unable to perform their duties or because the increased duration of the work will result in an increase in the software company's overhead costs attributable to the contract. Of course, a party to a contract is under a duty to mitigate his losses if the other party is in breach and, in this context, if the client's main computer is unavailable for a period of time, the software company should seek to re-deploy its employees to other duties (or perhaps continue to carry out part of the work using its own computers). In any event, the contract should make provision for an extension to the time for delivery and for additional costs plus a margin for overheads and profit necessarily resulting from the delay.

> Any delay to the performance of the work required of the Licensor under this agreement caused wholly or partly by the default or neglect of the Licensee shall entitle the Licensor to an extension to the time for performance and to additional payment for any attributable costs calculated in accordance with the schedule of rates. In the event of any such delay, the Licensor shall make every endeavour to minimise such additional costs by attempting to assign its employees or agents to alternative work associated with this agreement, or failing that, to other work, if available. Both the Licensor and the Licensee agree to keep a full record of the delay

and its consequences and to agree the extension of time for performance and the additional payment as soon as is practicable after the reason for the delay has ceased to be operative.

Although self-evident, the fact that detailed records should be kept is essential and can prevent heated disputes from occurring later (indeed, a comprehensive diary should be kept by both sides detailing the performance of the contract on a daily basis – this will aid agreement and, failing agreement, could be crucial in any subsequent arbitration, alternative dispute resolution or litigation). Equally important is the need to seek agreement as to the impact of the delay in terms of time and cost as soon as possible. The human memory is apt to distortion and this can result in some nasty arguments later which do neither party any good.

Another fact of life of writing software for a client is that the client will, more often than not, want to make changes to the specification during the performance of the contract. The client may suddenly see another use for the software, perhaps after seeing a prototype or part of the software under trial. For example, in our scenario, Squeers may decide that it would be useful to be able to provide its agents with small databases containing the customers who order goods through those agents. Perhaps the manager in charge of agents has been to visit some of them and has noticed that quite a few have their own personal computers. Any variation to the performance required by the software company must be agreed before the work associated with it is commenced. The two aspects of time and additional payment should be mutually agreed at the outset. Rather than rely on the schedule of rates for calculating payment, it is far better to ask the software company to submit a price and an estimate of the additional time required, if any, to carry out the additional work. This can then be the subject of negotiation between the parties before a formal order in writing is placed for the work. The agreement must include a term with the basic mechanism for dealing with variations to the contract.

> Variations to the work to be carried out under this agreement must be agreed in writing between the Licensor and the Licensee. The additional payment and extension to the time for performance, if any, shall be agreed between the Licensor and the Licensee before any work associated with any such variation may be carried out and appropriate officers of the Licensor and the Licensee shall sign and date a written variation order specifying the additional work, payment and extension to the time for performance, if any.

It is essential that both parties make the position as to variations clear to their own employees. Difficulties may arise where an employee of the client gives an oral order to carry out additional work and there is no agreement as to payment or extra time. In this situation, the software company could attempt to claim on the basis of the schedule of rates which will probably be more expensive than the price they would have agreed to in negotiations. There also could be difficulties resulting from misunderstandings about the nature and extent of the additional work required.

A similar term may be useful should the software company come across some unforeseen difficulty in performing the contract. To affect the payment or time for performance, the difficulty must be such that a reasonably experienced software company would not have anticipated it. For example, there may be an unexpected problem with the client's main computer operating system which was not published until after the contract was made and it will result in the software company having to modify its software accordingly. Such a term must not, however, be seen as carte blanche for an inexperienced software company to make up for its lack of experience. It is, regrettably, very difficult to lay down a precise test for when such an unforeseen difficulty should give rise to a claim for an extension of time and additional payment but some formulas such as "not reasonably foreseeable by an experienced software company" might be the best that may be achieved. The appointment of an experienced professional to supervise the performance of the contract can be useful in bringing some objectivity into deciding whether the problem was or was not foreseeable.

Renewal and termination

If the agreement is for a limited duration (less than the term of the copyright), there should be provision for renewal. This may be expressed as being by mutual agreement, at the request of either party or automatic subject to notice of termination not having been served by one party on the other. Renewal may be on the same terms (watch out for agreements that may be perpetually renewable unilaterally) but, usually, there will be provision for some variation in the fee to be paid. To avoid the danger of uncertainty allowing an escape route to one party, it is usual to have the fee for the new contract calculated by some index applied to the original fee (such as the retail prices index). Either party may require provision for termination for a breach of the agreement by the other but it would be unwise to allow one party to terminate for a trivial breach. Whilst provision for termination may be included in some of the relevant terms (for example, in relation to very late performance by the software company), a general term can be included.

> Either party may terminate this agreement, unless otherwise provided for herein, if the other party is guilty of a serious breach of the agreement having failed to remedy that breach (if remediable) after being given one calendar month's notice of the breach in writing by the party seeking to terminate the agreement. Notice of termination shall be served in writing and signed by a director or partner of the party seeking to terminate. Any monies due at the time of termination shall remain payable and become due immediately upon termination without prejudice to any other legal remedy available to either party.

It is both reasonable and advisable to allow the party guilty of the breach some time to remedy that breach. Some breaches may not be remediable such as a serious breach of confidence but the injured party will lose little by allowing one month before bringing the agreement to an end. Other legal remedies should be reserved. For example, where the software company has divulged information about the client's business secrets to a competitor, the client may want to sue the software company for breach of confidence in addition to terminating the contract and/or seeking damages under it. The client may also want to apply for an injunction against the competitor to prevent it using the secrets or divulging them to others.

Liabilities and indemnities

Liability can arise in a number of ways. The client may suffer direct damage because of a defect in the software (for example, it might underprice its goods) or through the software being out of commission for a period of time during which it must revert to slow and ponderous manual methods. If the software is out of action for substantial periods, it is only to be expected that the client will want some compensation for this. In either case, if the defect is attributable to the software company's negligence it seems reasonable that it should bear all or some of the loss. However, the software company will not want to expose itself to a plethora of unlimited claims and it will seek to limit its liability. We have seen that the complete exclusion of liability is unlikely to be deemed reasonable by the courts. See for example, *The Salvage Association* v *CAP Financial Services Ltd* [1995] FSR 654 and *St Albans City & District Council* v *International Computers Ltd* [1997] FSR 251.

The central issue as regards liability is which party realistically can obtain insurance against at a reasonable premium to cover the liability. The importance of insurance to the test of reasonableness is highlighted by section 11(4) of the Unfair Contract Terms Act 1977. It is not unreasonable to expect a software company to have professional liability insurance up to a maximum of at least £250,000 in any one claim. The maximum liability cover that can be obtained without substantially affecting the cost of developing and providing software of the kind envisaged should be obtained. Another useful guideline is what is normal in software companies developing software of that type. After evaluating these factors, the software company should obtain the necessary insurance cover and then insist on a term limiting its liability to that figure. The term must also reflect the scope of the insurance cover obtained. However, insurance is unlikely to cover every eventuality and cover for the Millennium bug and other date error problems is usually excluded. The licensor should take this into account and draft his limitation clause accordingly.

The software company will wish to avoid any claims for loss or damage caused by third party software and exclude or at least minimise its liability for any defects resulting from the negligence of others, including the licensee or any third party software supplier. Where third party software has been obtained by the software company, it should have used reasonable care and skill in selecting that software (if there is a choice of supplier) and, apart from that duty, which is implied by section 13 of the Supply of Goods and Services Act 1982, it should exclude liability.

> The Licensor warrants that it has exercised reasonable skill and care in developing and writing the Dispatch Software and in selecting and incorporating any included third party software and that it has made every effort to minimise errors and ensure that the Dispatch Software performs adequately and reliably.

> The Licensor shall not be liable in respect of periods not exceeding seven days during which the Dispatch Software is incapable of being used by the Licensee as a result of a defect in the Dispatch Software. The Licensor's liability for any longer period during which the Licensee is unable to use the Dispatch Software because of a defect attributable to the negligence of the Licensor shall be limited to £25,000 for each such period except as provided for below. The Licensor shall not be liable for any other non-use of the Dispatch Software howsoever caused.

> The Licensor shall not be liable for loss, damage or expense resulting directly or indirectly from errors attributable to any act, omission or input error of the Licensee, its employees, servants and agents or the Licensee's hardware or software or third party hardware or software or resulting

from any act, omission or input error of any third party beyond the control of the Licensor. The Licensor's maximum liability for loss, damage or expense resulting directly from the Licensor's negligence is limited to £250,000 in respect of any one claim or series of related claims except as provided for below. The Licensor shall not be liable for any other loss including any indirect or consequential loss, damage or expense nor any loss of profit howsoever caused except as provided for in this agreement.

The Licensor warrants that it has taken all due care to ensure that the Dispatch Software will be free from date errors and currency errors. The Licensor's maximum aggregate liability for any loss, damage or expense suffered by the Licensee and resulting from the Licensor's negligence in relation to date errors and currency errors wholly attributable to the Dispatch Software is limited to £25,000. All other liability of the Licensor in relation to date errors and currency errors howsoever caused is hereby excluded.

The Licensor does not warrant that any third party software included in the Dispatch Software nor any other third party software whether provided by the Licensee or otherwise is free from defects and whilst the Licensor has used all reasonable care to ensure that such third party software is free from defects and reasonably fit for its intended purpose the Licensor shall not be liable for any loss, damage or expense directly or indirectly attributable to any such defect or lack of fitness for purpose.

The Licensee warrants that it shall use the Dispatch Software in accordance with the Licensor's instructions and the Licensee shall indemnify the Licensor against any losses suffered by or claims made against the Licensor by any person other than the Licensee resulting from the loss, use or misuse of the Dispatch Software by or with the express or implied authority or consent of the Licensee.

There is always a possibility that the completed software infringes a third party right. For example, it may turn out that one of the software company's staff has, unknown to the company, made use of materials that he had retained from a previous employment and incorporated those materials in the finished software. This type of event may be difficult to guard against, bearing in mind the scope of copyright protection in relation to computer programs reaches to non-literal elements such as a program's structure. Alternatively, there may be an infringement of a trade mark in one of the screen displays or there may be an issue of an obligation of confidence owed to a third party. It should be remembered that some intellectual property rights may be infringed innocently, without knowledge of the existence of the right, and injunctive relief may be a possibility as might be an account of profits. Even damages may be awarded against "innocent" infringers as innocence is usually judged objectively, not subjectively.

Provision should be made to cover the above eventuality and the possibility that a third party could obtain an injunction and other remedies against the client preventing it from continuing to use the software. It is common to see liability limited to the total price paid by the client under the agreement. However, it may be that the problem is relatively easy to overcome and the software company should have an opportunity to re-write the offending part of the software or take other corrective action. If required, liability for the client's inability to use the software during this period of time could be covered by limitation clause similar to that above for non-use.

> In the event that the Dispatch Software is proved to infringe a third party's intellectual property rights, the Licensor shall make the necessary modifications without delay to prevent further infringement, if possible. Should the Licensee be prevented from using the software permanently and/or become subject to third party claims in respect of such infringement, the liability of the Licensor is limited to a maximum of total of the payments made to the Licensor under this agreement. If the Licensee becomes aware that the software infringes or is claimed to infringe a third party's intellectual property rights, the Licensee shall inform the Licensor of such at once in writing and provide the Licensor with such information and assistance to allow the Licensor to defend any claim made against it. The Licensor will indemnify the Licensee in respect of its costs in providing such information and assistance including legal costs.

Dispute resolution

It is inevitable that, in some cases, the parties will not be able to resolve a disagreement relating to the performance of the contract. If there is an independent professional supervising the contract then, despite his attempts to mediate, the parties still cannot agree. They may be breathing fire at each other. In this situation, either arbitration or alternative dispute resolution (ADR) may be used. ADR has become very popular and has an excellent track record in terms of settling disputes and it boasts some notable successes and can prove quick and inexpensive. One major advantage of ADR is that sometimes an imaginative solution is found which leaves both parties satisfied at the outcome. WIN-WIN solutions are possible. For example, in one case, a client modified the licensed software in a way which caused a number of errors, resulting in a dispute between the client and the licensor. The matter was resolved quickly by ADR. The licensor corrected the errors in return for a licence from the client in respect of the modifications which turned out to be quite good. Arbitration, on the other hand, can be expensive and drawn out and often results in a finding in which one party loses and the other wins. WIN-LOSE outcomes are probable. However, it may be that the complexity of the dispute and the technical issues call for this form of dispute resolution. One approach is to provide for ADR at the first instance and, if this proves unsuccessful, to go to arbitration.

Arbitration

Arbitration is an established and commonly used method of resolving disputes without having to go to the courts. The parties to the contract appoint an independent third party who will listen to both sides and then make a ruling. A major advantage of arbitration is that the arbitrator should have considerable knowledge of the technical area involved in the dispute. It is supposed to be quicker, cheaper and less formal that a court hearing although this is not always so. Parties to an arbitration are usually legally represented.

It is common for arbitration clauses to state that the arbitrator's decision shall be final and binding on the parties, and the courts will not interfere with an arbitrator's decision unless he has erred on a point of law. A court will accept the arbitrator's evaluation of the facts of the case as being conclusive. In practice, arbitration works well and the standard of arbitrators, who belong to the Chartered Institute of Arbitrators, is very high. If an arbitration clause is included in the agreement, the machinery for selecting an arbitrator should also be dealt with, the usual practice being to appoint an arbitrator agreed upon by the parties, or failing such agreement, a person to be nominated by the President for the time being of the British Computer Society which holds a register of suitably qualified arbitrators.

Alternative dispute resolution

ADR appears to hold great promise of speedy and fair resolution of disputes. Usually, a mediator will be appointed to assist and encourage the parties in the negotiation of a settlement to their mutual satisfaction. The mediator can take an active role and make suggestions for resolving the conflict. However, there is no legally binding obligation on the parties to continue with the process and they may abandon it at any time. The process itself is based on informality and consent and its claimed success rate is in the order of 90%.

One technique which may be used is for both sides to make a presentation before senior members of the organisations involved (who have not been involved in the dispute) who will then attempt to negotiate a settlement with the assistance of the mediator. Another ADR technique is adjudication in which a neutral third party gives a non-binding ruling on the case or certain aspects of the case. "Expert appraisal" is another possibility in which a technical expert assesses each of the party's cases for the purpose of assisting negotiations.

Any ADR clause in a licence agreement must make it clear that anything admitted, said or done in connection with ADR is without prejudice to the legal rights of the parties. The clause should make provision for the appointment of a mediator (who should be skilled in resolving disputes by negotiation), payment of his fees (usually these will be borne equally by the parties) and procedures to be adopted. The Centre for Dispute Resolution, 95 Gresham Street, London EC2V 7NA has a model mediation procedure and model ADR clauses and provides advice and ADR services.

Standard terms

The agreement will contain a number of general or standard terms (sometimes referred to as boiler-plate terms) dealing with such matters as notices, the fact that the licence represents the entire agreement, *force majeure*, and applicable law. Other issues that may need to be dealt with, depending on the nature of the software and the surrounding circumstances, are compliance with the Data Protection Act 1998, ownership of the copyright in any output produced by using the software or databases created by using the software and moral rights which may subsist in items of software other than computer programs or those created by employees. For example, the creator of a database may have asserted his moral right to be identified as the author of the database.

If the work to be carried out requires access to the client's computers or other items of software, it may be useful to require that the client gives express authorisation for access (and modification, where appropriate) of any programs or data. Such a term could also include a duty placed upon the software company to respect the security of any passwords disclosed by the client and to take care not to prejudice the security or integrity of any such programs and/or data.

The sample agreement in the Appendix includes a number of standard terms of the type mentioned above. Of particular importance is the requirement under the Data Protection Act 1998 for processors (which will include many software companies in respect of their developing software for clients) to be subject to security obligations which are in a written contract or evidenced in writing.

Specification

The importance of the specification for the work cannot be overstated. It is the yardstick by which the work will be measured and the performance of the software evaluated. The specification must be comprehensive, clear and to the point. In particular, it should not set vague and unrealistic targets as to the performance of the software. In addition to detailing what the software will do (for example, what reports it will generate, what files it will create and maintain) it should define the required performance of the completed software in such a way that it can be assessed easily and in a way that is free from doubt: for example, speed of operation, response times, file handling capabilities, freedom from date errors and currency errors should be based on a set of benchmark tests and other criteria. Allowance must be made where the software is installed on a main computer that may be performing other tasks at the time of testing. The use of dummy databases may be required to see the effects on the operation of the software when any databases used have grown to their expected maximum sizes. Retrieval in a database consisting of a few hundred records may be fast, taking no more than a couple of seconds. Yet, when that database reaches a few thousand records, retrieval times may be increased 20 or 30-fold; disproportionately to the size increase.

Professional supervision

Where the proposed software is complex or will take some time to develop or where there is a possibility of difficulties occurring during the work, it is sensible to take the lead of the construction industry and appoint an independent professional to oversee the work and make certain decisions during the performance of the contract. Architects and engineers have fulfilled this type of role very successfully for some considerable time. In some cases, the professional may actually be employed by one of the parties, but his professional code of ethics requires him to be neutral when making decisions concerning the interpretation and application of the contract. The professional can:

- supervise the work and ensure that it is carried out in accordance with the specification;
- make interim valuations and certify payments to be made under the contract;
- deal with variations, extensions to time and additional payments;
- act as first line arbitrator in the case of a dispute between the parties.

An independent professional could also be engaged to advise upon or even draw up the specification for the work and could help with the award of the contract; for example, by inviting tenders based on a detailed specification and a draft form of agreement. The same professional could then supervise the performance of the contract. He or she will not be cheap. However, the appointment of such a person could result in many advantages. The overall final cost could be much less than it would have been. The professional will have acted as a useful buffer between the parties and, at the end of the day it could make the difference between having software that works with both parties content at the conclusion of a successful contract or ending up with useless software and acrimonious claims and counterclaims, with the prospect of expensive litigation looming on the horizon. Of course, it is essential that any person appointed to supervise a contract in this way belongs to an appropriate professional body having recognised standards and appropriate ethics. A suitably experienced member of the British Computer Society and/or a chartered engineer should fit the bill.

Arrangements for payment of a professional supervisor will have to be agreed, although, at the end of the day, it will be the client that picks up the tab. Nevertheless, experience shows that it is a cheap price to pay. In *The Salvage Association* v *CAP Financial Services Ltd* [1995] FSR 654, the plaintiff client recovered its losses in wasted time (£139,672) but, in the end still did not have the software it so badly needed. Had a truly independent professional been involved from the start, the required software might have been up and running on the first agreed date for delivery.

Table 6.2 lists those terms commonly found in software licences together with some brief comment on those terms.

Table 6.2 Checklist of Common Terms

Type of Term	Term	Comment
Preliminary	Definitions	Word-saving and an aid to interpretation.
	Nature of agreement	Licence or assignment.
Software company's obligations	Grant and/or transfer necessary licences (or assignments) to client	Licence may be exclusive or non-exclusive and may be for a specific duration with possibility of renewal or may be for the term of the copyright.
	Deliver & install software	The specification will give full details of the software and a schedule may give a list of the software to be delivered together with dates for delivery, installation, testing and acceptance.
	Test software	The specification should contain details of tests to be satisfactorily completed.
	Date and currency compliance	A specific set of tests used to demonstrate that the software performs date operations and currency calculations and conversions accurately both at the time of testing and in the future.
	Provide copies of documentation	Increasingly likely to be electronic, on-disk, CD-ROM or even on-line.
	Provide training	Amount and nature should be specified, possibly with rates for additional training.
	Maintain software for specified period	May be a collateral maintenance agreement subsequently.
	Respect confidentiality of client's operations	May need to spell out what material is or is not confidential.

Type of Term	Term	Comment
Software company's obligations *(cont)*	Keep client informed during performance of contract	Formal system of notices may be provided for and progress meetings.
	Place copy of software & preparatory material with escrow agent (and pay initial fee)	If source code and other relevant design material is not delivered with software.
Client's obligations	Make payment	There may be a schedule detailing the payment mechanism.
	Provide facilities, access to equipment, sample data or other assistance	Include provisions for delays.
	To attend testing and accept the software	Deemed acceptance a useful provision but must be reasonable.
	Use, copy, disclose, transfer software in accordance with agreement	A duty may be placed on the client to protect software from unauthorised use, copying or disclosure.
	Respect confidentiality of software company's methods	A description of what information is confidential may be useful.
	Keep software company informed during performance of contract	Using agreed system of notices.
	Pay escrow agent's continuing fees	If escrow is used for source code and other materials.
Delays and variations	Late delivery	It is usual to provide for liquidated damages – there may be a long stop for excessive delay and/or a cap on the maximum payable.
	Late payment	Interest should be payable at specific figure above bank rate.

Type of Term	Term	Comment
Delays and variations (*cont*)	Extension of time for delivery and provision for additional payment	This should be available if the client causes delays or requires additional work or wishes to modify the specification during performance of the contract or an unforeseen difficulty is experienced.
Liabilities	Liability for defective software	Usual to limit liability to amount covered by insurance, say £250,000 – bear in mind Unfair Contract Terms Act 1977. Exclude liability for losses outside control of software company, for example, defects in third party software, default of client, etc.
	Liability for date and currency errors	May be limited to a lower figure reflecting the difficulty of obtaining adequate insurance.
	Indemnity for infringement of third party right (mutual)	The delivered software may infringe another person's right. There should be provision for software company to seek to modify software to avoid this problem. It is also important that the software company is notified immediately and assistance provided. Data provided by the client may be subject to the Data Protection Act 1998 and may give rise to a claim for compensation if it is wrong.
Miscellaneous	Termination	Under what circumstances will the agreement terminate or when may it be terminated unilaterally. To what extent should the defaulter be given an opportunity to remedy any breach?
	Data protection	The software company is likely to be classed as a processor under the Act and there will have to be a term in the agreement imposing obligations on the software company in relation to the security of personal data.

Type of Term	Term	Comment
Miscellaneous (*cont*)	Ownership of output	May be implied by law but express provision better if there is any doubt.
	Staff poaching	Two way obligation not to employ other party's staff for a period of time following completion of performance of contract.
	Force majeure	What happens to monies paid and due, etc.?
	Modification and error correction, decompilation	Can client do these acts or engage a third party to do any of them?
	Back-up copies	Cannot be prohibited in respect of computer programs if deemed necessary to lawful use. What about back-up copies of other materials, for example, a database?
	Moral rights	May subsist in items of software other than computer programs.
Schedules	Software and services provided	
	Delivery dates	
	Payment mechanism and dates	
	Schedule of rates and prices	
	Detailed list and schedules	
Specification	Detailed description of software and its performance	Important document. Essential that it is clear and unambiguous and sets realistic and achievable benchmarks that will satisfy the client that the software is acceptable. There may be two specifications, a functional specification (what the software will do) and an operational specification (how the software will do it and how well it will do it).

Chapter 7

Licences for Off-the-shelf Software

Licences for Off-the-shelf Software

Introduction

For ready-made software (often referred to as off-the-shelf software), different considerations come into play compared to bespoke software. Off-the-shelf software is pre-written and the person acquiring the software plays no effective part in the specification and design of the software. It is the software analogy of speculative building. This has a number of implications which may explain the type of licence agreement frequently found in such software packages. For one thing, the software company which has developed the software and owns the rights subsisting in it has no knowledge of the precise uses to which the software will be put to by persons acquiring it. To some extent, this means that the software company should be even more rigorous in testing the software but it could be argued that lack of foresight about the actual uses of the software (as opposed to the type of use) should let it off the hook, so to speak, as regards liability for defects in the software. It might also be said to place a duty on the software company to make it quite clear what uses the software may be put to and what its limitations are.

Off-the-shelf software covers an enormous range of types of software. It can be broadly classified as being either systems software (for example, MS-DOS, UNIX or Microsoft Windows, configuration and boot-up files) providing the computer's operating system or applications software such as word processing software, spreadsheet software and such like. However, some software may be difficult to classify in this way. For example, software designed to handle the scheduling and priority of a number of applications running concurrently. Word processing software can be used to create or modify configuration files and batch files used to make the appropriate operating system settings before loading applications software. Nevertheless, the distinction is not of particular importance as regards licensing and the same concerns apply to either type of software.

Nature of the agreement

The nature of contracts under which off-the-shelf software is obtained has proved somewhat of a puzzle. Some commentators have argued that they are, essentially, sale of goods contracts and, as such, governed by the appropriate implied terms, particularly as to quality and fitness for purpose. Chapter 4 contains a general discussion of the legal environment of software licences, including off-the-shelf software. We can now take that discussion further by considering the particular manner in which this form of software is obtained. The person wishing to acquire a copy of the software will walk into a computer software retail outlet and ask for a copy of, say, a particular word processing package. As mentioned in Chapter 4 (p 90), the person acquiring the copy of the software must have a licence from the owner of the copyright subsisting in the software because simply loading it into a computer memory (whether onto a hard disk or into the computer's volatile memory) will require the performance of an act restricted by copyright.

The approach favoured by the author is to identify three separate contracts involving three separate individuals, the software company that developed the software and owns the copyright in it (or has an appropriate licence or licences from the copyright owner or owners), the supplier and the person acquiring a copy of the software, the customer. Between the software company and the supplier there is a sale of goods contract in relation to the physical items provided, that is, the disks, packaging, manuals, etc. As between the supplier and the customer, there is an equivalent sale of goods contract in relation to those same items. Between the software company and the customer, there is a licence agreement (and/or appropriate sub-licences) together with a collateral warranty based on the terms, express or implied, in the licence agreement (of which more later). The supplier is acting as the software company's agent in respect of this contract. The arrangement is shown diagramatically in Figure 7.1.

If the disks are faulty and the software is corrupted as a result or cannot be loaded into the customer's computer, then the customer will have remedies under the Sale of Goods Act 1979 against the supplier. If the software is faulty because of, say an error in the computer program, the customer's redress will be against the software company under the licence on the basis of an express or implied term that the software should work, that is, be fit for its purpose. This can be seen as a collateral warranty.

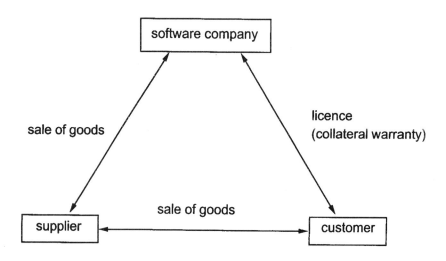

Figure 7.1 Off-the-shelf Software Contract

Atiyah discusses collateral warranties in *Sale of Goods* (London: Financial Times Pitman Publishing, 9th ed, 1995 at 227) where he suggests that a statement of fact made in literature by a manufacturer of goods which was intended to influence potential customers could be relied upon by buyers on the basis of a collateral contract. However, Atiyah does comment on the paucity of English law on the point, and he reflects that "there is room for the development of the law here" noting that, in *Lambert* v *Lewis* [1980] 2 WLR 289, the Court of Appeal declined to hold that statements made in a brochure by a manufacturer could be construed as a collateral contract although, in the United States, the implication of a collateral contract in such cases appears not to be a controversial issue. There may be some assistance to be had by an analogy with guarantees which may be deemed to be collateral contracts, although here again, the matter is not without some doubt.

"Shrink-wrap" licences

Given that the person acquiring an off-the-shelf software package must have a licence to use it brings us to the question of the validity of standard form licence agreements so often to be found amongst the material provided. The term "shrink-wrap" is often used to describe such licences because it was, at one time, not uncommon for the licence to be exposed to view on the outside of the box, as an outer wrapper. This would give the person acquiring the software an opportunity to inspect the terms of the licence before deciding to "buy". Nowadays it is more common for the licence to be inside the box containing the disks and manuals. The problem should be immediately apparent. As the licence cannot be seen until after the contract has been concluded, has it any contractual relevance? Unless it has been drawn to the attention of the buyer of the software who has been given an opportunity to read it (whether or not he takes the opportunity) then the software company's licence agreement can have no force under English law. A golden rule of contract law is that it is not possible to introduce a term into a contract after it has been made; see for example, *Thornton* v *Shoe Lane Parking Ltd* [1971] 2 QB 163 and *Olley* v *Malborough Court Ltd* [1949] 1 KB 532. The only other way the terms in the licence agreement could be incorporated into the contract is on the basis of knowledge of the terms through a previous course of dealing though the case of *McCutcheon* v *David MacBrayne Ltd* [1964] 1 All ER 430 sheds some doubt as to whether a prior written contract can be so imputed into an oral contract.

How might a software company seek to ensure that its standard terms are incorporated in the contract? One way is to require the supplier to show a copy of the licence agreement to the customer and ask him to sign it before he buys. This simple expedient could be a practical possibility although suppliers might resist having to deal with more paperwork. In any case, it will not be practical because software is not always obtained "over the counter". There is a thriving mail order business in computer software and some software is available by electronic mail or over the Internet. One way in which many software companies attempt to resolve the situation is to place the disks containing the programs and associated computer files and databases in a sealed envelope with a notice on it to the effect that breaking open the seal on the envelope signifies acceptance of the terms of the licence agreement. The effectiveness of this approach is, under English law, doubtful although, as it is usual to offer the customer his money back if he does not like the terms as long as he returns the software with the envelope unopened to the software company, this practice demonstrates that software companies believe in the collateral licence approach to off-the-shelf software contracts.

Resolution of this problem was attempted in the Scots case of *Beta Computers (Europe) Ltd* v *Adobe Systems (Europe) Ltd* [1996] FSR 367, discussed in Chapter 4 at page 92. However, Scots contract law is not the same as English contract law, the former being based on Roman law and the decision depended to some extent on the manner in which a third party (the copyright owner and licensor) was given rights under the contract to acquire the software. In England, the doctrine of privity of contract would seem to prevent this but one way in which *Beta* v *Adobe* could work in England and Wales would be to take the following approach:

- there are two contracts, one between the customer and the supplier with respect to the tangible items and one between the customer and the owner of the rights in the software, this latter contract being a licence agreement;
- both contracts are conditional upon the customer agreeing to the terms of the licence which he signifies by opening the sealed packet containing the disks or CD-ROM on which the software is stored;
- until the time that the customer agrees to the terms of the licence, neither contract is made and the customer can return the package containing the software and other items to the supplier and insist on his payment being refunded;
- although acceptance normally has to be communicated to the person making the contractual offer (in this case the supplier and the owner of the rights in the software are making an offer) acceptance can arise from conduct and in the case of a shrink wrap licence, the conduct is opening the sealed packet, installing and using the software.

Whether such an approach will be taken by the English courts remains to be seen. There still seems to be something of a judicial fixation on the perverse notion that it is a sale of goods contract. However, there are signs that some judges are beginning to see the light. Certainly, Lord Penrose in *Beta* v *Adobe* was happy to accept that a contract for shrink-wrap software was not a sale of goods contract. The few cases there have been in England on this issue have not been before any of the more experienced intellectual property judges in the Chancery Division of the High Court.

Some pre-prepared software may be very expensive such as that written for mainframe computers. It may be systems software or applications software. Where this type of software is licensed it is more practicable to have the licence agreed and signed at the time the contract is made. Such licences more closely resemble those applicable for bespoke software and there may even be some room for negotiation. However, standard form contracts are common here as well but it must be noted that it is not advisable to use a standard United States agreement for use in the United Kingdom even with some modification. In *Andersen Consulting* v *CHP Consulting Ltd* (unreported) 26 July 1991, Chancery Division, the judge strongly criticised the phraseology of the plaintiff's licence which was based on its original United States form of agreement. The licence used the phrase "... exclusive owner of the programs which are proprietary and copyrighted" which was described by the judge as being an obscure phrase followed by an Americanism. Because of the unsuitability of the licence in terms of English law the judge, in refusing to grant the injunction sought by the licensor, found it difficult to determine whether there was a breach of contract or whether there was any *prima facie* defence to it.

If the standard form licence is of no effect, the entire licence agreement must be implied. It is difficult to speculate but it is likely that a court would look at the type of terms commonly found in such agreements on the basis of what is customary in the trade. Most of them are fairly innocuous such as limiting the number of copies that may be made of the software, stressing the licensor's intellectual property rights and, not surprisingly, limiting the liability of the software company for losses arising out of the use of the software.

Concerns of the software company and the "customer"

If an off-the-shelf software licence is of doubtful validity the relevance of the terms in the licence must be questioned. From the customer's point of view, why should he bother to even look at the licence? Why should the software company trouble itself to take any care drafting the licence unless it is going to ensure that it is properly incorporated into the contract? The answer must lie in the court's power to imply terms into contracts. Two factors are important and may influence the court in deciding what terms are appropriate for implication. The first is based on trade custom. What is customary in the business of supplying off-the-shelf software? The nature of the terms commonly found in such licences will be helpful though not necessarily conclusive. Another factor might be the terms of the particular agreement. One fact that might greatly enhance the possibility that these terms might be implied is where the customer has been given an opportunity to return the software if he is not happy with the licence terms. At least it could be said that the customer has, by not taking up that option, impliedly assented to those terms, morally if not legally. Whether this could give rise to an equity against him if he later seeks to do something inconsistent with the terms and deny their validity is a moot point though the concepts of acquiescence and estoppel could be appropriate. In any case, eventually, an English court will be able to follow *Beta* v *Adobe*, at least partially and hold that licences in off-the-shelf software are valid.

Most software licences contain a limitation on the number of persons that may use the software and this is particularly true of off-the-shelf software. The norm is the single user licence where the software may be used by the customer and no-one else. From this baseline various other options may be available. For example, a network licence may be available, limiting the use of the software to a specified number of terminals, users or file servers. Alternatively a site licence or organisational licence may be available. There has been a great deal of publicity to the alleged misuse of software, typically by an organisation obtaining a copy of software under a single user licence and then making numerous copies which are distributed and used throughout the organisation. A number of Anton Piller Orders have been obtained to "raid" such organisations and large out-of-court settlements agreed, usually on the basis of the cost of the appropriate multi-user licence. The fact that the "victims" of these orders seem to have been prepared to settle demonstrates that they accept that the licence agreement carries some force and that their copying and use in excess of that permitted by the agreement was an infringement of copyright subsisting in the software. Even an implied licence would not permit unrestricted copying.

Even if the terms of the licence can only have force as a basis for implied terms, persuasively (because of common usage), it still is important for both the software company and the customer to be aware of them. Notwithstanding the contractual difficulty with shrink-wrap licences, some of the terms contained within them may be relevant as regards tortious liability, subject to section 2 of the Unfair Contract Terms Act 1977. It will be useful for both parties to consider what terms will serve their needs and expectations and then to check the licence for such terms.

First, what would be important for the software company. Generally, terms dealing with the following aspects would be deemed to be desirable:

- the use that the customer can make of the software, in particular, the number of copies that may be made, the number of persons who can use the software and the duration of the agreement (if not for the term of the copyright), bearing in mind provisions such as sections 50A to 50D of the Copyright, Designs and Patents Act 1988 and regulation 19 of the Copyright and Rights in Databases Regulations 1997, preventing the prohibition or restriction of certain acts;
- liability for defects in the software or losses caused by the customer's misuse of the software;
- copyright and other intellectual property rights subsisting in the software;
- transfer of the software and licence to a third party;
- whether and under what circumstances a customer can modify the software. It is usual to include a term requiring that the customer does not decompile or disassemble any programs (this must now be subject to the decompilation permitted act in section 50B of the Copyright, Designs and Patents Act 1988).

From the customer's point of view, he will be concerned, primarily, with the performance of the software. Frequently, persons acquiring off-the-shelf software do not rely heavily on any representations made by the software company or software retailer but tend to evaluate the performance independently by referring to computer magazines and trade journals which frequently carry out comparative tests on new items of software. Word of mouth is also effective and there is nothing better than to talk to an experienced current user of the software. This could have implications in terms of any claim for misrepresentation (most licences for off-the-shelf software include an "entire agreement" term) as in *Attwood* v *Small* (1838) 6 Cl & Fin 232 where the buyer of a mine who did not rely on the vendor's exaggerated statements and who sought independent advice was refused an application for rescission of the contract. The terms that will be of interest to the customer will be:

- the number of copies that can be made and how many users the licence allows;
- whether upgrades and enhancements will be available in the future and their likely price;
- the level of support offered and the position with error correction. The presence of a thriving user group might be an important factor;

- how well the software will interface with other software the customer now has or intends to obtain in the future;
- whether the software company is one of the market leaders and will still be around in years to come;
- whether the software can be transferred to a third party in the future – this may be especially important if the customer intends to outsource his IT operations in the future;
- "quiet enjoyment". The position in respect of third party rights and whether there is provision for an indemnity should it be later found that the software infringes a third party's intellectual property rights;
- if the software is development software, to be used by the customer to create new software applications which the customer will then distribute or licence out, what the position is in respect of run-time licences.

Some of the above aspects will be more relevant to the decision to choose a particular software package rather than to the licence itself. Of course, in the great majority of cases, there will be no scope for modifying the licence, the software will be available on a "take it or leave it" basis. Some of the terms that may be found in licences for off-the-shelf software are discussed below with examples.

Particular terms

Licences for off-the-shelf software vary somewhat but most contain a limited warranty. There is a much welcome attempt by some software companies, notably Borland, to write their licences in simple "no-nonsense" English. However, this approach needs care and analogies made in such licences, for example, "you must treat this software just like a book" could have unexpected consequences. Many licences start with a basic statement about the nature of the agreement. As a basis for the terms suggested below, imagine that the software is for a database development system with a compiler called G-Base. Greysoft Ltd is the licensor and the owner of all the intellectual property rights subsisting in the software. It is used to design database systems. Users can create and modify databases and specify the forms and reports to be used with those databases. The compiler produces a "stand alone" system that can be run without the G-Base software but it incorporates modules from within G-Base (a "run-time" system). This allows the customer to create new applications which then may be licensed to others by the customer.

Definitions

As usual, some definitions usefully may be included, normally at the beginning of the licence agreement. The fact that the licensor is the owner of the copyright in the various items provided is stressed.

> "G-Base software" means all the software items supplied in this package including programs, dictionaries, indexes, data files, tutorial programs and files and sample programs, databases, forms and reports.

> "Related Items" means the printed matter and disks supplied in this package.

> "Greysoft Ltd" is the owner of the copyright and other rights in the G-Base software and related items and is, accordingly, the licensor of the G-Base software and related items.

> "Customer" is the person acquiring the G-Base software and is, accordingly, the licensee in respect of it.

Licence agreement

It is common to find a term spelling out the nature of the agreement. The opportunity is taken to deal with copying of the software including making back-up copies and the labelling of such copies. A duty to take precautions to prevent unauthorised use or copying is placed on the licensee.

> Greysoft Ltd grants the customer a licence to use the G-Base software. It may be copied onto one or more computers being used solely by the customer (whether or not on a network) and one back-up copy of the G-Base software may be made by the customer. The customer must ensure that any copies of the G-Base software are clearly labelled as such as include a prominent notice to the effect that Greysoft Ltd is the copyright owner.

> The customer shall take all reasonable precautions and measures to protect the G-Base software and related items from unauthorised use, access, copying, modification, reproduction, distribution or publication.

Permitted uses

Provisions as to the use of the software are important, particularly in terms of how many persons may use the software concurrently. Such provisions will probably be effective no matter what the precise legal nature and validity of the agreement. Note that, to be reasonable and to reflect what will probably happen anyway, the licensor has allowed the software to be loaded on a number of computers though limited to those being used solely by the customer. Many persons acquiring software for their own use will want to install it on more than one computer (typically where they use a desk top computer in the office and a portable or notebook computer when working away from the office).

The licence has to address the fact that the software may be used to create "stand-alone" programs and associated databases, format and report files that may be distributed to third parties. Programs written by the licensee will be compiled into executable form and, in this case as is common, requires a run-time program for the compiled programs to operate. The licensor grants permission to the licensee allowing distribution of the run time program GRUN.EXE along with such compiled programs and associated databases and files. A notice must be given to any person to whom a compiled program is made available setting out the copyright position and limiting the acts that might be performed and disclaiming the licensor's liability (the licensor has included a term later requiring an indemnity from the licensee in respect of use by such persons).

> The G-Base software may NOT be used by ANY PERSON OTHER THAN THE CUSTOMER OR AN EMPLOYEE OF THE CUSTOMER IN THE COURSE OF HIS EMPLOYMENT BY THE CUSTOMER. However, the run-time program GRUN.EXE may be copied and/or distributed in accordance with this agreement.

> The customer may write and compile programs using the G-Base software to be distributed internally or to third parties in executable form only without payment of any additional licence fee to Greysoft Ltd. Apart from the programs compiled by the customer, the customer may also distribute to persons to whom the customer's compiled programs are made available a copy of the G-Base run-time program GRUN.EXE without any additional payment to Greysoft Ltd.

> The customer must include a notice with any copies of the customer's compiled programs and GRUN.EXE setting out that the copyright in the compiled programs (and associated databases, forms and reports files) belongs to the customer and the copyright in GRUN.EXE belongs to Greysoft Ltd and that none of the programs may be copied, decompiled, disassembled or otherwise modified except as permitted by sections 50A and 50B of the Copyright, Designs and Patents Act 1988. The notice must also set out that Greysoft Ltd. has not written the customer's compiled programs (and associated databases, forms and report files) and accepts no responsibility for any of the programs or other software items delivered by the customer. The customer must state that the compiled programs and any

associated databases, format and report files have been created using the G-Base software (quoting the particular release date and number).

The copyright in programs, databases (and/or database structures), format and report files will, *prima facie*, belong to the customer. Greysoft is not seeking to claim any rights in these items.

Prohibited uses

The prohibited uses are spelt out (although some may be implied in the absence of express statement). The licensor has been careful not to include any terms that would be void under the Copyright, Designs and Patents Act 1988. The licensor has allowed the licensee to transfer the software and assign the licence to a third party in the future. Presumably the software has been obtained by the customer for a single payment and there is no difficulty associated with enforcing a contract with a third party, such as there might be where annual payments were to be made for the software. Note the precaution of requiring a note signed by the transferee (which may be binding in equity) and notification of transfer which will enable the licensor to send details of upgrades to the transferee together with any relevant information. The restriction on decompilation, etc is repeated as, in the clause above, it relates only to compiled programs and the run-time program, GRUN.EXE.

In terms of copyright law, under section 18 of the Copyright, Designs and Patents Act 1988, the licensor loses control over copies of his work that have been sold by or with his consent on the basis of the doctrine of exhaustion of rights. However, this does not apply to rental and lending which the licensor will seek to control. Normally, the licensor will prohibit rental and lending as it could adversely affect his sales. It is difficult to prevent a person to whom software has been rented or lent from making and retaining unauthorised copies of the software.

> The customer may not make copies of the software items except as provided above and may not, under any circumstances, make copies of the related items.

> Unless provided for above in terms of compiled programs, the customer must not rent, lease, lend, share, disclose, transmit or transfer the G-Base software and related items except that the customer may transfer all the G-Base software items and related items including any copies made in accordance with this agreement together with this licence agreement to another person under a written agreement signed by that other person. The

written agreement must include a statement to the effect that the transferee agrees to abide by the terms of the licence agreement as the customer. The transferor of the G-Base software and related items must give Greysoft Ltd written confirmation of such a transfer within 14 days of it taking effect together with a copy of the signed written agreement hereinbefore referred to. Greysoft Ltd will keep the transferee informed of future upgrades and enhancements to the G-Base software.

The customer must not decompile, disassemble or otherwise modify the software except as provided for by this agreement and section 50B of the Copyright, Designs and Patents Act 1988, as amended, and the Copyright and Rights in Databases Regulations 1997.

Duration and termination

The duration of licences for off-the-shelf software is not a controversial issue as a lump sum payment usually is made with a statement that the licence is to endure for the term of the copyright. This could have the effect of bringing about a perpetual arrangement as new upgrades made available to the customer (whether or not for payment would keep on extending the copyright term assuming copyright subsists in such new items). Some software companies specify a particular time, such as 25 years or 50 years from the commencement of the licence. It is conceivable that the software may be acquired under an annual renewable licence in which case similar considerations that apply in such cases to bespoke software are relevant. Termination is invariably dealt with, though seldom happens. The licensor has taken the sensible decision to limit termination by him to occasions where there has been a serious or irremediable breach. The licensee would not want the software to be "taken away" from him for some minor transgression that can be quickly remedied, such as taking a photocopy of some pages of the written documentation included in the related items. Of course, policing is a major problem in terms of detecting unauthorised use. Co-operation with the Federation Against Software Theft may help in this respect.

This agreement shall endure for as long as copyright subsists in the United Kingdom in any of the G-Base software items unless terminated earlier. The customer may terminate this agreement at any time by returning all the original items of G-Base software and related items supplied together with all copies made of the G-Base software or after sending written confirmation that all such original items and copies made have been permanently destroyed. Greysoft Ltd may terminate this agreement at any time following a serious or irremediable breach of this agreement and/or a serious infringement of Greysoft Ltd's copyright.

Liability

The licensor will be especially concerned to make sure that he does not leave himself open to claims for loss or damage caused by use of the software. Whereas, with bespoke software the courts have taken a strong view on limitation clauses, with off-the-shelf software it would be reasonable to expect that severe restrictions or even exclusions of liability would be effective and deemed to be reasonable within the Unfair Contract Terms Act 1977. The main reasons are that the software has been designed on the basis of the software company's own specification (based on speculative and hypothetical examples of potential use) and that the software company has absolutely no control over how the software will be used by the customer. Other factors include the difficulty that the software company would have in insuring against losses by users of the software (primarily because of lack of control and knowledge of specific intended uses of the software made by the customer) and the fact that many persons obtaining off-the-shelf software do not rely on the software company's representations as to the performance and capabilities of the software. They normally seek independent advice from an information technology specialist, from software tests in magazines and journals or from colleagues. At least, they ought to.

Even if the standard form licence agreement has little or no contractual significance for reasons mentioned earlier, the term on liability could be important as regards the giving of a notice in respect of tortious liability, bearing in mind the control over such notices by section 2 of the Unfair Contract Terms Act 1977. In our example, liability is limited to the physical items provided which will be replaced providing notification is given within 90 days. For example, if a disk containing some of the software was defective and it was impossible to run the programs, a replacement would be given. This warranty is probably not particularly important because, if the software company refused to replace the disk, the software as a whole would probably not work at all and this would be viewed as a total failure of consideration.

A statement is made to the effect that statutory rights are not thereby prejudiced. Although it is difficult to predict precisely what those rights might be because of the difficulty in classifying a contract for off-the-shelf software, this term makes sure that, whatever the position, the licensor will not commit a criminal offence by trying to interfere with statutory rights.

> Greysoft Ltd warrants that the physical related items provided by Greysoft Ltd are free from defects for a period of 90 days from the date of purchase and that Greysoft Ltd will replace any such items proving to be defective provided notice of the defect has been received in the said 90-day period.

> The customer is entirely responsible for determining the suitability of the G-Base software for his purposes and for the use that he makes of the G-Base software. The customer is entirely responsible for the quality and fitness for purpose of any software distributed to third parties containing programs compiled by the customer using the G-Base software and for any guidance, instruction or training of such third parties in respect of distributed software. The customer shall save harmless and indemnify Greysoft Ltd against claims from third parties in respect of the customer's compiled programs and associated databases, format and report files, GRUN.EXE and other items delivered by the customer to third parties

> Greysoft Ltd is not liable for any loss or damage, direct or indirect, arising from the use of the G-Base software and related items, however caused.

> This agreement is without prejudice to the customer's statutory rights, if any.

Entire agreement

It is common to include an entire agreement term to insulate the software company against any difficulties caused by representations made in any advertising literature (which should also contain a statement that the specification can change without warning and no representation is made as to functions, facilities, performance, etc) or by the retailer supplying the software.

> This agreement represents the entire agreement between Greysoft Ltd and the customer and supersedes all previous agreements or representations whether written or oral.

Applicable law

Software is sold the world over and it is important to specify the applicable law. It may be advisable, if the software is being distributed in a number of countries to have appropriate licence agreements drawn up for those other countries, reflecting differences in the law there. Although, for all the Berne Copyright Convention countries, the basic principles of copyright law will be similar (there can still be substantial differences particularly in respect of sound recordings, films, rights in performances, etc. which may need to be addressed – CD-ROM software could include all those rights in addition to other copyrights) but the laws of contract and tort can be very different. In this case, we have an agreement subject to the laws of England and Wales so the following simple statement will suffice.

> This agreement is subject to the laws of England and Wales and subject to the exclusive jurisdiction of the courts in England and Wales.

The Civil Jurisdiction and Judgments Acts of 1982 and 1991 implement the Brussels Convention and the Lugano and San Sebastian Conventions which may allow an action to be brought in another country in some circumstances, for example, in the case of a breach of contract the action can be brought in the country in which the contract was to be performed or in relation to a tortious act the action can be brought in the country where the harmful event took place. In some cases, a plaintiff will have a choice of countries in which to commence an action. Nevertheless, the exclusive jurisdiction clause may be helpful, especially as regards countries not in those conventions. Where a court has some discretion in whether to accept jurisdiction, this clause could swing the balance in favour of the English courts. After all, that is what the parties agreed.

The terms used above by way of example were designed for the situation mentioned. In other cases, different or additional terms may be required. For example, what if the software company is itself a licensee in respect of some of the software it is now licensing? The customer in our example would need to think carefully before drafting a licence agreement for any applications software created using G-Base that it intends to license out. It is always a question of designing the agreement in the light of the particular circumstances. Other terms that might be relevant are those dealing with arbitration, ownership of output, the position with respect to upgrades and transfer to certain countries. If the software includes databases or other information containing personal data, the provisions of the Data Protection Act 1998 must be adhered to. If the software is to be transferred to a country or territory outside the European Economic Area the rules governing when such transfers may be made, if the country or territory in question does not have an adequate level of protection for personal data, must be examined closely.

Chapter 8

Issues in
Software Procurement

Issues in Software Procurement

Introduction

Obtaining software is not always simply a matter of reading a few magazine articles to find out what the available software products are and how they compare before setting off to visit a computer shop to buy a copy of the package selected. Off-the-shelf software will not be a realistic option in many cases and a software company will have to be engaged to write the required software. Often, the decision to engage a particular software company to write software is the end of a long preliminary process involving consultation with computer professionals and lawyers to advise on the specification of the software, to draw up the necessary agreements, etc. Even in terms of off-the-shelf software, it is often sensible to engage someone to advise on the most appropriate software package where, for example, it is to be the standard package to be used in a large organisation. The initial stages in acquiring software can be the most important. If the software is to be specially written for a client, it is essential that care is taken to engage a competent software company and that the required software is fully specified. It should not be forgotten that what the client wants is fully operational software that performs all its specified tasks efficiently and reliably and that was delivered on time for the cost originally agreed. The software company wants to be paid adequately for the work and to have had a good working relationship with the client which will lead to more work with the client in the future and enhance its reputation generally. This chapter looks at some of the preliminary stages in the acquisition of software and their significance.

Feasibility studies

If the proposed software is complex or has to perform novel tasks or there is some other aspect about it that is impossible or at least very difficult to predict, it may be worthwhile carrying out a feasibility study. This may be carried out by the client's own software engineers and information technology experts where the client has such staff or it may be a matter of engaging an expert consultant to perform the study. This may be advisable even if the client has appropriately qualified staff as an outside expert will bring objectivity into the exercise. If the client's own staff are to collaborate or work alongside the consultant, it is worth explaining to the staff why the consultant has been engaged. Internal staff often can be upset at the appointment of a consultant to carry out work that they themselves feel competent to do. Some diplomacy may be required.

The choice of consultant is critical. The person engaged must be truly independent and it is best not to hire a person who is tied up with a particular software company or supplier in any way. The client must have fully objective advice if it is to be equipped to make a decision that will have important repercussions for years to come. The choice of inappropriate software can eventually be the cause of or a significant contributor in the demise of a business organisation. If it is decided not to appoint an independent consultant the client must ask itself how it is to evaluate the findings of any feasibility study. The importance of this was spelt out in *The Salvage Association* v *CAP Financial Services Ltd* [1995] FSR 654, where the client did not appear to have any staff capable of evaluating the strategy study undertaken by a software company. The case is also instructive in that the company carrying out the study was also the company to be given the work of developing the software concerned and its objectivity may have been questionable.

A feasibility study should properly take into account the client's existing hardware and software installations and any potential changes to them. The operating system software and other applications software that the client has will be particularly important in this respect. The tasks that the proposed software is to carry out must be fully defined and, again, any potential changes must be investigated. The feasibility study should look carefully at the existing methods of carrying out the tasks concerned, whether by manual methods or software implementation. A company may have used a particular method of working for years without ever questioning its efficiency and it is not unheard of for an awkward and unduly complex manual method of working to be built into the software. In many respects, the feasibility study should give an opportunity to evaluate the existing methodologies employed. Care too must be taken not to suggest the abandonment of something which turns up to have a good *raison d'être* some time later. If the tasks to be carried out by the software are new to the client, this leaves the consultant with a clean sheet and much more work to do and responsibility to shoulder. In either case, the assistance and collaboration of the client in defining the software's functional, operational and performance-related aspects is of the utmost importance.

The feasibility study can be seen as the first major step in the procurement process. Quite often, it will include the development and writing of a detailed specification for the software which may then be used to obtain quotations or as a basis for the invitation of tenders. In either situation, it may then form the basis of the agreement for writing the software and be the yardstick by which its performance is measured. If things go wrong, the determination of liability may be largely dependent on the specification. From the consultant's point of view, carrying out a feasibility study carries a heavy burden to ensure that it is done proficiently and the resulting report is comprehensive, accurate, contains sound advice and a consideration of all the options together with estimates of costs and time-scale and is, above all, easy to understand so that the client can evaluate the options and their implications. Such a person will almost certainly carry professional

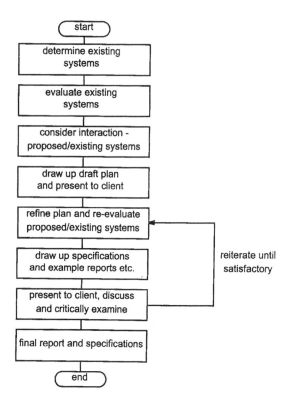

Figure 8.1 Feasibility Study for New Computer Software

indemnity insurance and should not be engaged without it. Figure 8.1 shows the steps in a typical feasibility study for software to automate an existing manual system.

Carrying out a feasibility study may involve something known as prototyping. This is where software is written to demonstrate and test what the finished software will look like, what it will do and how it will perform. It may be particularly useful where the client is not quite sure of his requirements or where there are a number of alternative methods of implementing the software.

Prototyping

This is useful if the client is unable to define precisely the exact requirements at the outset or several alternative implementations of the proposed software are possible and it is required to have some parts written in prototype form so that they can be compared. A consultant and/or software company will commit resources to developing skeleton or partial software systems with the assistance and advice of the client so that different methods and techniques can be experimented with and their effects studied and evaluated. Prototyping is often a deductive process in that a very general idea of the system is the starting point and by applying a generalised model to particular data more detailed software solutions suggest themselves or show themselves to be the most satisfactory. The full co-operation of the client is essential and the staff who are likely to be involved with operating the proposed software should be involved. After a while, it should be easier to write a full specification, to draw up a draft agreement for the proposed software and then to decide how to select a software company to carry out the work.

A sense of direction is essential in prototyping. The absence of final and intermediate goals together with a lack of discipline may mean that a large amount of time and money is spent with little to show for it at the end of the day. There should be clearly defined targets and a programme of work should be drawn up. Meetings should be held at appropriate intervals to review progress, to evaluate findings to date and to decide and agree upon future work and resource allocation. The agreement under which the prototyping is carried out should have provision for termination should it become clear that it will lead nowhere, which it might do without it being anybody's fault (appropriate compensation could be provided for in the agreement).

Payment for prototyping work will usually be on a time and

materials basis. Prototyping work should be continually reviewed and assessed. Objectives should be clearly stated. Firm leadership is essential otherwise it will be difficult to reconcile the differing priorities of the persons involved in the work on both sides of the camp. Differences between the members of one party's team are not unknown.

Sometimes, rather than seeing the development of a prototype as an intermediate stage in the software procurement process where it is useful to develop a detailed specification, it can be continued through to final delivery of the software. This is fraught with problems. Usually, the agreement will contain only broad statements of what is expected: it cannot do otherwise. One difficulty is determining liability for defective software or software that performs poorly. As the client's own staff will have been deeply involved in the process of developing the software, attributing blame for deficiencies in the software may be virtually impossible. Another problem is that it will be open-ended in terms of cost. The client does not know at the outset what the final bill will be. From the software company's point of view, as the agreement is on a time and materials basis, it should make a profit but then there is little incentive to complete the work more quickly or efficiently. In fact, if it has little work elsewhere, it may be tempted to drag the work out for as long as it can, constantly making proposals for additional features.

Nevertheless, it must be accepted that prototyping to final installation can be very successful and provide the client with software that performs all the tasks the client wished for (probably plus some others that the client had not thought of when the work started). Gone also are the problems caused by a client that changes its mind half way through the performance of the contract and wants "just a couple of extra reports" or "a little bridge to my accounts software". It is also argued that the relationship between the parties is more likely to be one of co-operation rather than being adversarial or confrontational. However, a meeting where the cost is already higher than that first envisaged with little sign of the work being finished can be fairly confrontational! Also the time taken to test, debug and add the final touches to software can easily surprise a client who might get irritated at the additional time and expense for little obvious benefit. The software company must spell out the necessity for full testing and for the fact that little finishing touches can take a lot of time. Another disadvantage is that if the costs are starting to run away the client may have little option but to terminate leaving itself with no software after substantial expenditure. No one wants to commission the Sydney

Opera House of software, no matter how good, if it takes five times longer to finish than originally anticipated and costs 15 times the original estimate.

Tenders

A client requiring computer software may invite tenders for the development and installation of the software. Tenders are very common in the public sector but some private organisations also make use of this method of letting contracts, particularly where the work is substantial. Indeed, inviting tenders may be compulsory in the case of large schemes under EC rules on compulsory competitive tendering. The legal significance of a general invitation to submit tenders is that it is deemed to be an invitation to treat; see *Spencer* v *Harding* (1870) LR 5 CP 561. There is no obligation to accept any of the tenders. For example, if tenders are invited for the writing of software, there is no obligation to accept the lowest or any tender. However, if the invitation includes a term to the effect that the lowest (or highest depending on the circumstances) bid will be accepted then the invitation to submit tenders is an offer as in *Harvela Investments Ltd* v *Royal Trust Co of Canada* [1986] AC 207. Otherwise, the persons submitting tenders are the offerors and, consequently, the persons submitting tenders have to bear the costs of preparing their bids. This can be a considerable expense where the project is complex.

The documents normally made available to persons submitting tenders will include a detailed specification (it has to be sufficiently detailed to allow the persons submitting tenders to calculate the work and risk involved with some degree of certainty) and a form of agreement (so that the contractual consequences such as the apportionment of liabilities can be determined). The form of agreement will deal with all the issues discussed in Chapter 6 together with any others peculiar to the project. Of particular significance will be the time for completion of the work and the quantum of liquidated damages for late delivery. It is common for there to be provision for a performance bond to be arranged by the successful tenderer. This may be arranged with a bank or insurance company and can be called on by the client if the software company fails to complete the work. The money (typically, 10 per cent of the total tender figure) can be used to cover the additional expense involved in appointing a new company to complete the work.

By inviting tenders in this way, the client takes full responsibility for the quality of the specification. If there are problems later, the successful tenderer will look for deficiencies in the specification; for example, arguing that some particular work now required was not specified and, therefore, not included in the original bid and that an additional payment and extension of time for completion is now justified. Alternatively, the client may include only a functional specification, outlining the tasks the software will have to perform, leaving it to the companies invited to submit tenders to draw up their own detailed operational and performance-related specifications which will be included in the documents returned to the client. This can, however, make it difficult to compare final bids. It is sensible to include a schedule of rates to be completed by tenderers, to be used to calculate the price of any additional work.

In many cases, the time for completion will be completed by the client before the tender documents are sent out (if there is provision for liquidated damages for late delivery, this is usually to be completed by the client). In some cases, particularly where the client is unable to fix a realistic time for completion, it may be left to be completed by the companies submitting tenders.

Tenders may be open or selective; in the former the invitation to tender is usually advertised in the press or appropriate trade journal or *Official Journal of the European Communities* and any company interested may submit a bid. In the case of selective tendering, a small number of software companies will be selected by the client (perhaps after seeking professional advice) and these will be invited to submit a tender. By using selective tendering, the client can make sure that only software developers competent in the relevant field are considered. Under the normal rules of tendering, the companies submitting tenders must not modify the tender documents in any way (all must bid on precisely the same basis), a deadline is set (tenders will not be opened until after the passing of the deadline) and late bids will be rejected. These rules have developed as a way of minimising the possibility for unfair practices and corruption. However, there are some problems with tendering which may be exacerbated in tenders for software:

- not all tenderers may be able to comply precisely with the specification and some may submit tenders based on an alternative or modified specification. This makes comparison of bids very difficult;
- the client is taking on himself responsibility for the quality of

the specification (at least the functional specification). An eager software company will pounce eagerly on deficiencies as a way of obtaining further payment and extensions of time. If the client provides a functional or outline specification, asking tenderers to submit a detailed specification with their bids, this may make it difficult to compare the submitted tenders;

- the terms in the proposed agreement may frighten off some tenderers (for example, it may impose liability on the software developer for delays caused by or faulty work of a sub-contractor or supplier specified by the client or provide for an unrealistic time for completion or heavy liquidated damages for late delivery – or both);
- mistakes in working out the final tender figure may be difficult to deal with, particularly where the mistake is apparent to the client such as where the tenderers have submitted a list of rates or extended sums and there are some arithmetical errors which should have been spotted by the client.

Nevertheless, if the client is confident that he has the ability to produce a good set of tender documents, inviting tenders may be the best way to obtain the required software at as low a price as possible. A software company with a low order book is likely to submit an attractive price. Tenders may also be invited for the supply of computer equipment, consumables or services over a period of time either for a specified amount of items or services or as and when required. An example would be an annual software maintenance contract based on a schedule of rates, work to be carried out only as and when the software needs attention. Such tenders are known as standing offer tenders.

The legal implications of a standing offer for unspecified quantities of goods or services is that acceptance may, anomalously, not create a binding contract because there is no guarantee that any goods or work will be required. Acceptance is complete when a definite quantity of goods is requisitioned or an order is placed for some particular work; *Percival Ltd* v *London County Council Asylums* (1918) 87 LJKB 677. Effectively, each requisition or order creates a separate binding contract. In the absence of express provision otherwise, the party who accepted the tender is not bound to place any order at all and cannot, therefore, be sued for breach of contract if he fails to place an order. However, on the other hand, the company that submitted the successful tender can also withdraw it at any time before a definite order is placed unless it has bound itself otherwise. When an order is placed, that creates a binding contract in respect of that order and the successful tenderer is bound to fulfil that order but remains free to revoke at any time as to future orders; *Great Northern Railway Co* v *Witham* (1873) LR 9 CP 16. Of course, one way to overcome the uncertainty of whether a future order will be accepted is to pay a retainer, perhaps annually.

As an alternative to inviting tenders, the client may simply ask for quotations based on a description of the client's requirements. Quotations are normally expressed as not being offers. Also, they will be less easy to compare as each company quoting may base its quote on different approaches and solutions, and different forms of contract.

Independent advisors

An independent advisor may be engaged to advise on the procurement of software and/or to draw up the tender documents including the specification. That advisor may do further work, such as advising on the choice of companies to be included in a list for selective tendering and managing the tendering process. This can be useful as, with a complex operation, some of the companies submitting tenders may raise a number of queries during the process of assessing the project and calculating their bids. Some may even want to submit tenders based on an alternative scheme (the normal method of dealing with this is to allow it, providing it is a reasonable alternative subject to the submission of another tender based on the original scheme). Other tenderers should be informed that an alternative bid is being submitted by one company and given a description of the basis for the alternative in broad terms (the others may wish to do likewise). The advisor may then assist in selecting the successful tenderer. A few points should be mentioned here. The client may have established rules for dealing with the award of contracts, such as a senior officer of the organisation putting a proposal to accept a particular tender to a committee who makes the final decision. Assessment of tenders is not always easy. It is not necessarily a matter of selecting the cheapest, particularly where open tendering has been used. The company submitting the least expensive tender may be inexperienced in the type of work envisaged or there may be a mistake in the arithmetic. Other problems are where the tenderer has based his tender on a modified specification or contract. For example, the form of agreement may require a fixed price bid but the tenderer insists that his bid is on a fluctuating price basis. Alternative tenders may also have to be assessed. In short, a suitably qualified and experienced consultant can prove very helpful at this stage in choosing the best blend of price and performance. For certain large schemes, EC rules on tendering may be applicable.

Following the award of the contract, the consultant's role may continue. As has been noted in Chapter 6, the use of an independent professional to supervise the work, certify payments, check on quality and deal with problems such as variations, can be very beneficial to both parties and aid the smooth running of the contract. Apart from anything else, such a person should bring a welcome breath of objectivity and calmness to the performance of the contract. His role as an intermediary should not be underestimated. In terms of the client getting the best software at a reasonable price, this arrangement can be well worth the expense of paying such a person. One thing to be considered, however, is that the person appointed should be suitably experienced and professionally qualified, typically being a member or fellow of the British Computer Society and a chartered engineer. He will also need some basic legal knowledge as part of his duties will involve interpreting and applying the terms in the contract and dealing as a first line mediator or "arbitrator" in the case of a dispute.

Of course, it could be argued that such a person cannot be independent if he is paid by the client, as will normally be the case. However, a true professional will make sure that he stands apart from both parties and that he maintains his objectivity and sense of fairness.

Chapter 9

Negotiating Software Agreements

Negotiating Software Agreements

Introduction

Where software is being developed specifically for a particular client in line with his requirements it is likely that some negotiation is necessary (and desirable) before the final form of the agreement is arrived at. One of the parties will draw up a draft agreement to form the basis of negotiation. Usually, it will be the software company which will do this but, in some cases, particularly where the client is a large organisation, such as a local authority, the client may prepare the first draft. Some organisations attempt to impose their standard form contract on the other. This is a mistake where the work involved is not straightforward. In fact, it can backfire and render the contract subject to section 3 of the Unfair Contract Terms Act 1977.

The existence of preliminary negotiations *per se* does not escape section 3 which subjects terms excluding or restricting liability for breach of contract to a test of reasonableness where, *inter alia*, the contract is made on written standard terms of business. This was held to be so in *St Albans City & District Council* v *International Computers Ltd* [1997] FSR 251, where although there were some preliminary negotiations concerning the contract, the defendants written standard terms of business remained effectively untouched. At first instance, ([1995] FSR 686) Scott-Baker J said that not all terms had to be fixed in advance by the supplier and there may be negotiations as to the contract price, for example. However, where there are negotiations and subsequent alterations to the written standard terms of business to reflect the particular circumstance of the client, that might take the case outside section 3; see Potter J in *The Flamar Pride* [1990] 1 Lloyd's Rep 434. A crucial point is whether there has been any modification of the terms excluding or restricting liability.

Negotiation is something we all do from time to time. It may be a negotiation with an employer about a pay rise, time off work or the timing of a holiday. Negotiating the price of a house or a motor car is an important negotiation for most of us. To some extent, most people already have some basic negotiating skills but these can always be improved. The first thing to consider is what is the goal to be achieved.

What is negotiation about?

In the context of software licensing, negotiation is transactional and, unlike the case where the goal is to settle some dispute such as an alleged infringement of copyright, the process is constructive. The ideal is to arrive at a form of contract that satisfies both parties. This can seem an odd goal at first and it could be argued that the goal should be to get the contract terms that most favour the party the negotiator represents. However, if the contract ends up being too lopsided, this can lead to difficulties when it comes to perform the contract. For example, if the client has managed to get the software company to agree to a time for completion that is too tight, the latter will be likely to look for any reason it can to justify extensions to that time or may claim that the software is acceptable when he knows some errors remain to be fixed. Of course, this does not mean that a firm approach should not be taken to the negotiation and there are dangers in being too conciliatory.

In many cases, one party will already have a standard form of agreement which it wants to impose on the other. There may be good reasons for this, for example, the terms are familiar and the agreement appears to have worked well in the past. However, it may impose onerous conditions on the other party or may be based on an inappropriate mechanism as far as the other party is concerned. It may seek to reduce or eliminate the risk of one at the expense of the other. In many cases, some modification may be desirable which can be best achieved by negotiation. The aim of both parties should be to draft an agreement which is balanced and fair, provides appropriate mechanisms for performance-related issues and any problems that might arise and it should properly allocate risk. This should mean that the performance of the contract is supported by the agreement, rather than having one or other party relying on the agreement to excuse poor contractual performance.

Before the negotiation

Consideration should first be given to the technical objectives. For example, what does the client want the software for, what computers will it be installed on, what other software must it operate with and when should delivery take place? Another issue to consider is the desired provisions for maintenance. Will the client or the software company maintain the software? The consequences of failing to reach an acceptable agreement also ought to be thought through – this may condition expectations and make the parties more realistic.

Effective negotiation comes only with thorough preparation. This involves:

- identifying objectives and requirements and reflecting on the realities of the situation;
- identifying and analysing the relevant facts and the legal constraints;
- identifying the issues and ranking them;
- preparing a SWOT analysis – Strengths Weaknesses Opportunities Threats;
- considering the other party's position and its objectives, strengths and weaknesses;
- categorising the issues in terms of whether concessions can be made and what concessions from the other side they could be traded for;
- deciding how the negotiation should be handled including structure and strategies.

This will enable a plan to be drawn up which can be taken to the negotiation to help as an *aide-memoire* and to form a framework for the negotiation. For example, the plan will include statements of:

- the objectives;
- the facts or background information;
- an analysis of the relevant law;
- strengths, weakness, opportunities and threats;
- supposed objectives of other side and their strengths and weaknesses;
- possible concessions;
- relevant calculations;
- possible structure for the negotiation.

Objectives

The client may hold expectations which may or may not be realistic. For example, the client wants the source code in a situation where it is not normal to deliver the source code. It may require that the software is delivered in an unreasonably short time. The software company may want to lock the client into a maintenance agreement and not allow any other company to maintain the software. It is important that some realism is adopted. However, there may be some objectives that cannot be compromised. If the client wants the source code so that it can maintain the software itself or use third party software maintenance providers but the software company has a rigid policy of never releasing the source code to clients, then any negotiation seems doomed to failure. If this is a possible scenario (it is the most common and irreconcilable difference) the client should consider whether there are other software companies that do hand over source code and which can write the software concerned. If there are none, the client should add to his objectives an escrow agreement. The software company should also consider this as a possible means of resolving the issue.

Facts or background information

Some basic fact finding will help the client to discover whether there are any appropriate standard forms of contract and what the norms are for the type of software development concerned. Any standard or typical forms should be studied and compared to get a feel for what is usual and what is sensible to ask for. It does not help a negotiation to keep asking for unrealistic concessions from the other party.

From both parties' points of view it is important to do some background research on the other party. For example, does the proposed client pay invoices quickly and what is its reputation amongst suppliers and other contractors? The client will be concerned to satisfy itself that the software company is proficient. This may involve talking to other clients of the software company. Questions such as the length of time the software company has been established and its shareholding could be important. For both, it will be worthwhile carrying out a company search and checking its credit-worthiness. Some software companies are quite small and have only a programmer or two who have set up a company for tax reasons. Whilst this does not necessarily mean that it will not be able to carry out the work, it will be an important factor in deciding whether to engage that company for a large contract.

Analysis of the relevant law

The legal constraints should be identified and their implications considered. For example, does the work involve personal data and thus require inclusion of an appropriate term in relation to security measures? What is likely to be considered reasonable as a limitation clause for defects? What types of terms does the law make void and unenforceable? There is no point including terms in a contract that are likely to be caught by the Unfair Contract Terms Act 1977 or made void by the Copyright, Designs and Patents Act 1988. Both parties need to be aware of such legal issues and, particularly where the parties are negotiating round an old form of contract, they need to be vigilant in respect of how recent changes in the law may have impacted upon that agreement. There are likely to be implied terms also to consider, such as section 13 of the Supply of Goods and Services Act 1982.

Strengths, Weaknesses, Opportunities and Threats

An essential stage in the preparation for negotiation is to consider the strengths, weaknesses, opportunities and threats. Table 9.1 contains an example of a SWOT analysis for both sides based on preparation for a hypothetical negotiation of a software licence.

Table 9.1 SWOT Analysis

SWOT	client	software company
Strengths	• high profile, large plc • reputation for prompt payment	• established for a number of years • some important clients • experienced programmers with good knowledge of latest techniques and networking
Weaknesses	• there are not many software companies operating in this field • not very experienced in the acquisition of software of the type concerned	• currently have cash-flow problems • some of the most experienced programmers are threatening to set up in business in competition • difficulties in recruiting good staff
Opportunities	• software, if developed quickly and effectively, could give a market edge	• developing a long term relationship with client, maintaining software and, as client is likely to be thinking of embarking on "e-commerce" in the future, securing further important contracts
Threats	• main competitor is rumoured to be considering similar software • if software turns out to be unsatisfactory, this could be disastrous as it is tied into the launch of a new service	• client has a reputation for litigation • may be too stretched if awarded contract

Where appropriate, the factors should be ranked to identify their relative importance.

Objectives of other side and their strengths and weaknesses

It is vital that the perspective of the other party is also considered so that relative "bargaining power" may be assessed. Consider what concessions the other party is likely to be prepared to make. This may assist in selecting an appropriate strategy.

It may be that the market is very limited and most software companies use similar standard form agreements. In such a case, the client may be in a relatively weak negotiating position and the software company may be prepared to make minor concessions only. On the other hand, the client may be a large local authority or prestigious company and there may be the opportunity to gain further substantial work in the future, including software maintenance.

Possible concessions

The basic rule is never make a concession without getting anything in return. This rule should be adhered to unless there are special reasons to depart from it and the negotiator is particularly skilled.

Items which are likely to come up for negotiation should be classified as:

- things of minor importance that can be conceded readily;
- things that can be conceded but only in return for appropriate concessions from the other party;
- things that must not be conceded under any circumstances.

In some cases, items in the first category may be usefully sacrificed, perhaps as a way of getting the negotiation going or restarted from an impasse. This needs care, however, unless something in return is obtained. Alternatively, they may be used singly or collectively to obtain concessions from the other party. In some cases, a minor concession might be quite important to the other party, in which case it should be negotiated on the basis of its worth to the other party. Consideration should also be given to the possible timing and sequence of concessions.

Relevant calculations

It may be appropriate to have some figures worked out beforehand, such as what constitutes a reasonable royalty or fee or a reasonable timescale for performing a contract (identifying critical points as in a critical path analysis) or the manner in which variations and additional work can be calculated. Even though some of the figures may be tentative at this stage, they should be helpful assessing the consequences, financial or otherwise, of any agreement that may be reached.

Structure

It may be sensible to deal with the most important issues first because if agreement cannot be reached on these there is little point in spending time over minor issues involving things that are likely to be readily conceded. It would be useful to have a proposed agenda to work to and, if possible, agree upon this before negotiation commences.

Negotiating

It is likely that any negotiation will involve technical persons as well as lawyers. Both parties must have persons involved who are capable of understanding the technical issues and this goes for the lawyers also. How can they assess the legal implications of a particular contractual term if they do not know what the technical implications are?

It can be helpful to have the contribution of those persons who will be responsible for developing the software and for using it once it is finished. All negotiators should have clearly defined responsibility and authority in relation to the negotiation which should be carried out in a structured manner. Some degree of flexibility will probably be required of both sides. It is advisable to minute a negotiation and maintain a professional, though amicable, atmosphere.

There are two main negotiating styles:

- adversarial or competitive, starting from a strong opening position, demanding concessions and being slow to concede anything in return; keeping one's cards close to one's chest, or
- co-operative, more open, looking for common interests and proposing reasonable offers in return for reasonable concessions.

Both may be suitable where the parties are in dispute but in relation to negotiating the terms of a software licence, the latter is more appropriate. The approach to be adopted may be:

- positional, determining the "bottom line" (that is, the worst position you would agree to) and the opening position to be adopted, or
- problem-solving, looking at the situation from both points of view and evaluating all possible outcomes.

A mixture of the two approaches may be used. For example, a positional approach may be adopted in the determination of the price to be paid whilst a problem-solving approach might be useful when considering whether the source code is to be delivered to the client.

From the client's perspective, the positional approach might involve deciding on a best position, an opening position and a bottom-line (below which he will "walk-away"). In terms of the price to be paid for the software, the decisions should be informed by looking at comparable agreements, where these exist, quotations, bids or proposals from other software companies willing to perform the contract. For example, if a price around £200,000 is usual, the client may choose a best position of £170,000, an opening position of £150,000 and a bottom line of £235,000. The opening position should be lower than the best position to give the client room to manoeuvre and something to concede whilst still achieving his optimum position. Some flexibility is required as the negotiation proceeds, for example, the other side may propose the inclusion of additional features in the software which could mean that the above figures must be re-appraised. It is important, however, not to depart from the chosen positions and criteria without thinking through the implications carefully. This may require a break from the negotiation process.

Each party should seek to clarify the authority of the other party's negotiators to make decisions and conclude the agreement. If the agreement is subject to the approval of someone higher up, this fact should be made clear. Sometimes, having an agreement subject to approval by someone not taking part can be a ploy to make live a term that had apparently been agreed. It is far better to have all the persons who can authorise the agreement present and involved in the negotiation. It is essential that any agreement reached is properly and accurately recorded.

A useful opening is for each party to state their view of the licence to be agreed, setting out their objectives and perceptions, concentrating on mutual interests, where there is likely to be agreement already, as this will engender a cooperative atmosphere.

Tactics

Apart from deciding what strategy to use, it is important to decide on matters such as the timing of concessions, what to reveal and what to conceal. Do you want to make the first move or would it be more appropriate for the other party to do so? One party may hope to grind the other down by pedantically sticking to minor details at the outset and, for example, refusing to agree to something which is trivial, arguing that it is more important than it really is. Another approach, common in licence negotiations is the "take it or leave it" scenario. Both need careful use and may be counterproductive in many cases.

A basic rule is never to simply accept a "stonewall" approach as it seldom turns out to be so rigid if progress can be made in other areas. Try to find ways to explain that such an approach is not necessarily in the other side's own interests. For example, in terms of a written standard form agreement, the intransigent side may be exposing themselves to section 3 of the Unfair Contract Terms Act 1977. Alternatively, it could be pointed out that stubbornness and inflexibility will derail the negotiation and, if other software companies have expressed interest, the negotiation will be suspended for a while. This may allow time to sound out some other companies about their willingness to negotiate the particular issue causing deadlock. Other responses to deadlock include:

- take a break;
- summarise progress made thus far and stress common interests;
- put the issue on the back-burner for a while and look at something else more likely to be agreed;
- replace one or more negotiators; or
- as a last resort, appoint a mediator.

Soon after commencement of the negotiation, one party may make some minor concession without asking for anything in return in order to foster a good atmosphere. This needs great care and, as a tactic should only be used sparingly and then only by very experienced negotiators. The other party might eagerly accept the concession then refuse to concede anything in return. From then on, the negotiation will be an uphill fight. Another tactic to be aware of is bringing the negotiation to a premature end, hoping that the other will be anxious to agree outstanding matters.

Less important concessions may be exchanged for more important ones. For example, a client prepared to settle invoices quickly may be able to obtain a much greater concession from a relatively new software company which probably will have cash flow problems.

Ample time should be allowed for the negotiation with appropriate breaks, for example, for inter-team discussions or for obtaining further information. Avoid rushing into accepting a poor agreement simply to get the negotiation over with. This might be tempting when the other party has been very difficult or unpleasant to negotiate with. No deal is better than a bad deal.

Other tactics to be aware of include:

- a shock opening offer or demand – do not be thrown by this;
- just when agreement seems close, a negotiator makes a new demand for an additional and important concession;
- important and sensitive looking information left lying around, for example, during a break from negotiation – it may have been left deliberately and be misleading;
- a surprise concession is made that was not even contemplated – take a break and consider it carefully – after such consideration it may be appreciated that it is nowhere as good as it first seemed;
- a negotiator making lots of little demands – he should be asked to set them all down, rather than trying to deal with them individually;
- "good guy/bad guy" – a team of negotiators includes one member who is unpleasant in manner and who will not agree to anything. Another member of the team is charming and appears helpful – the danger is that you may concede more than you should to the "good guy";
- other tactics such as intimidation and emotional outbursts should be seen for what they are and it should be made clear that they are unacceptable.

Summary

Finally, just to recap some key points in negotiation, some basic guidelines can be stated as follows:

- Each team of negotiators must be well briefed. They must know what the software is intended to do and what standards of performance are required. They must know what is or is not acceptable in such matters as time for delivery, time and manner of payment, etc. They must also be aware of what leeway is reasonable.

- Each member of the team must know what his role is within the team and what the scope of his authority is vis-à-vis the other members. For example, can a particular team member agree a certain point during negotiation or will he have to refer it to other team members or to other officers of the company not present? A negotiating team should not be worried about asking for a break so that it (and the other team) can discuss a particular issue in private.

- Team members should avoid being confrontational. After all, the reason the teams are in a negotiating position is that they hope to do business with each other.

- Team members should be good listeners and hear the other team's points and explanations.

- A team should be prepared to concede some points as this may help it to win other points that are more important.

- Team members should never lose their composure and good nature. If the other team will not agree a particular point, it should be put on one side until later when some other less difficult points have been agreed. An attempt should be made to develop an air of mutual progress.

- It is worth considering using just one or two members of a team to concentrate on finding a compromise to a very difficult issue whilst the rest of the team looks at less controversial issues. The sub-teams may manage to agree and then submit their proposal to the whole of both teams. This approach can be helpful if one member of a team is being particularly awkward or obstinate.

- Timing is all. A team should not concede a point before it has to – the other team should be made to think that any concession is generous. Nor should a team gloat over a point conceded by the other team. This should not be treated as a victory, rather it is just one more step in the process of coming to a conclusion that is satisfactory to both teams and that can form the basis of a fruitful relationship between the parties.

Facilities Management

Facilities Management

Introduction

A situation whereby a contractor provides services to a client in respect of information technology may be described as outsourcing or facilities management. The two terms are often used interchangeably though theoretically, there is a narrow distinction between them. A dictionary definition of outsourcing is "to obtain (goods, etc) by contract from an outside source" (*Oxford Concise English Dictionary*, Clarendon Press, 9th ed, 1995). "Facilities management" occurs where an outside contractor takes over the operation, maintenance and future development of a particular facility of the client, such as the information technology systems. In this chapter, generally though not exclusively, the term "facilities management" will be used.

It is becoming increasingly common for organisations to outsource certain of their functions and processes by engaging specialist contractors. A typical area for outsourcing is information technology and there are numerous specialist companies that specialise in taking over and running an organisation's information technology facilities and functions. Facilities management operations may range from simply running the client's computer ("platform operations") to full applications operations where the contractor takes complete responsibility for all the client's information technology operations up to and including help desk facilities (Hallahan, "Should you hand over your computer room", *Computing*, 17 September 1993, p 33).

There are a number of claimed advantages enjoyed by an organisation engaging a specialist information technology facilities management company such as:

- the facilities management company is likely to have specialist skills and knowledge and efficient and up to date hardware and software;
- the cost to the organisation is likely to be less than if it continued to operate its own information technology department; there are likely to be efficiency gains and some sharing of equipment and software used in relation to data

processing carried out by the facilities management company for a number of clients;

- the organisation's information technology staff may be transferred to the facilities management company which will then take on responsibility as their employer, including ensuring that the staff are fully and regularly trained to high standards;
- the expertise of the facilities management company may result in more effective, imaginative and powerful use of the organisation's data and processing operations;
- the facilities management company is more likely to be able to respond to change and technological development than might be the case if the organisation retained its data processing activities in-house;
- the organisation may be freed from future large capital expenditure on new computer equipment;
- the organisation will be freed from the problems of hardware and software maintenance;
- systems management and development is likely to be more coherent and coordinated.

Of course, outsourcing information technology facilities will not be appropriate in all cases and some organisations with specialist or sensitive data processing operations may, if they have appropriate equipment, software and staff, prefer to keep their information technology function in-house.

A facilities management contract is likely to be considered, in the main, to be a contract for services within the Supply of Goods and Services Act 1982. There will be, therefore, the implied terms of "reasonable skill and care" and in relation to time for completion and payment where there is no provision for such in the agreement itself. There may also be aspects related to changes of ownership of hardware or software or rental or licensing.

The contractual framework for facilities management is usually through a service level agreement which has to provide for the overall control and management of the outsourcing operation. It has to deal with transfers of staff, equipment and software, performance, control, supervision and monitoring, payment, change to the services provided, impacts on third parties, liabilities, insurances and indemnities, intellectual property and other rights and termination, amongst other things. Of course, the agreement will be heavily influenced by the particular circumstances and it is not possible to predict every aspect that should be covered in the service level agreement. The purpose of this chapter is, therefore, to consider some of the common issues that are likely to be found in the outsourcing of information technology functions and operations.

Some of the main issues that must be addressed by the service level agreement are:

- the level and nature of the service provided;
- what is to be transferred to the facilities management company from the client (equipment, software, staff, licences, etc);
- the mechanism for payment to the facilities management company;
- the mechanism for agreeing and implementing modifications to the service provided and the impact of such modifications on the duration of the agreement and payments due;
- how the service can be implemented (hopefully in as seamless a way as possible) and how it can be transferred if, in the future, another facilities management company is appointed or the client decides to revert to running its information technology operations in-house again;
- the provisions for supervision of the contract and its performance and for assessing targets and service levels and whether they are being achieved;
- the mechanism for dispute resolution.

There follows a discussion of some of the terms commonly found in facilities management contracts.

Definitions

As with most forms of agreement it is useful to start with important definitions. This is particularly important in terms of facilities management contracts due to the great number of issues involved, for example where existing equipment or software is being transferred to the facilities management company. The definitions must be quite precise, dealing with model numbers, release numbers and the like. Where the service is being provided wholly or partly on the client's premises the extent of the premises and other facilities being made available should also be specified. In many cases, the definitions may refer to schedules of equipment and software.

Things provided by the facilities management company

First and foremost, it will be the services provided by the facilities management company that will be of prime interest to the client. A schedule to the agreement will be usual to specify the services provided in some detail. Apart from the day-to-day running and maintenance of the information technology facilities, there may also be training and "help-desk" facilities available to the client's staff who are the end users of the relevant applications systems. Other services may include advising on enhancements and further uses of the computer facilities and computer data and the further development of those facilities. The client is likely to want strategic guidance ranging from the acquisition of additional software (which may be written by the facilities management company on behalf of the client) to a wholesale review of the client's use of information technology now and in the future.

Computer technology is continually developing and improving, not just in terms of processing speed and power but also in relation to networking and shared or pooled access to data and software. It is important that the agreement provides for periodical reviews and studies of available technology and the uses it could be put to in the context of the client's present and future requirements otherwise the client could find that its use of information technology is stagnating and it is being left behind by its competitors.

Depending on the circumstances, the facilities management company may use its own equipment and software for the benefit of the client. It may even use another client's hardware and software on a shared basis to provide the services to the client. Again, this must be spelt out and provision included to deal with upgrades, new applications and other changes.

Things provided by the client

It is common for the client to transfer its existing hardware and software to the facilities management company. This will entail a sale of the equipment (alternatively, it may be hired), an assignment or licensing of copyright in the client's own software and a transfer of any licences in third party software (assuming this is possible). Where the client owns the rights in software to be used by the facilities management company it makes good sense for a client to grant a licence for the duration of the facilities management contract and which terminates when that contract terminates.

If the service is provided wholly or partly on the client's premises, this must be dealt with together with any implications in respect of occupier's liability and insurances. It may be that the agreement operates to license or even lease the relevant premises to the facilities management company for the duration of the contract. This could be useful in determining any changes to the payments due should it later be decided to move off-site, for example, to the facilities management company's own premises.

It is likely that the client has subsisting contracts with third parties which may be affected by the change to facilities management. For example, the client may have current hardware or software maintenance agreements with third parties. These will have to be transferred to the facilities management company (that is, the benefit of these agreements assigned) if this is possible. Alternatively, novation of these agreements may be a possibility. However, it may not be possible to assign these existing contracts or novate them in all cases and provision must be made for this occurrence and any financial implications. It may be sensible to explore the possibility of transferring such contracts before the facilities management contract is executed. Where there remains any doubt, a term may be included to the effect that the client will use his best endeavours to secure the transfer or, failing that, to obtain equivalent goods or services by other means. The agreement may provide that, in such a case, the client bears the cost, at least in relation to the remaining period that the contract in question was to run.

In most cases, where a client outsources his information technology operations for the first time, there will be a transfer of staff to the facilities management company. Where this is so, the effect of the Transfer of Undertakings (Protection of Employment) Regulations 1981 must be borne in mind. These regulations apply to secure the contractual and statutory employment rights of transferred employees. Although the regulations have been criticised because of their limitations, for example, by being confined to the transfer of commercial undertakings, they will apply in many cases. Additionally, other employment legislation may apply such as the Employment Rights Act 1996. If an employee is subsequently dismissed, the dismissal will be treated as unfair automatically unless, it can be shown that the dismissal was based on economic, technical or organisational reasons requiring a change in the workforce.

There will be other cases where the transfer is outside the provisions of these regulations. In *Betts* v *Brintel Helicopters Ltd* [1997] ICR

792, KLM won an outsourcing contract with Shell which had previously been enjoyed by Brintel. It was held, following the European Court of Justice's ruling in a German case, *Süzen* v *Zehnacker Gebäudereinigung GmbH Krankehausserive* [1997] ICR 662, that there has to be a transfer of significant assets for a change of contract to be a transfer within the provisions. There must be a transfer of significant tangible or intangible assets or of a major part of the workforce. In *Betts* the new service was provided with assets that were largely different to those used by Brintel. However, many facilities management contracts will involve a significant transfer of assets or the workforce and, therefore, be subject to the regulations. Note that a significant transfer of intangible assets may be sufficient, such as where a substantial amount of software is transferred.

A distinction must be made, however, between the loss of a customer and a loss of a business and between the transfer of an activity and the transfer of an undertaking. In *ECM (Vehicle Delivery Service) Ltd* v *Cox*, *The Times*, 10 June 1998, it was held by the Employment Appeal Tribunal that where employees were dedicated to servicing a particular contract without which they would have no employment and that contract was transferred to a competitor, then there was a transfer of an undertaking for the purposes of the regulations. The implication of this is that if company A has staff dedicated to a particular facilities management contract and that contract is lost to company B, then there is an obligation on company B to take over the employment of those staff of company A dedicated to servicing that contract. However, if the staff servicing the contract for company A also work on other contracts and the contract is lost to company B but no significant transfer of tangible or intangible assets or staff occurs, then there is no such obligation. As Morison J said in the *ECM* case, the rationale behind the European Directive on which the regulations are based is to protect them when the business to which they were dedicated was transferred and a new employer came on the scene; it did not seek to protect employees from the "chill wind of redundancy".

As regards the staff transferred, they must be offered the same terms and conditions and there may need to be specific provision for the transfer of pensions and other benefits.

Duration

A fixed period of time should be set for the provision of the service. It may range from one to several years. It may be subject to automatic renewal subject to certain basic parameters to determine changes to payment and services provided. The client will not want to be left high and dry so there should be a deadline for renewal some time before the expiry of the agreement. Six months would not seem unreasonable, allowing the client to engage another contractor in sufficient time to take over the facilities management without major disruption. The process of renewal can be seen as a major and important exercise requiring considerable evaluation, planning and negotiation between the parties. The ideal outcome is for the parties to establish a good, mutually beneficial, long-term relationship.

Payment

An agreed and specified payment mechanism is essential so that the client can budget effectively for his costs. However, if the contract lasts more than one year, it is likely that the facilities management company will want payment to be linked, for example, to the retail prices index. Furthermore, it is almost inevitable that further services or extended services will be required and there should be some mechanism for agreeing the impact on payment. One technique may be for the parties to agree the payment for each year based on a precisely specified level and scope of service, perhaps payable in monthly instalments in arrears and to include a schedule of rates to cover any additional services or provision of software as *agreed by the parties beforehand*. Percentage uplifts can be set where any additional work includes the provision of further equipment or software, bought or hired in. Some mechanism for adjustment in the case of late or defective provision of services would also be sensible, provided delivery and response times and the level and quality of services can be adequately defined to enable unsatisfactory performance to be clearly identified.

Typically, the client will want a reduction in the payments due to the facilities management company in respect of any downtime, when the computer facilities are not available for use. In some cases, even if the computer systems are unavailable for a short period, the consequences for the client's operations may be quite serious.

Change

Given the complexity of many facilities management contracts it is almost inevitable that changes will be required to the level of service and its nature. The client may find that, on reflection, it would be desirable to enhance the level of service or to automate another of its functions. Alternatively, it may be that there is to be a change in the computer equipment or software to take advantage of the latest technology. A decision may be made to move the service provision off-site to take advantage of the facilities management company's own equipment. Given the nature of information technology, it is likely to be very difficult to predict all the changes that may occur even over a relatively short period of time, and some of the changes may be substantial. If a major change is anticipated which could not reasonably be envisaged and provided for in the initial agreement, the parties may find that they have to engage in some significant negotiation, perhaps with the facilities management company submitting costed proposals for discussion. Of course, change does not necessarily mean increased costs. In many cases as computer technology becomes more sophisticated and powerful, there might be significant reductions in costs coupled with improvement in the service provided.

In some cases, the changes may be implemented by means of a variation to the contract. In other cases, the changes may be so fundamental and radical that the parties might want to consider a novation of the contract with a new agreement drawn up to reflect the radical changes in the service provided. In other cases it may be a matter of modifying the service level agreement by mutual agreement the next time the contract is renewed.

Warranties

Both parties will be expected to provide warranties. The facilities management company is likely to include the following warranties:

- that it will use reasonable care and skill in the provision of its services to the client (this will be implied anyway under section 13 of the Supply of Goods and Services Act 1982);
- that it will engage competent staff who are adequately trained (such training to be updated and enhanced as appropriate) on the provision of the services;
- that it has the right to use any software provided or acquired for the purposes of providing the services to the client;
- that any software provided by or used by the company in the provision of the services will be free from serious errors including date errors and currency errors.

The client may be subject to the following warranties:

- that the client owns the rights in any software it will transfer (by assignment or licensing) to the facilities management company or, if not, it has the benefit of appropriate licences which are transferable;
- where licences and third party contracts are transferred to the facilities management company (assignment of the benefit), there are no subsisting or unresolved breaches of the licences or contracts;
- that there are no outstanding claims by employees to be transferred with respect to salaries, wages or other benefits nor any outstanding unfair dismissal or wrongful dismissal claims;
- that any software transferred to the facilities management company is free from serious errors including date errors and currency errors.

As a rule of thumb, all software contains errors, many of which may be quite minor and insignificant. It may be unreasonable to warrant that software is completely error free and the presence of minor errors does not necessarily mean that the software concerned is not fit for its purpose; see *Saphena Computing* v *Allied Collection Agencies* [1995] FSR 616. Of course, this fact should not remove any obligation to correct errors even if they are minor, bearing in mind it may prove impossible to remove some trivial errors, particularly if resulting from the interaction between the software and the hardware. A better approach may be to limit the warranty to serious errors and have some form of liquidated damages associated with them if they cause the software to be inoperable for a significant amount of time. A serious error may be defined in the agreement in terms of its consequences for the client's use of the computer systems.

There may be other warranties, for example, in respect of the condition or performance of equipment or software to be transferred.

Performance monitoring

The facilities management contract should be subject to continuing assessment and quality control so that performance against agreed targets can be checked and the need or desirability for changes, if any, can be identified. Persons from both parties should be allocated to this role and a series of regular meetings arranged at which performance and need for change can be evaluated. Technical and managerial personnel should attend such meetings and be of sufficiently high rank to have the authority to agree variations to the agreement and increases or decreases in any sums due to the facilities management company. Depending on the circumstances, the client may need access to the facilities management company's premises and software to inspect the operation of the services provided. Normally, such access would be conditional upon the client giving formal notice.

At performance meetings, any failure to meet targets or provide the agreed level of service can be addressed and remedies considered. It may involve an adjustment to the sums payable to the facilities management company. Of course, any failures may be outside the control of the company and may have been caused by the acts or omissions of the client or a third party unconnected with the facilities management company (which will, of course, remain liable for failures caused by its own suppliers or sub-contractors). The contract should include provisions to cover such matters and mechanisms for resolving any dispute about the consequences on the future performance of the contract.

Bespoke software

The facilities management company, as part of its service, may develop and write software tailored to the client's requirements. Where this is so, the ownership of the copyright and other rights (for example, the database right) is an issue. In most cases, the client will want the rights assigning to him so that, if another facilities management company is engaged after the termination of the present contract, the software can continue to be used by the client or on his behalf. Where, as will usually be the case, the software or any part of it does not exist when the contract is made, it is a simple matter to provide for the assignment of the prospective rights. Under section 91 of the Copyright, Designs and Patents Act 1988, where the agreement to assign the future copyright is signed by or on behalf of the prospective owner of the copyright then when the copyright comes into existence, it will automatically vest in the assignee.

For existing software, the equivalent requirement is a written assignment signed by or on behalf of the present owner of the copyright. Assignments are normally made with "full title guarantee".

The contract should describe "future copyright and other rights" as copyright, database right and all other intellectual property rights which will or may come into existence in respect of software specifically written for the client during the provision of the service by the facilities management company. If there is any likelihood of third parties being engaged in the writing of the software, there should be provision for the facilities management company to use its best endeavours to acquire such rights and to do everything necessary to make such rights effective, to assign them to the client, to execute any necessary documents and register any registrable transactions.

Data protection

Where personal data are involved, as will almost certainly be the case, the position of the facilities management company will be that of a data processor under the Data Protection Act 1988. That being so, the agreement must contain provision for security arrangements in respect of the personal data. Paragraph 11 of Part II of Schedule 1 to the Act (interpretative provisions in respect of the data protection principles) requires that a data processor must provide sufficient guarantees in respect of the technical and organisational security governing the processing and, under paragraph 12, the data processor must carry out the processing under a contract made or evidenced in writing which requires the data controller to act only on instructions of the data controller (the client in this case). Furthermore, the contract must require that the data processor complies with security obligations equivalent to those imposed on the data controller.

Thus, the facilities management company must ensure a level of security appropriate to the harm that might result from unauthorised or unlawful processing or accidental loss or destruction of, or damage to, the personal data, bearing in mind the nature of the data (for example, its sensitivity). Account may be taken of the state of technical development and the cost of implementing the security measures. The data processor must also take reasonable steps to ensure the reliability of any employees having access to the data. Some form of indemnity may be usefully included in the agreement to cover a failure of the facilities management company to ensure the required level of security of the data.

In some cases, it is possible that the facilities management company may be deemed also to be a data controller which is defined in the Act as "... a person who (either alone or jointly or in common with other persons) determines the purposes for which and the manner in which any personal data are, or are to be, processed"; section 1(1). As a data processor is defined as "... a person, other than an employee of the data controller who processes data on behalf of the data controller", it may be a question of the amount of freedom of choice and discretion that a facilities management company has in relation to the data processing. For example, if the contract is such that the facilities management company has a brief to be innovative in determining new uses for the client's data, subject to the client's approval, it may be that both parties are deemed to be data controllers.

The general practice under the previous legislation, the Data Protection Act 1984, appears to have been to treat facilities management companies as computer bureaux (which will fall into the wider definition of data processors under the 1998 Act), not "data users" (equivalent to "data controllers" under the 1998 Act). However, as the services provided by facilities management companies become more sophisticated and their contribution to the client's use of information technology becomes more proactive, this practice may change. Certainly, where the facilities management company is involved with forward planning of the client's information technology needs on a cooperative basis or is given wide-ranging discretion in the design of new computer systems and uses for the client's data, it is possible that facilities management companies could be classed as data controllers and data processors in respect of the client's personal data.

Data controllers have a duty to notify their computer processing of personal data to the Data Protection Commissioner. They are also under numerous obligations under the Data Protection Act 1998, including a duty to inform data subjects (individuals who are the subject of personal data) under certain circumstances and to allow them subject access. Data subjects also have a number of other rights in respect of the processing of data relating to them and can prevent processing of their data for the purpose of direct marketing and where the processing is likely to cause substantial damage or substantial distress. They also have certain rights in relation to automated decision-taking.

Where the facilities management company is likely to be perceived as a data controller jointly with the client, the contract should allocate responsibility for informing data subjects and with respect to other obligations under the Act. The facilities management company will also be required to notify under the Act in respect of its processing of the client's data (of course, the company will have to notify in respect of its own processing activity such as that relating to its employees). Of course, in many circumstances, the facilities management company will simply be a data processor but the point at which it becomes also a data controller is not clear, especially when the definitions in the Act are considered and, of course, there is no guidance as at the time of writing. It may be that the Data Protection Commissioner will issue guidelines appropriate to facilities management operations.

Other terms

The contract will have a number of other terms dealing with matters such as liability for defective performance, perhaps liquidated damages for tardy performance, insurances, staff poaching, whether the benefit of the agreement can be assigned, confidentiality, arbitration (or more appropriately in a facilities management contract, alternative dispute resolution), termination and force majeure, applicable law and jurisdiction.

Depending on the circumstances, other terms may be included. For example, it may be that the client requires a bond to cover the situation where the facilities management company is no longer able to complete the performance of the contract, perhaps because of its insolvency. There should also be terms dealing with security arrangements including back-up facilities, disaster recovery, password systems and their maintenance.

Postscript: at the time of writing it appears that the main provisions of the Data Protection Act 1998 will not come into force until some time in 1999. It should have been brought into force by 24 October 1998, as required by the Directive.

Example Licence Agreement for Bespoke Software

Verisopht Ltd, having its registered office at 123 New Street, Westhampton (hereinafter called "Licensor"), hereby grants Squeers Ltd, having its registered office at 77 Sunset Strip, Easton-on-Sea (hereinafter called "Licensee"), an exclusive licence to use the Dispatch Software package as described in the specification annexed to this agreement (hereinafter referred to as "Dispatch Software") and all other rights hereinafter described all in accordance with this agreement.

Definitions

For the purposes of this agreement the following definitions have effect:

"software" includes computer programs, data files, databases, data and other related information stored on computer media or otherwise and any associated printed documentation;

"hardware" includes computers, terminals, printers, input and output devices, modems and cabling;

"currency error" means any error in storing, retrieving, calculating, manipulating or converting currency or sums of money but not including any normal rounding operation, any error resulting in whole or in part from software other than the Dispatch Software or any hardware or input error;

"date error" means any error in storing, retrieving, calculating or manipulating dates but not including any error resulting in whole or in part from software other than the Dispatch Software or any hardware or input error;

"input error" means any error in data or information submitted to the Dispatch Software in software form or entered via a keyboard or other input device by any person using the Dispatch Software and includes erroneous data or information originating from any person other than the person entering it or submitting it to the Dispatch Software;

"date of acceptance" is the date at which the Licensee signifies acceptance of the Dispatch Software or the date of deemed acceptance whichever is the earlier and "acceptance" may be actual or deemed acceptance in accordance with this agreement;

"Postal Database" means the database of postal addresses supplied by Matalini Data Services Ltd, version 2.1 or such later version as may become available at the discretion of the Licensor;

"Cassandra" means the Cassandra fourth generation development software package supplied by Kenwigs Software plc, version 4.5 or such later version as may become available at the discretion of the Licensor, to be used to develop the Dispatch Software;

"CCA" means the subscription credit reference database service provided to the Licensee under a separate agreement between the Licensee and Cheeryble Credit Assessors Ltd;

"CES" means CES Ltd, which provides source code escrow services.

Licensor's obligations

Licence

The Licensor grants to the Licensee an exclusive, non-transferable, licence in respect of the Dispatch Software to be used throughout the Licensee's organisation. The licence will endure for the term of the copyright subsisting in the Dispatch Software programs and databases created by the Licensor unless terminated earlier in accordance with this agreement. The Licensor agrees to grant to the Licensee a non-exclusive sub-licence in respect of the Postal Database and the benefit of a non-exclusive run-time licence in respect of Cassandra. The Licensor reserves the right to use modules contained in the programs in programs or software other than the Dispatch Software.

Licensor to provide

The Licensor agrees to deliver and install the Dispatch Software, Postal Database and run-time version of Cassandra on the Licensee's main computer no later than six calendar months following receipt of a written order to carry out the work from the Licensee. Within a further two months, the Licensor undertakes to test the operation of the Dispatch Software and to demonstrate its compliance with the specification, including demonstrating that it is free from date errors and currency errors. The Licensor also undertakes to deliver to the Licensee no later than the date of acceptance of the Dispatch Software by the Licensee one copy of the Dispatch Software, Postal Database and run-time version of Cassandra on magnetic disk together with 12 copies of the user manual.

The Licensor undertakes to deliver to CES within three months of the date of acceptance of the Dispatch Software one copy of the source code for the programs contained in the Dispatch Software together with the design materials for said programs and to pay the initial deposit fee to CES.

The Licensor agrees to provide training in the use of the Dispatch Software to three of the Licensee's employees for a period of not more than four days to be completed within one month of the date of acceptance of the Dispatch Software.

The above dates and periods may be varied only in accordance with this agreement.

Maintenance

The Licensor undertakes to maintain the Dispatch Software and correct any errors therein following written notice of such errors from the Licensee for a period of 12 months commencing from the date of acceptance. The Licensor undertakes to make every effort to commence work on correcting such errors within 24 hours of receipt of notification and will make every endeavour to correct the error and install the modified software on the Licensee's main computer within a reasonable time. The Licensor reserves the right to charge if it is discovered that there is no error in the Dispatch Software of the kind notified by the Licensee or if the error is due in whole or in part to any act, omission or input error of the Licensee, its employees, servants or agents or is attributable to the hardware or to software other than the Dispatch Software.

Licensee's obligations

Payment

The Licensee undertakes to pay to the Licensor the sums stated in Schedule 1 within one calendar month of receipt of invoices to be submitted by the Licensor after the occurrence of the events stated in Schedule 1 less a retention of 10 per cent of the sums due. Half of the retention monies so retained by the Licensee shall become due following acceptance of the Dispatch Software, the remainder becoming due upon satisfactory completion of the period of maintenance subject to there being no outstanding errors in the Dispatch Software previously notified by the Licensee awaiting correction by the Licensor. Interest shall accrue in respect of late payment in accordance with Schedule 1.

Facilities, etc provided by Licensee

The Licensee shall provide the Licensor with all facilities, assistance and information reasonably required by the Licensor for the installation and testing of the Dispatch Software. In particular, the Licensee shall provide appropriate access to its main computer for installation and testing following 24 hours written notice given by the Licensor and the Licensee shall provide appropriate test data to enable the Licensee to test the Dispatch Software thoroughly. The Licensee shall ensure that details of and an explanation of the operating system of its main computer will be available to the Licensor and that access to the CCA database will be afforded to the Licensor as and when required.

Whilst on the Licensee's premises, the Licensee shall make available to the employees and agents of the Licensor reasonable access to photocopying, telephone, facsimile machines as reasonably required for the performance of this agreement. The Licensee shall be responsible for keeping a record of the use of such equipment and the Licensor agrees to pay for its use thereof at cost.

The Licensee agrees to provide access to its canteen and rest-room facilities to the employees and agents of the Licensor whilst they are on the Licensee's premises, such employees and agents to pay for any food or drink provided to them by the Licensee.

Acceptance

The Licensee agrees to attend acceptance testing of the Dispatch Software following a minimum of 48 hours written notice of such and to accept the Dispatch Software upon its satisfactory completion of the acceptance tests stated in the specification notwithstanding that there may remain some minor work to be carried out by the Licensor providing that the Dispatch Software is in a state such that it may be used to perform all of its main functions adequately and reliably. The Licensor undertakes to complete all outstanding work within the following calendar month. If the Licensee fails or refuses to attend properly notified acceptance testing operations it shall be deemed to have accepted the Dispatch Software unless it submits in writing good reason why it is not acceptable within seven days following notification of testing. In any event, if the Licensee commences using the Dispatch Software in relation to its business activities, the Licensee shall be deemed immediately and unconditionally to have accepted the Dispatch Software if the Licensee has not previously accepted it.

The Licensee shall at its own expense immediately before acceptance testing back up all its own software including any software belonging to any third party stored or situated on its main computer. During testing for date errors the Licensee agrees to stop all other work on the main computer and to suspend the use of all software on the main computer. If the Licensee fails to take these necessary precautions the Licensor can accept no responsibility for any damage, modification or erasure of any of the Licensee's software caused directly or indirectly by testing the Dispatch Software for date errors in accordance with the specification. The Licensee also agrees at its own expense to test the operation of its own software (and arrange for the testing of any third party's software) during or immediately after the testing for date errors in the Dispatch Software and to inform the Licensor immediately if any problems are discovered. If the Licensee fails to perform any of its duties under this clause, the Licensor at its entire discretion may elect not to check the Dispatch Software for date errors and will not be liable for any damage or loss resulting directly or indirectly from any such date errors.

Use of software by Licensee

The Licensee undertakes to use the Dispatch Software only in accordance with this agreement for its own business purposes and otherwise not to copy, modify, disclose or transmit it and not to decompile or disassemble the programs without prejudice to sections 50A, 50B and 50D of the Copyright, Designs and Patents Act 1988 and regulation 19 of the Copyright and Rights in Databases Regulations 1997.

Furthermore, the Licensee agrees that it will not transfer the Dispatch Software or any part thereof to any other person or organisation nor will it sell, rent, lend or otherwise distribute or dispose of copies of the Dispatch Software or any part thereof nor use it or any part thereof to provide services to other persons or organisations without the prior written consent of the Licensor signed by a Director of the Licensor.

The Licensee agrees to monitor the use of the Dispatch Software and to take reasonable precautions to ensure that copies of it or any part thereof are not sold, rented, loaned, disclosed or transmitted or otherwise made available to any other person or organisation. Any copies of the Dispatch Software made under this agreement are to be clearly labelled as back-up copies and an appropriate copyright notice denoting the Licensor as owner of the copyright is to be attached. Such copies are to be stored in a secure place.

Escrow payment

The Licensee agrees to pay the annual escrow fee to the CES escrow service in return for CES holding a copy of the source code of the Dispatch Software programs and associated preparatory materials. In the event that:

(a) the Licensor is unable to continue to maintain the Dispatch Software as a result of entering into liquidation (whether compulsory or voluntary) other than for purposes of solvent reconstruction or amalgamation or if the Licensor has a receiver appointed over all or any part of its assets or undertaking or if the Licensor ceases to be able to pay its debts within the meaning of section 123 of the Insolvency Act 1986, or

(b) is in breach of its error correction or other maintenance obligations within 10 days of receipt of a written notice from the Licensee stating the breach and requesting it be remedied forthwith, or

(c) the Licensor assigns the copyright subsisting in the Dispatch Software and fails within 10 days to obtain equivalent undertakings from the assignee in respect of the escrow arrangement,

CES will upon written request from the Licensee together with evidence that any of the above events have occurred and the necessary release fee deliver to the Licensee a copy of the above mentioned source code and other materials in accordance with the conditions of escrow.

In the event that the Licensee fails to pay the annual escrow fee to CES within four weeks of receiving a final written demand from CES for payment, the escrow arrangement shall come to an end forthwith and all deposited source code and other materials shall be returned to the Licensor.

Performance related issues

Liquidated damages for late performance by Licensor

Should the Licensor fail to deliver, install and test the Dispatch Software to the acceptance of the Licensee within eight months from the date of receipt of the Licensee's written order or such later date as provided for by an extension of time in accordance with this agreement, the Licensor shall pay to the Licensee the sum of £1,250 per week by way of liquidated damages. Periods of less than one week shall not be taken into account in calculating liquidated damages.

Termination for extreme late performance

Should the Licensee fail to deliver, install and test the Dispatch Software to the acceptance of the Licensee after six months following the period of eight months from the date of receipt of the Licensee's written order or such later date as provided for by an extension of time in accordance with this agreement, the Licensee may at its discretion treat the failure as a breach of condition (or, in Scotland a material breach) and terminate the agreement forthwith notwithstanding its claim for damages under the agreement.

Delays caused by Licensee

Any delay to the performance of the work required of the Licensor under this agreement caused wholly or partly by the default or neglect of the Licensee shall entitle the Licensor to an extension to the time for performance and to additional payment for any attributable costs calculated in accordance with the schedule of rates. In the event of any such delay, the Licensor shall make every endeavour to minimise such additional costs by attempting to assign its employees or agents to alternative work associated with this agreement, or failing that, to other work, if available. Both the Licensor and the Licensee agree to keep a full record of the delay and its consequences and to agree the extension of time for performance and the additional payment as soon as is practicable after the reason for the delay has ceased to be operative.

Variation orders

Variations to the work to be carried out under this agreement must be agreed in writing between the Licensor and the Licensee. The additional payment and extension to the time for performance, if any, shall be agreed between the Licensor and the Licensee before any work associated with any such variation may be carried out and appropriate officers of the Licensor and the Licensee shall sign and date a written variation order specifying the additional work, payment and extension to the time for performance, if any.

Renewal and termination

Either party may terminate this agreement, unless otherwise provided for herein, if the other party is guilty of a serious breach of the agreement having failed to remedy that breach (if remediable) after being given one calendar month's notice of the breach in writing by the party seeking to terminate the agreement. Notice of termination shall be served in writing and signed by a director or partner of the party seeking to terminate. Any monies due at the time of termination shall remain payable and become due immediately upon termination without prejudice to any other legal remedy available to either party.

This Licence may be terminated forthwith by notice in writing signed by the Licensor if the Licensee becomes insolvent or ceases trading or commits an act of bankruptcy or is adjudicated bankrupt or enters into liquidation, whether compulsory or voluntary, other than for the purposes of an amalgamation or reconstruction, or makes an arrangement with its creditors or petitions for an administration order or has a receiver or manager appointed over all or any part of its assets or generally becomes unable to pay its debts within the meaning of section 123 of the Insolvency Act 1986.

Termination of this Licence will automatically terminate any support obligations of the Licensor in respect of the Dispatch Software all copies of which in the possession of the Licensee are to be delivered forthwith to the Licensor.

Warranties and indemnities

The Licensor warrants that it has exercised reasonable skill and care in developing and writing the Dispatch Software and in selecting and incorporating any included third party software and that it has made every effort to minimise errors and ensure that the Dispatch Software performs adequately and reliably.

The Licensor shall not be liable in respect of periods not exceeding seven days during which the Dispatch Software is incapable of being used by the Licensee as a result of a defect in the Dispatch Software. The Licensor's liability for any longer period during which the Licensee is unable to use the Dispatch Software because of a defect attributable to the negligence of the Licensor shall be limited to £25,000 for each such period except as provided for below. The Licensor shall not be liable for any other non-use of the Dispatch Software howsoever caused.

The Licensor shall not be liable for loss, damage or expense resulting directly or indirectly from errors attributable to any act, omission or input error of the Licensee, its employees, servants and agents or the Licensee's hardware or software or third party hardware or software or resulting from any act, omission or input error of any third party beyond the control of the Licensor. The Licensor's maximum liability for loss, damage or expense resulting directly from the Licensor's negligence is limited to £250,000 in respect of any one claim or series of related claims except as provided for below. The Licensor shall not be liable for any other loss including any indirect or consequential loss, damage or expense nor any loss of profit howsoever caused except as provided for in this agreement.

The Licensor warrants that it has taken all due care to ensure that the Dispatch Software will be free from date errors and currency errors. The Licensor's maximum aggregate liability for any loss, damage or expense suffered by the Licensee and resulting from the Licensor's negligence in relation to date errors and currency errors wholly attributable to the Dispatch Software is limited to £25,000. All other liability of the Licensor in relation to date errors and currency errors howsoever caused is hereby excluded.

The Licensor does not warrant that any third party software included in the Dispatch Software nor any other third party software whether provided by the Licensee or otherwise is free from defects and whilst the Licensor has used all reasonable care to ensure that such third party software is free from defects and reasonably fit for its intended purpose the Licensor shall not be liable for any loss, damage or expense directly or indirectly attributable to any such defect or lack of fitness for purpose.

The Licensee warrants that it shall use the Dispatch Software in accordance with the Licensor's instructions and the Licensee shall indemnify the Licensor against any losses suffered by or claims made against the Licensor by any person other than the Licensee resulting from the loss, use or misuse of the Dispatch Software by or with the express or implied authority or consent of the Licensee.

In the event that the Dispatch Software is proved to infringe a third party's intellectual property rights, the Licensor shall make the necessary modifications without delay to prevent further infringement, if possible. Should the Licensee be prevented from using the software permanently and/or become subject to third party claims in respect of such infringement, the liability of the Licensor is limited to a maximum of total of the payments made to the Licensor under this agreement. If the Licensee becomes aware that the software infringes or is claimed to infringe a third party's intellectual property rights, the Licensee shall inform the Licensor of such at once in writing and provide the Licensor with such information and assistance to allow the Licensor to defend any claim made against it. The Licensor will indemnify the Licensee in respect of its costs in providing such information and assistance including legal costs.

Miscellaneous

Assignment and sub-licensing

The licensee shall not assign or sub-licence this agreement or any of the rights, obligations, benefits or interests granted under this agreement.

Confidentiality

Both parties agree not to disclose confidential information obtained or received by them from the other party without the prior written consent of the other party. This obligation is to continue after termination of the agreement until such time as the other party grants a written release or the information enters the public domain other than by default of the party owing an obligation of confidence to the other party.

Force majeure

Neither party shall be liable to the other for any delay in or failure to perform its obligations as a result of acts, omissions, events, accidents or Acts of God beyond the reasonable control of the party to perform. If such delay or failure continues for at least six months, either party may terminate the agreement by notice in writing.

Data protection

Both parties agree to comply with the provisions of the Data Protection Act 1998 and secondary legislation made under it in relation to the notification requirements, the collection, use, storage, processing, disclosure and transfer of personal data. Where the Licensor has access to the Licensee's personal data, the Licensor agrees to guarantee to take all appropriate security measures as required in Schedule 1 to the Act.

Computer viruses

Both the Licensor and the Licensee agree to check their disks and tapes at regular intervals for computer viruses using an up-to-date virus check program and to immediately inform the other if a virus is detected and to give details of the action to be taken to erase the virus and to check other disks and tapes for the presence of the virus.

Moral rights

The Licensor warrants that it has or will ensure that all moral rights under copyright law, if any, in the Dispatch Software have been waived.

Notices

Any notice given under this agreement by either party to the other must be in writing and delivered personally or by recorded delivery post.

Entire agreement

This agreement represents the entire agreement between the parties and no variation of the terms of this agreement shall be effective unless in writing and signed by a director of each of the parties to this agreement

Dispute resolution

If any dispute arises in connection with this agreement, the parties agree to attempt to resolve such dispute by negotiation. In the event that a negotiated settlement cannot be reached, the parties agree to attempt to settle it by mediation in accordance with the model procedure of the Centre for Dispute Resolution. Neither party may commence court proceedings or arbitration until the mediation process has been exhausted and a settlement has not been reached.

Applicable law

This agreement shall be governed by and construed in accordance with English law and subject to the jurisdiction of the courts of England and Wales.

Headings

Headings to the clauses of this agreement are for guidance only and not to be used in the construction of any of the provisions of this agreement.

SIGNED .... for and on behalf of ....

SIGNED .... for and on behalf of ....

DATE ....

Schedule 1

Schedule of payments to be made by Licensee

Total fee payable = £87,500.00 (eighty-seven thousand and five hundred pounds)

Payment No	Event at which payment becomes due	Amount (as percentage of total fee payable)
1	Receipt of order from Licensee to commence work	10%
2	Installation of Dispatch Software on Licensee's main computer	40%
3	Acceptance of Dispatch Software by Licensee	50%

All fees and charges are exclusive of VAT and similar taxes. All such taxes are payable by the Licensee and will be applied in accordance with UK legislation in force at the tax point date.

Any additional payments becoming due under the agreement to be paid in accordance with the Schedule of rates (Schedule 2).

All invoices shall be payable net one calendar month from receipt by the Licensee after deduction of 10 per cent retention monies. Half of retention monies to become due on acceptance of the Dispatch Software by the Licensee.

Overdue payments shall remain payable together with interest for late payment from the due date at a rate of $1\frac{1}{2}$ per cent per annum above the base rate for the time being of [Bank Name] to accrue on a daily basis and payable on demand.

If the Licensor or Licensee shall become entitled to terminate this agreement for any reason any sums due will immediately become payable in full.

Schedule 2

Schedule of rates

Analysts, programmers, technicians, etc (hourly rate includes all on costs and profit subject to note below)

Description	Hourly rate £
Team leader	45.70
Senior analyst	37.00
Analyst	31.00
Senior programmer	29.75
Programmer	24.90
Senior technician	22.45
Technician	20.35
Trainee	13.75

The above rates do not include subsistence costs in respect of employees or agen. working further than a 30-mile journey from Licensee's head office. A daily subsistence rate of £95.00 for senior staff and managers and £80.00 for other staff is payable in addition to the above rates together with necessary travelling expenses (standard class rail fare or £0.42 per mile for travel by car).

Materials and equipment supplied at cost (including all discounts and taxes) plus 5 per cent.

Example Licence Agreement for Off-the-shelf Software

Definitions

"G-Base software" means all the software items supplied in this package including programs, dictionaries, indexes, data files, tutorial programs and files and sample programs, databases, forms and reports.

"Related Items" means the printed matter and disks supplied in this package.

"Greysoft Ltd" is the owner of the copyright and other rights in the G-Base software and related items and is, accordingly, the licensor of the G-Base software and related items.

"Customer" is the person acquiring the G-Base software and is, accordingly, the licensee in respect of it.

Licence agreement

Greysoft Ltd grants the customer a licence to use the G-Base software. It may be copied onto one or more computers (whether or not on a network) and one back-up copy of the G-Base software may be made by the customer. The customer must ensure that any copies of the G-Base software are clearly labelled as such as include a prominent notice to the effect that Greysoft Ltd is the copyright owner.

The customer shall take all reasonable precautions and measures to protect the G-Base software and related items from unauthorised use, access, copying, modification, reproduction, distribution or publication.

Permitted uses

The G-Base software may NOT be used by ANY PERSON OTHER THAN THE CUSTOMER OR AN EMPLOYEE OF THE CUSTOMER IN THE COURSE OF HIS EMPLOYMENT BY THE CUSTOMER. However, the run-time program GRUN.EXE may be copied and/or distributed in accordance with this agreement.

The customer may write and compile programs using the G-Base software to be distributed internally or to third parties in executable form only without payment of any additional licence fee to Greysoft Ltd. Apart from the programs compiled by the customer, the customer may also distribute to persons to whom the customer's compiled programs are made available a copy of the G-Base run-time program GRUN.EXE without any additional payment to Greysoft Ltd.

The customer must include a notice with any copies of the customer's compiled programs and GRUN.EXE setting out that the copyright in the compiled programs (and associated databases, forms and reports files) belongs to the customer and the copyright in GRUN.EXE belongs to Greysoft Ltd and that none of the programs may be copied, decompiled, disassembled or otherwise modified except as permitted by sections 50A and 50B of the Copyright, Designs and Patents Act 1988. The notice must also set out that Greysoft Ltd has not written the customer's compiled programs (and associated databases, forms and report files) and accepts no responsibility for any of the programs or other software items delivered by the customer. The customer must state that the compiled programs and any associated databases, format and report files have been created using the G-Base software (quoting the particular release date and number).

Prohibited uses

The customer may not make copies of the software items except as provided above and may not, under any circumstances, make copies of the related items.

Unless provided for above in terms of compiled programs, the customer must not rent, lease, lend, share, disclose, transmit or transfer the G-Base software and related items except that the customer may transfer all the G-Base software items and related items including any copies made in accordance with this agreement together with this licence agreement to another person under a written agreement signed by that other person. The written agreement must include a statement to the effect that the transferee agrees to abide by the terms of the licence agreement as the customer. The transferor of the G-Base software and related items must give Greysoft Ltd written confirmation of such a transfer within 14 days of it taking effect together with a copy of the signed written agreement hereinbefore referred to. Greysoft Ltd will keep the transferee informed of future upgrades and enhancements to the G-Base software.

The customer must not decompile, disassemble or otherwise modify the software except as provided for by this agreement and section 50B of the Copyright, Designs and Patents Act 1988, as amended, and the Copyright and Rights in Databases Regulations 1997.

Duration and termination

This agreement shall endure for as long as copyright subsists in the United Kingdom in any of the G-Base software items unless terminated earlier. The customer may terminate this agreement at any time by returning all the original items of G-Base software and related items supplied together with all copies made of the G-Base software or after sending written confirmation that all such original items and copies made have been permanently destroyed. Greysoft Ltd may terminate this agreement at any time following a serious or irremediable breach of this agreement and/or a serious infringement of Greysoft Ltd's copyright.

Liability

Greysoft Ltd warrants that the physical related items provided by Greysoft Ltd are free from defects for a period of 90 days from the date of purchase and that

Greysoft Ltd will replace any such items proving to be defective provided notice of the defect has been received in the said 90 day period.

The customer is entirely responsible for determining the suitability of the G-Base software for his purposes and for the use that he makes of the G-Base software. The customer is entirely responsible for the quality and fitness for purpose of any software distributed to third parties containing programs compiled by the customer using the G-Base software and for any guidance, instruction or training of such third parties in respect of distributed software. The customer shall save harmless and indemnify Greysoft Ltd against claims from third parties in respect of the customer's compiled programs and associated databases, format and report files, GRUN.EXE and other items delivered by the customer to third parties.

Greysoft Ltd is not liable for any loss or damage, direct or indirect, arising from the use of the G-Base software and related items, however caused.

This agreement is without prejudice to the customer's statutory rights, if any.

Entire agreement

This agreement represents the entire agreement between Greysoft Ltd and the customer and supersedes all previous agreements or representations whether written or oral.

Applicable law

This agreement is subject to the laws of England and Wales and subject to the exclusive jurisdiction of the courts in England and Wales.

Bibliography

"Agreement on Trade-Related Aspects of Intellectual Property Rights" [1994] 11 EIPR 1

Atiyah, P S, *Sale of Goods* (London: Financial Times Pitman Publishing, 9th ed, 1995)

Bainbridge, D I, *Introduction to Computer Law* (London: Financial Times Pitman Publishing, 3rd ed, 1996)

Bainbridge, D I, *Intellectual Property* (London: Financial Times Pitman Publishing, 4th ed, 1998)

Bandey, B, *International Copyright in Computer Program Technology* (Birmingham: CLT Professional Publishing, 1996)

Centre for Dispute Resolution, *Model ADR Clauses*, 95 Gresham Street, London EC2V 7NA

Forrester, I S, "Software licensing in the light of current EC competition law" [1992] 1 ECLR 5

Henry, M, *Publishing and Multimedia Law* (London: Butterworths, 1994)

Institute of Purchasing and Supply, *Model Form Agreements*, Easton House, Easton on the Hill, Stamford, Lincs PE9 3NZ

Klinger, P & Burnett, R, *Drafting and Negotiating Computer Contracts* (London: Butterworths, 1994)

Lloyd, I, *Information Technology Law* (London: Butterworths, 2nd ed, 1997)

Megantz, R C, *How to License Technology* (New York: John Wiley & Sons, 1996)

Morgan, R & Steadman, G, *Computer Contracts* (London: FT Law & Tax, 5th ed, 1995)

Powell, M, "Drafting software licences in light of EEC competition rules" [1993] 9 CLSR 254

Rennie, M T, *Computer Contracts* (London: Sweet & Maxwell, 2nd ed, 1994)

Smith, G, "Software Contracts" in Reed, C (ed), *Computer Law*, (London: Blackstone, 3rd. ed, 1996) at 55 et seq

Tapper, C, *Computer Law* (London: Longman, 4th ed, 1990)

Glossary

Computer Programming Language: a set of words, letters and numbers which, according to the particular syntax of the language, describe a computer program, directly or indirectly, to a computer. A programming language may be a high-level language such as BASIC or COBOL or in a low-level language, normally termed assembly language. The distinction between high-level languages and low-level languages is that one statement of the former represents many statements in machine language while one statement of a low-level language is directly equivalent to one statement of machine language.

Computer Program: a series of instructions which control or condition the operation of a computer. Programs may be contained permanently in the computer, on integrated circuits, or stored on magnetic disks or tapes, or punched cards, etc.

Conversion of a Computer Program: The object code version of a computer program is produced by *compiling* the source code version. A computer program, known as a compiler program is normally used for this task. To retrieve the source code version from an object code program, a reverse process known as *decompilation* is used. Again, another computer program is used to perform this task. In terms of the hierarchy of programming languages, compilation converts a program expressed in a higher level language into a lower level language version, whereas decompilation converts a program expressed in a low level language into a higher level language version. It is in this way that decompilation is defined in section 50B of the Copyright, Designs and Patents Act 1988.

Data and Database: data comprises information stored in a computer or on storage media such as magnetic disks or tapes. A database is a collection of data; for example, it may be a collection of clients' names and addresses or a collection of poems, photographs, paintings or other works stored digitally. A database is used in conjunction with a computer program which accesses and manipulates the data contained in it. A computer software system often contains a number of linked computer programs and databases. The databases may be *relational*; that is, they are linked together by a relationship that is used to extract and combine data from a number of databases. A database will normally have an index or dictionary file that may be used to assist or speed up retrieval from the database. It may also have other associated files which define the format of screen displays or reports to be generated from the database. In some cases, a database may contain executable code.

Digital Representation: any item of information can be represented digitally; that is, using binary arithmetic. A bit is a single unit of information which may be "1" or "0". A graphic work can be mapped into digital form (for example, by a fax machine or optical reader), sound can be represented digitally as, indeed, can moving pictures (for example, as in video tape or CD-ROM). Letters and numbers are represented by combining a number of bits together. Computers usually use 8 bits to represent letters, numbers and other characters. 8 bits allows a total of 2^8, that is, 256 different combinations, equivalent to 0 to 255 in decimal numbers. A standard system of representing letters, etc is ASCII code. For example, the letter "F" is represented by 01000110 which is decimal 70.

Expert System: a computer system designed to provide advice at or approaching the level of an expert. Expert systems contain knowledge in a database of rules and facts which is accessed and manipulated by computer programs. An important feature of an expert system is its ability to provide an explanation for any advice it produces. In most basic form this may be a list of the rules used and answers given to provide a particular item of advice.

Fourth-Generation Language (4GL): a programming and system development environment. It may be used to generate an application without writing computer programs. The user specifies the application; for example, by describing the data to be stored together with details of entry screens and reports to be generated. Additionally, 4GLs usually have a built-in query language, allowing the user to query the database direct. For more complex applications, the system developer will also write a number of computer programs to enhance and complement the available features of the 4GL. Examples of 4GLs are dBaseIV, Oracle and Ingres.

Object Code Program: the form of the program which can be executed directly by the computer's processor. Generally, computer programs are made available in object code. This is difficult to modify. It can be "reverse engineered" to retrieve the source code and this process is usually termed "decompilation". More usually, all that can be retrieved is an assembly language version of the program.

Software: includes computer programs and data stored in a computer, preparatory design materials, computer programming languages and also associated documentation, such as user guides and manuals. It may also include computer output in digital and paper form. Particular types of software include applications software (such as word processing and spreadsheet software) and operating system software (such as MSDOS and Windows). All computers have an operating system which is the environment in which applications programs operate.

Source Code Program: a computer program in the form in which it is written by the programmer. Source code programs are written in a high level language, such as BASIC or COBOL or a low level language known as assembly language. The computer's processor cannot execute source code programs and they must be converted to object code by a process known as compiling (strictly speaking with a program written in assembly language, the process is known as assembling though this has no legal significance – both are within the meaning of making an adaptation which is an act restricted by copyright).

Index